# Discourse Syntax

Discourse Syntax is the study of syntax that requires an understanding of the surrounding text and the overall discourse situation, including considerations of genre and modality. Using corpus data and insights from current research, this textbook is a comprehensive guide to this fast-developing field. It takes the reader "beyond the sentence" to study grammatical phenomena, such as word order variation, connectives, ellipsis, and complexity. It introduces the core concepts of discourse syntax, integrating insights from corpus-based research and inviting the reader to reflect on research design decisions. Each chapter begins with a definition of learning outcomes, provides results from empirical articles, and enables readers to assess data visualizations critically. Complete with helpful further reading recommendations and a range of exercises, it is geared toward intermediate to advanced students of English linguistics and is also essential reading for anyone interested in this exciting, fast-moving discipline.

**Heidrun Dorgeloh** is Professor of English Linguistics at the Heinrich Heine University Düsseldorf with many years of experience in teaching English syntax, discourse analysis, and the corpus-based study of language use. She has published books and journal articles on word order, syntactic variation, and genre and register.

**Anja Wanner** is the Enid H. Anderson Professor of English and an award-winning teacher at the University of Wisconsin–Madison. A syntactician by training, she teaches classes on the structure of English and grammar in use and has published monographs and co-edited collections on English syntax, syntactic variation, and genre.

# Discourse Syntax

## English Grammar Beyond the Sentence

HEIDRUN DORGELOH
*Heinrich Heine University Düsseldorf*

ANJA WANNER
*University of Wisconsin–Madison*

CAMBRIDGE
UNIVERSITY PRESS

# CAMBRIDGE
## UNIVERSITY PRESS

University Printing House, Cambridge CB2 8BS, United Kingdom

One Liberty Plaza, 20th Floor, New York, NY 10006, USA

477 Williamstown Road, Port Melbourne, VIC 3207, Australia

314–321, 3rd Floor, Plot 3, Splendor Forum, Jasola District Centre, New Delhi – 110025, India

103 Penang Road, #05–06/07, Visioncrest Commercial, Singapore 238467

Cambridge University Press is part of the University of Cambridge.

It furthers the University's mission by disseminating knowledge in the pursuit of education, learning, and research at the highest international levels of excellence.

www.cambridge.org
Information on this title: www.cambridge.org/9781108471053
DOI: 10.1017/9781108557542

© Heidrun Dorgeloh and Anja Wanner 2023

First published 2023

*A catalogue record for this publication is available from the British Library.*

*Library of Congress Cataloging-in-Publication Data*
Names: Dorgeloh, Heidrun, author. | Wanner, Anja, author.
Title: Discourse syntax : English grammar beyond the sentence / Heidrun Dorgeloh, Anja Wanner.
Description: Cambridge, United Kingdom ; New York, NY : Cambridge University Press, 2022.
Identifiers: LCCN 2022032520 | ISBN 9781108471053 (hardback) | ISBN 9781108457040 (paperback) | ISBN 9781108557542 (ebook)
Subjects: LCSH: English language – Syntax. | English language – Discourse analysis. | BISAC: LANGUAGE ARTS & DISCIPLINES / General
Classification: LCC PE1361 .D67 2022 | DDC 425–dc23/eng/20220810
LC record available at https://lccn.loc.gov/2022032520

ISBN 978-1-108-47105-3 Hardback
ISBN 978-1-108-45704-0 Paperback

Additional resources for this publication at www.cambridge.org/DiscourseSyntax

# Contents

Additional resources can be found at www.cambridge.org/Discourse
Syntax

# Figures

# Tables

# Acknowledgments

This book is the result of many years of teaching courses in English linguistics on syntax, discourse analysis, and syntactic variation. We often wished there would be a textbook that would situate such variation in the context of the surrounding text, while keeping a focus on grammar and syntactic form. We didn't find that textbook, and so we have written it. The book reflects what we appreciate about textbooks – providing a coherent framework and systematic terminology, making results from influential research accessible, and guiding students toward designing their own research projects.

This book is also the result of many years of collaborating on topics in syntax, register studies, and genre variation. We thank our colleagues at Heinrich Heine University Düsseldorf and the University of Wisconsin–Madison, who made it possible that we could consistently teach courses that led to the development of this book, and our families, who supported our work every day, throughout a global health crisis. We owe you. We thank Lynn Zhang for her wonderful illustrations and insightful comments on all data visualizations, Sara Asher and Sally Kolasa for their proofreading, and the student assistants at the Department of English Linguistics at Heinrich Heine University Düsseldorf for being our test readers. Further support was provided by the College of Letters and Science and the Wisconsin Foundation and Alumni Association.

We are also grateful to Helen Barton and the Cambridge University Press team for their enthusiasm and support for this book from inception to finish and to Gordon Lee for his exceptional work as copy editor.

Most importantly, we thank our students, whose questions about where the study of syntax ends have kept us on our toes and who, over the years, have developed many fantastic projects showing that, yes, there is always something new to learn about English grammar. We hope this book will contribute to other students doing the same.

# PART I

# Foundations

# 1 | *Introduction*

In this chapter, we provide an overview of what this book is about, how it connects with what you likely already know about English grammar, and how each chapter is structured to lead you from learning new concepts and skills to applying those concepts and ultimately to designing your own research projects.

## 1.1 What This Book Is About

"Discourse syntax" is the cover term for the study of all aspects of syntactic form that we can only explain with reference to the surrounding discourse. The objects of study are syntactic forms, constructions, or phenomena that can only be fully accounted for by taking the surrounding discourse (also referred to as "text," regardless of written or spoken mode) into consideration. This is where this book is fundamentally different from a general introduction into English syntax, which first and foremost deals with the structure of English sentences without considering any surrounding discourse. For example, in an introductory English syntax class, one would discuss that in English the subject position cannot be left empty (hence we have "dummy subjects," like *there* or *it*), that the object comes after the verb, and that questions require subject–auxiliary **inversion**. One might also discuss that under certain circumstances the object may come first in the sentence and one might introduce the name for such a construction (**topicalization**). Example (1a), taken from the freely available Corpus of Contemporary American English (COCA; Davies 2008), illustrates this construction; Example (1b) would be its canonical syntax counterpart.

(1)  a. The second batch I only microwaved for 4 minutes covered and that seemed to work. (COCA, Blog, 2012)
     b. I only waved the second batch for 4 minutes covered and that seemed to work.

What one normally does not study in such a class is under which discourse conditions topicalization occurs, which can leave the impression that word-order variations like topicalization are simply a stylistic choice. But that is not the case! We cannot give a proper account of topicalization without specifying the discourse conditions that warrant it. The same holds for other constructions that you are probably already familiar with, like passivization, inversion, or left dislocation, which are all, in some way, non-canonical clauses, that is, clauses that are derived from more basic, or canonical, patterns through a change of word order or the addition of extra lexical material. Canonical and non-canonical patterns of a clause typically share the same propositional meaning (or **proposition**), which is to say that they underlie the same truth conditions. There are no circumstances under which only sentence (1a) would be true, but not (1b), and vice versa. The second kind of phenomena considered in discourse syntax are constructions and elements that cannot be described as variations of another pattern but whose very function is to hold the discourse together and weave connections beyond the sentence, such as **conjunctions** and **coordinators**. We refer to the first set of phenomena as *grammar in discourse* and the second as *grammar of discourse*. Discourse syntax is therefore a field of linguistic study that describes and investigates patterns of syntax in language use, with the focus on illuminating the role of the surrounding text, rather than on the role of the speaker's individual preferences or choices.

## 1.2 How This Book Connects with What You Already Know

Perhaps you are working with this book because it has been assigned as the textbook or supplementary reading for one of your classes. If that is the case, the chances are that you already have some knowledge of English syntax. You have probably studied parts of speech (nouns, verbs, adjectives, conjunctions, etc.), tests for the constituency of phrases (noun phrases, verb phrases, and so on) and functions they take in the clause (subject, object, adverbial/**adjunct**). You know that *before* in (2b) is a preposition, which makes the italicized sequence in (2b) a preposition phrase, while *before* in (2a) is a subordinator (conjunction), which makes the italicized sequence in (2a) no phrase at all.

(2)  a.  We've got about 10 weeks *before the trial* comes up in January.
       (COCA, Movies, 1996)
     b.  By its very definition, any expertise a juror gained *before the trial*
         cannot be extrinsic. (COCA, Academic, 2017)

You are likely familiar with the distinction between simple and complex
sentences and the functions that subordinate clauses can take. The *that*-
clause in (3a) is a content clause (traditionally also known as an object
clause), while the one in (3b) is a relative clause (modifying the noun *plan*).

(3)  a.  He said that the progress of the action plan will be reviewed by him
         every month. (COCA, Web, 2012)
     b.  Choose the plan that's right for you. (COCA, News, 2019)

You also probably know that English is a language that has the
requirement that the subject position be filled (in finite, or tensed,
clauses) and that this is the reason we have sentences like (4b), with a
dummy subject. What you may not have studied are the circumstances
under which speakers may choose to produce a sentence like (4a), with
the *what*-clauses serving as a subject, rather than the construction
known as **extraposition** in (4b).

(4)  a.  What had happened was clear. (COCA, Magazine, 1993)
     b.  It was perfectly clear what had happened. (COCA, Web, 2012)

You may also have heard that English is considered a strict word
order language. The function of a phrase is indicated by its position in
the clause rather than by a case-marking affix, as in other Germanic
languages. In German, unlike in English, the function of a phrase can be
expressed through morphology. For example, in (5), it doesn't matter if
we put the phrase *den Jungen* (the boy) in a preverbal or postverbal
position. The accusative case marking *-n* indicates that the phrase
functions as the direct object.

(5)  a.  Den Jungen kenne ich nicht.
         The$_{ACC}$ boy$_{ACC}$ know$_{1ST-PERSON-PRESENT}$ I not.
         "I don't know the boy"
     b.  Ich kenne den Jungen nicht.
         I know$_{1ST-PERSON-PRESENT}$ the$_{ACC}$ boy$_{ACC}$ not.
         "I don't know the boy"

English used to be like that. Old English, the earliest recorded form of
English (roughly from the fifth to the eleventh century), was a language in

which grammatical relations could be expressed through inflection. However, by around the twelfth century, much of the case inflection in Old English had become optional. How and exactly why this happened is a complicated question, due to the limited availability of data. What we do know is that this "deflexion" (Allen 2016) happened most rapidly in the northern parts of England, where there was close contact with Scandinavians. It seems, therefore, that language contact is an accelerating factor, if not the initiating one. The further loss of inflectional morphology during the Middle English period led to a decrease in flexibility in word order for **canonical sentences**, which ultimately paved the way for non-canonical patterns to be associated with specific communicative purposes. One example would be the increase of constructions that allow for non-agents to fill the subject position and become the entity that the sentence is "about" (also known as the **topic**), such as passives, cleft sentences, and middle constructions (*This jam spreads easily*). In other words, in a language with a strong sense of canonical syntax, non-canonical patterns have to be motivated, and, more often than not, that motivation lies in the surrounding text. As unlikely as it sounds: A language with strict word order, like Modern English, is the perfect ground to study syntax beyond the sentence boundary.

## 1.3 How This Book Is Structured

This book is divided into three parts: Part I: *Foundations* (Chapters 1 and 2) introduces the concept of canonical and non-canonical syntax in English and situates the book in the context of variationist linguistics – the idea that linguistic variation does not occur at random, but is highly structured and influenced by linguistic and extralinguistic factors. Of all those factors, we will focus on the role of the surrounding discourse of different registers and on **genre** conventions. As a reference model for linguistic terminology, we will use the *Cambridge Grammar of the English Language* (Huddleston & Pullum 2002), which also comes in a less comprehensive student version (Huddleston & Pullum 2005). Another grammar we will often refer to is the *Grammar of Spoken and Written English* (Biber et al. 2021), which provides rich usage data on grammatical features in four register varieties (conversation, fiction, news, and academic prose). There is also a student version of the previous edition (Biber et al. 1999) of this grammar (Biber, Conrad & Leech 2002).

Reference Grammars of English

There is a myriad of grammars of the English language. While they all, in theory, describe the same facts, they do not all have the same goal. Some grammars intend to provide guidance to learners, some resemble style guides, and some use rather idiosyncratic terminology. We are choosing the *Cambridge Grammar of the English Language* as our point of reference because it is a comprehensive, synchronic account of English grammar, written with the goal of incorporating "as many as possible of the insights achieved in modern linguistics" (Huddleston & Pullum 2002: xv), without assuming great familiarity with theoretical linguistics. Using the *Cambridge Grammar* as our **reference grammar** means that we will adopt its terminology along with the premise that the role of the linguist is to "describe and not prescribe" (Huddleston & Pullum 2002: 2). By contrast, we will use the *Grammar of Spoken and Written English* (henceforth *GSWE*, Biber et al. 2021) mostly as a resource on usage data. The *GSWE* is based on data from a proprietary **corpus** (40 million words of text representing four main register categories) and, along with a description of the linguistic system, also provides information, including quantitative data, on how a grammatical feature is used in a particular situational variety of English. The *GSWE* itself closely follows Quirk et al.'s *A Comprehensive Grammar of the English Language* (1985) in its terminology. An earlier version of the *GSWE* was published as the *Longman Grammar of Spoken and Written English* (Biber et al. 1999). As you can see, a lot of thought goes into the writing of grammars, and the analysis of grammar writing has become a linguistic field in its own right, called "grammaticography."

Part II: *Grammar in Discourse* (Chapters 3–5) focuses on grammatical phenomena *in* discourse and looks at how syntactic patterns that you are most likely already familiar with (like **topicalization** or **particle shift**) are realized in different discourse situations. The underlying assumption here is that the reason for choosing one syntactic option over another lies in the surrounding discourse. The three chapters in this part move from phenomena that affect the beginning of the sentence (such as any kind of fronting operation, Chapter 3), over phenomena in the core sentence (anything from subject to object position, Chapter 4), to complex sentence endings (any kind of construction that shifts material toward the end of the sentence, like extraposition, Chapter 5). If the names of these constructions don't mean anything to you at this point, don't worry, every construction that we highlight will be defined and illustrated with data from linguistic corpora (and we will also show you how to work with these corpora).

Part III: *Grammar of Discourse* (Chapters 6–9) looks at the grammar *of* discourse, in particular the way in which sentences are connected, and also discusses syntactic phenomena conditioned by or brought about by genre conventions. Chapter 6 deals with the most obvious way of connecting sentences, namely through extra linguistic material known as "**connectives**" (such as coordinators). Chapter 7 looks at how we can underspecify information in a given sentence (through the use of **pronouns** and elliptical constructions) because it refers to something already mentioned before. Chapter 8 introduces the concept of "**discourse markers**," a series of elements (not necessarily unified in their appearance or syntactic behavior) that have the function of structuring the discourse. Lastly, Chapter 9 goes beyond the local discourse and discusses the role that register or genres as varieties of discourse have for shaping the syntactic characteristics of a text. You will see that certain constructions and phenomena may be used not so much because of any relationship with the surrounding discourse, but because the text is part of a whole discourse situation, and the relationship between discourse participants or the purpose of the text may determine the use of syntactic constructions. For example, in scientific abstracts we have an overrepresentation of passive-**voice** constructions because in many scientific fields there is still a convention to make the object of inquiry (the thing that is studied) the subject of a sentence, rather than the person who led the inquiry (the **agent**).

We like clarity in the classes that we teach and have aimed to achieve the same in this book. Each chapter will start with a definition of learning outcomes for the chapter. Each chapter will then introduce core concepts and questions necessary for the subsequent discussion, such as non-canonical word order or discourse grammar and **cohesion**. This introductory part is followed by a discussion of two or three selected syntactic phenomena or constructions that illustrate the concept under discussion, plus one subsection presenting exemplary empirical work (mostly based on corpus data, but occasionally also on experimental data). That way, you will gain insight into what is being studied in a field without being overburdened with all the complexities around the issue right away. References come both from recent work and from classics in the field. The chapters conclude with a summary, recommendations for further reading, and two kinds of exercises: level-one exercises will help you practice your analytic skills by applying the concepts introduced in the chapter, and level-two exercises will ask you to create or interpret data and guide you toward thinking about designing your own research. Throughout the text we will let you know when you should be ready to take on which exercise with this study icon:

For these exercises, we do not presuppose any prior experience with corpus-linguistic methodology or statistics and we include practical information on carrying out corpus-based research (how to do it, how to present and interpret data, but also which problems to watch out for) throughout the book. These tips will be marked with the toolbox icon.

The chapters are rounded out with squibs on interesting, but adjacent questions of language usage, clearly set apart from the main text in boxes labeled "Good to Know," marked with the owl icon:

The index and glossary at the end will help you with studying specific concepts (terms that are printed in bold in the text when occurring for the first time have their own entry in the glossary). The index focuses on those pages where a concept is introduced or elaborated on. Overall, the chapter structure of the book makes it possible to cover the whole book in the course of one semester or to cover selected parts and use the book as a secondary textbook or resource book.

As the linguistic world we live in continues to develop, presenting us with new words, new modes of expression, and new communicative needs, we hope you will share our excitement about studying syntax beyond the sentence. It is our goal to empower you to pursue projects of your own that show that syntax is a lot more than a set of rules holding a sentence together.

## Further Reading

• The developing field of grammaticography is discussed in Ameka, Dench & Evans (2006). Articles in this edited volume deal with aspects like the role of linguistic theory in grammar writing and the distinction between native and non-native speakers.
• If you are interested in learning more about the language-internal and external factors that made English the strict word order language it is today, you will find the articles in *The Cambridge Handbook of English Historical Linguistics* (Kytö & Pahta 2016) useful, especially Cynthia Allen's article "Typological change: investigating loss of inflection in early English" (2016). The book also offers overviews on theoretical frameworks, such as historical pragmatics or generative grammar, and on methodologies, such as corpus linguistics and philological methods.

# 2 | Concepts, Data, and Methods

## 2.1 Introduction: Why Discourse Syntax?

In introductions to linguistics, we all learn that syntax is the study of rules that form sentences. If you are used to tree diagrams to visualize syntactic structures, you know that they never go beyond the boundary of a sentence. But we don't speak in isolated sentences (actually, we often don't speak in sentences at all) and syntactic phenomena do not stop at the sentence boundary. To demonstrate how strongly the structure of sentences is influenced by the surrounding discourse, let's look at the sentences in Figure 2.1, taken from the beginning of an op-ed in *The New York Times* (August 2020) and numbered arbitrarily. Let's put them in the order that seems most natural to you. Note that this text is an opinion piece – it does not recount a series of events. Therefore, in arranging the sentences, you cannot rely on your extra-linguistic knowledge of how certain types of events unfold (for example, we know that in a car accident the crash comes before anyone is taken to the hospital). Rather, you will apply your intuitive knowledge about discourse syntax. Keep track of the markers that you rely on for making your choice and write down the sequence of numbers that seems right to you.

Perhaps your thought process looks something like this: Sentence #6 does not make a good first sentence – a connective like *and* would typically not be the first word in a text. You also probably did not put sentence #4 first – a demonstrative pronoun like *that* needs to have an antecedent and it wouldn't be clear what *that* refers to if sentence #4 came first. Similarly, you probably ruled out sentences #1, #3, and #5 as potential first sentences because they have personal pronouns (*it, her, she*) whose reference would be equally unclear. Sentence #8 is an elliptical structure (there is no verb in the main clause), which points to this sentence not being the first sentence in this text either. This leaves us with sentences #2 and #7. Sentence #2 has an indefinite noun phrase as its subject (*Hundreds of thousands of*

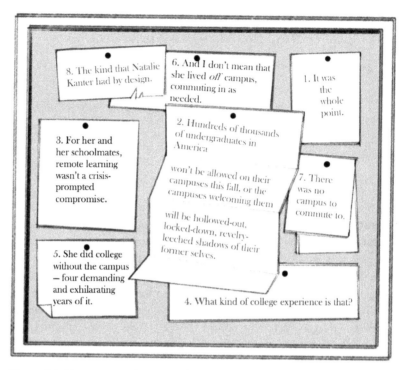

**Figure 2.1** Deconstructed paragraph
(Bruni, 2020)

*undergraduates in America*) and tells us something about them. This is achieved through the use of a **passive construction** (*won't be allowed*). Sentence #7 uses a dummy pronoun (*there*) as a subject and thus does not really establish an entity the text could be about. That makes #2 the most natural first sentence. Once the topic of students and their return-to-college experience is established, sentence #4 is the one that is the best continuation of that topic. Sentence #4 is in question format, and sentence #8 is the best answer to that question because it picks up on the same topic, choosing the same noun, *kind*, but this time with a definite article, *the*. And so on.

Go to Exercise 1 to see if your sequence matches the one of the original op-ed. There will also be the opportunity to reconstruct another paragraph.

It is this kind of syntax – constructions and grammatical devices that are chosen to integrate a sentence into the surrounding discourse – that we will focus on in this book. Studying discourse syntax means (a) making ourselves aware of options that speakers have to express an event or a statement, and (b) looking at the role the discourse has on choosing one of those options. For example, you probably know that almost all active voice sentences can be converted to passive voice sentences, but why is it that speakers choose one or the other option? You probably know that we can "front" almost any type of phrase in English, but why is it that speakers would choose a word order that is so different from what English normally looks like? On its own, a sentence like (2) sounds awkward, because it does not follow the canonical word order of English (Subject–Verb–Object), as exemplified in (1), but put into **context**, as in (3), the non-canonical word order is just right.

(1)  You would never soak lentils.
(2)  Lentils you would never soak.
(3)  A:  When you make white bean soup, you might want to soak your beans first so that they don't have to simmer so long.
     B:  What about lentils?
     C:  *Lentils, you would never soak first,* you just put them in the soup.

Studying discourse syntax, therefore, requires us to look at grammar beyond the question of what is canonical and what is not. What is non-canonical in an isolated sentence (e.g., the choice of passive voice) may be the preferred pattern in a specific discourse situation. "Discourse syntax" is thus the cover term for the study of all aspects of syntax that we can only explain with reference to the surrounding text, which itself is embedded in a situation. In this chapter you will learn how to investigate those patterns – the type of questions that are asked, the type of constructions that are looked at, the methodologies that are employed.

Good to Know: Discourse Syntax vs. Discourse Analysis

You may also have heard of the term discourse analysis, which applies to a different subfield of linguistics. In discourse analysis, the properties and patterns of different kinds of texts are investigated, the basic unit under investigation being then the entire text or discourse itself. Typical research questions in this field include how texts perform specific acts of communication (e.g., an apology, an invitation) or reflect issues of society (e.g., discourses of migration or discourses of sustainability), and how they receive their **coherence**.

As you just saw above, one concept that is central to the study of discourse syntax is the concept of **syntactic variation**. This may at first glance seem like a contradiction to what we said in Chapter 1, where we discussed English as a language with rather strict word order. However, it is precisely this strict word order that makes syntactic variation such a powerful tool in English.

Let's talk a little bit more about what we mean when we say "syntactic variation." Most speakers are probably more familiar with the concept of language variation in the domains of lexical choices or pronunciation. One person's *soda* is another person's *pop*. Dialects can also have distinctive grammar features. For example, some Southern dialects in the United States consistently make use of double modals (*might could*), as exemplified in (4), while speakers from other regions may never use this feature, and African American English uses invariant *be* as a marker of habitual aspect, as in (5), a line from a song by American songwriter will.i.am.

(4)    . . . we'll never live up to the impossible standards so many in the world have for us. But, for the first time in my life, I think we might could do it. (COCA, Blog, 2012)

(5)    All the time she be working working working (will.i.am, *Mona Lisa Smile* 2013)

We will not deal with dialects or other speaker-based variation in this book. Rather, we will look at syntactic choices speakers make based on the discourse situation. For example, the language used in spoken conversation among friends is quite different from the language used in newspaper articles. A grouping of language chosen in accordance with the discourse situation is referred to as a "**register**." Registers can be defined at a very high level (for example, the *GSWE* is based on the four registers: news writing, academic writing, fiction, and conversation) or more locally, as sub-registers (for example, news writing includes the sub-registers international news and business news). Register analysis is concerned with syntactic patterns and choices motivated by the discourse situation. For example, since newspapers report past events, the language used in newspapers shows a high number of past tense verbs and time adverbials, as in the sentence in (6).

(6) The storm *began Tuesday night*, with snow starting *first* in most areas and changing to a wintry mix, *then* ice, *then* drizzle, starting south of Chicago. *At 6 a.m.*, weather spotters throughout the area *reported* trace amounts of snow at O'Hare. (COCA, News, 2019)

Methodologically, it follows that register variation studies work with large corpora of data based on similar discourse situations. Register-based corpora typically consist of many excerpts from similar types of texts (including spoken texts), without much information about the speakers who produced them.

A note on our example sentences: Most sentences that we use for illustration in this book are taken from English language corpora, i.e., they are authentic attestations of the constructions we deal with, and not examples that we thought up. We do not want to imply that constructed sentences would not also work to illustrate a syntactic phenomenon, but we want you to get into the habit of working with corpus data, because for many research questions, quantitative data – how often a construction occurs – will be relevant. Section 2.4 will discuss in some detail how to access and gather data from a corpus. Individual search strategies for constructions, including some necessary shortcuts, will be presented in later chapters.

In this book, we will mostly be concerned with studying the role of the context in making linguistic decisions limited to the area of syntax, including, but not limited to, word order variation. As we have seen, one important component of the situation is the text itself, which for each and every sentence determines the precise contextual conditions at the moment of its use.

In the following, we will introduce core concepts and methodological considerations for the study of discourse-based syntactic variation. We will discuss several key contrasts that lead you step-by-step to an understanding of discourse syntax and the phenomena and research questions studied in this field: (a) sentences in isolation as opposed to discourse as a whole, (b) **context** vs. **co-text**, (c) **discourse type** and **register**, (d) **given** as opposed to **new information**, and (e) the difference between two perspectives on the relationship between syntax and discourse. We'll refer to these two approaches as the variationist vs. the text-linguistic perspective, following influential work by corpus linguist Douglas Biber (e.g., Biber 2012). We will also introduce you to methods of data gathering and presentation common in this field.

After reading this chapter, you will be able to:

- identify the different properties of a discourse and of the discourse situation (co-text and context);
- describe how discourse syntax is shaped by the distribution of information within the sentence;
- carry out first searches in a corpus for gaining data on natural language use and make decisions on how best to visualize your findings;
- develop a basic research design for each of the main two perspectives employed in the study of discourse (variationist and text-linguistic perspective).

## Concepts, Constructions, and Keywords

*complement clauses, context, corpora, co-text, discourse type, functional linguistics, given/new information, predictor variable, rate of occurrence, register analysis,* that-*omission, utterance, variationist/ text-linguistic approach*

## 2.2 Sentences vs. Utterances

So far, we've focused on the "syntax" part of discourse syntax. Let us now turn to the "discourse" part. Discourse might be understood either formally, as all language elements larger than the sentence, or, functionally, as any language unit serving a communicative purpose. Let us illustrate those two different meanings through an example. Imagine that somebody wants you to go and clean your room. That person might try to bring this event about by uttering a single sentence such as (7). The communicative purpose of the sentence would be quite clear. However, more often than not, a slightly longer sequence of sentences (let's assume for a moment that people speak in sentences) will be produced, perhaps something like the sequence in (8). By the formal definition, only (8) would constitute a discourse (because it is larger than a sentence), while from a functional, communicative point of view, both examples are units of language use with a communicative purpose and would therefore both constitute a discourse.

(7)    Go and clean your room.

(8)    Listen! I told you a hundred times. You need to clean your room. Please do it now!

For a clear definition of discourse and its relation to syntax, the problem therefore arises that, on the one hand, discourse can comprise just a single sentence, perhaps even less (for instance, a verbless phrase like *Never!*). On the other hand, when we see discourse as a communicative event, it comes to involve numerous and non-linguistic aspects, such as the interlocutors, their relationship, the mode of communication, the social and cultural background, and so forth. From a functional perspective, then, discourse is a very complex phenomenon to analyze. In this book, following a prominent approach in the field (based on early work by discourse linguist Deborah Schiffrin, e.g., Schiffrin 1990), we adopt a third view of discourse, focusing on sentences or other syntactic units together with their context of occurrence. We define discourse through **utterances**, which means that the sentence in (7) also qualifies as a (short) discourse.

Sentences from that point of view are called utterances: units of language structure bound to a given context. One and the same formal sentence easily gives rise to different utterances, in the sense that it is possible that the same sentence can be spoken, or written, or repeated, or quoted under different conditions. For instance, the same sentence *I told you a hundred times* can be thought of and used in many different utterances. Its ultimate communicative meaning can vary from being aggressive, ironic, or a lie, to a warning, and so on.

By the same logic, any sentence that has been used, or is likely to occur, as an utterance is bound to its discourse. For example, the sentences *I'll give you some money* and *I'll give it to you*, with *it* referring to *the money*, are likely to be uttered under different discourse conditions. The latter would more likely be used when money has already been talked about and the focus is now on the transfer. This is what discourse syntax is all about, viewing syntax as being discourse-driven, and it rests upon defining discourse as consisting of utterances.

"I'll give you some money."

Think of utterances as sentences anchored in specific discourse situations.

As we saw in Chapter 1, a sentence, whether simple or complex, is generally considered the largest unit of analysis in syntax. Within the sentence, we have a hierarchical structure of constituents (for example, NPs inside of PPs, which in turn can be inside VPs), but discourse is not made of elements that are part of such a systematic structural hierarchy. Instead, what connects pieces of discourse in the first place are semantic and pragmatic relations, which are expressed only partly via language. This is also why you have probably seen the structure of a sentence represented as some kind of diagram, but the structure of discourse is not represented in this way.

Within a discourse, every sentence is an utterance within the surrounding text, also called "co-text" (discussed further below), as well as the situational context. The text excerpt in (9) comes from an article in *USA Today* and compares the Japanese snowboarder Ayumo Hirano to Shaun White, an American snowboarder, who, like Hirano, began his career very young, at the age of 13, and became a professional at the age of 17.

(9)    Air apparent: Ayumu Hirano might challenge Shaun White
       Moments before he put down an X Games run that would make him
       the youngest medalist ever, Ayumu Hirano crashed hard enough to

crack his helmet. From 13 feet up, he hit the deck of the halfpipe before falling another 22 feet to the flat bottom. He was sore, getting the wind knocked out of him, but not concussed. At his first X Games, Hirano, then 14, could have easily walked away. The snowboarder would have plenty more chances to compete in an event he'd watched on DVD at home in Japan as a kid, his coaches told him. [...]. (*USA Today*, December 10, Axon 2013)

A longer piece of discourse such as this one is not free of what we might consider as structure. For example, the sequence of tenses and the interpretation of pronouns depend on each other, and information is built up gradually. In the last sentence the past perfect (*he'd watched*) is used, because the event that it expressed (Hirano watching a DVD when he was a kid) precedes the event that this excerpt is about (Hirano winning his first medal at an internationally broadcast extreme sports event). However, the interpretation of each sentence within the excerpt does not result from structural relationships based on a limited set of functions within a larger whole, like being a subject, object, or modifier in the sentence. Still, there are meaning relations across sentence boundaries, which often connect considerable stretches of discourse, that need to be interpreted. This is what readers or listeners can do by using information from the surrounding text or the discourse situation. For example, the first sentence in (9) refers to Hirano via the pronoun *he*, making use of the presence of a headline. The cues for the retrieval and connection of information within a discourse are therefore given within the sentence but their motivation often lies beyond the sentence. What kind of cues are available for constructing discourse? And how do speakers interpret them with reference to the discourse? These are the kind of questions that linguists seek to answer in the field of discourse syntax.

Before we move on to discuss in greater detail the properties of discourse and the discourse situation, you should go to Exercise 2 to apply the distinction between sentences and utterances.

While sentence structure follows rules that substantially limit the number of patterns that are grammatical, variation in the actual use of grammar in discourse is the rule rather than the exception. When speakers are asked to tell the same kind of story, for instance, a picture story, a cartoon, or a film, in all likelihood no two speakers choose exactly the same wording. Try it for yourself: How would you narrate what you see in the simple cartoon in Figure 2.2? Ask a friend or a classmate the same question. Do they pick the same words and sentences?

**Figure 2.2** Bunny cartoon

Apart from many individual preferences that go into a person's re-telling, there are also systematic reasons for presenting roughly the same content in one way or another. These principles are generally referred to as strategies for "packaging" information within the sentence. To explore this kind of variation in detail over the chapters to come, we need to keep the grammatical form of a sentence apart from its meaning. Strictly speaking, we only deal with a case of true syntactic variation when the basic meaning of two alternative grammatical realizations remains the same. As introduced in Chapter 1, this basic meaning of a sentence is called its proposition, referring to the truth value carried by the sentence. For example, the sentence *I gave you the money* is true under exactly the same conditions as those for the sentence *I gave the money to you*. The proposition mainly results from the relation of the verb to its core **arguments** (*I*, for example, being the agent of the act of giving, *you* being the recipient), which is here not affected by the change of sequence of the direct and the indirect object.

The separation of sentential meaning in the sense of the truth value and of the many other meanings that are also expressed by packaging information into grammar (attitudes, emotions, indirect intentions) is relevant for the study of discourse syntax because we are interested in options here that do not change the basic meaning of the sentence. Choosing one option is not motivated by a change in propositional meaning, but by the discourse situation. In that sense, looking at grammar in discourse means analyzing situated syntactic decisions. But what exactly determines the discourse situation of a sentence? There are several levels to consider here. First, there is the concrete surrounding, that is, preceding and subsequent, text, which is commonly referred to as the co-text. Second, there is also a wider kind of discourse context, namely the nature of the overall discourse (or, possibly, of just a discourse segment). This is the level of the type of discourse, which involves, for example, the choice of a certain rhetorical mode (e.g., narration or argumentation) or of a given genre (e. g., a blog entry, movie review, essay, and the like). More on the interaction of grammar and genres will be discussed in Chapter 9. In the broadest sense of the conditions that surround sentences as utterances, any discourse is placed within a given situation, commonly referred to as the proper context. This context is, for example, governed by the channel or medium, the relationship between the speaker and the hearer, a private or institutional setting, a specific topic or purpose of the discourse, the formality of the situation, and the like.

Situational varieties and their patterns of language use have their own area of research, which is the study of registers. A register analysis investigates linguistic features in functional varieties of language use. It takes place at different levels of specificity for classifying discourse, ranging from widely studied, rather general varieties, such as conversation, academic writing, or fiction, to specific sub-registers like article introductions or office hour consultations (e.g., Biber & Conrad 2019). Throughout this book, our discussion will highlight that register variation also plays a substantial role in the study of discourse syntax. Chapter 9 in particular examines the role of register and genre. However, you should note that, in this book, situational varieties are not the object of interest *per se*; instead, we are dealing with the use of grammar as governed by the discourse as a whole, that is, on all levels discussed above. This means that the focus of our analysis lies on the context-bound nature of grammatical constructions, not so much on specific situations, such as the situation you find yourself in right now, as a student who is reading this text (see Figure 2.3).

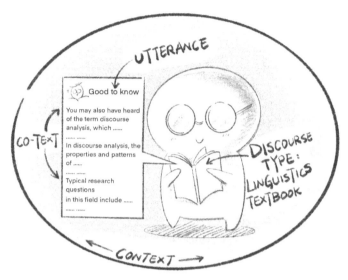

**Figure 2.3** Three levels of the discourse situation for sentences as utterances

Throughout this book you will see how elements of grammar or certain patterns of sentences depend on these different levels of the discourse situation, that is, how sentences become utterances. Often, the starting point for this discussion is the observation that a sentence follows a non-canonical syntactic pattern. As introduced in Chapter 1, a non-canonical clause is a clause that can be derived from a more basic pattern, that is, from the sentence that we would expect based on our knowledge of the general rules of English grammar. A deviation from the canonical pattern is usually motivated by reasons that lie in the discourse. For example, in English the object follows the verb, it does not precede it, so that a transitive verb will be followed by an object. Now, a sentence in which the object comes before the subject (as is the case in (2), *Lentils you would never soak*) will have to be motivated. The same holds for the passive construction (*Lentils are never soaked*), which enables you to drop the agent of an event and turns the former object into the subject. Constructions like these result from a decision about which of the verb's arguments should come first and in which order and how densely you want the informational content to be packaged. Looking at sentences as utterances therefore means looking at the reasons for their variant forms in the surrounding discourse, and not just in the rules of grammar.

## 2.3 Discourse Syntax and the Functional Tradition in Linguistics

The interest in syntactic usage dates back quite far in the history of linguistics. It came up with an early movement of what is now-adays called "functionalism" in linguistics, which is commonly seen in opposition to *form*-based approaches to syntax. The origins lie in the work of some linguists working in Prague in the 1920s, who referred to the packaging of information in the sentence as the "functional sentence perspective" (Newmeyer 2001). With that, the Prague School linguists were, in a way, syntacticians with an early interest in utterances. For example, they were already discussing that given and new material in the sentence is not distributed randomly, but that information which is familiar to the addressee (which they termed "thematic") tends to come first, while new information (referred to as "rhematic") is presented later in the sentence (a thorough discussion of the distribution of **given and new information** follows in Chapters 3 to 5). This characteristic sequence of information was found to apply to many languages, especially those with a flexible word order system, such as Russian or Czech.

The functional view of syntax emphasizes that syntactic patterns are not arbitrary because they are a means of communication. We saw above that syntax is not self-contained, but substantially influenced by how it is situated in a discourse situation. If syntax responds to and is shaped by the surrounding discourse, we will expect that it is not rigid, but will allow for some kind of variation, even in a language like English. If it were random, linguistic variation would indeed not be economical. Let's turn to an example for illustration: Examples (10) and (11) have similar propositions (something is located between $x$ and $y$), expressed by two different sequential arrangements of sentence elements. In (10), where speaker B's statement is a canonical English sentence, the location follows the grammatical subject, while in (11) its position is in front of the subject:

(10)  A:  Where is Sherman, Connecticut?
      B:  Sherman's about halfway between Long Island Sound and Massachusetts, right on the state line that we share with New York. (COCA, Spoken, 1999)

(11)    In the heart of the South Pacific Ocean, just about halfway between
        South America and Australia, lies a very small island called Hikueru.
        (COCA, Fiction, 2010)

According to a functional perspective on syntax, the grammatical
subject *Sherman* in (10) is positioned early in the sentence because it
 has been introduced in the co-
text, that is, in the preceding inter-
rogative (*Where is Sherman, . . . ?*)
and is therefore given information. By contrast, in the sentence
in (11), which is the very first sentence of a fictional narrative, there
is no previous information on the
story available. With this lack of
co-text, the sentence sets the scene
for the discourse: The reader gets
to know that the story will take
place on *a very small island called Hikueru*. In this position in the
discourse, the grammatical subject (*a very small island*) carries new
information, which is why the noun phrase is moved to the end of the
sentence. We could also say that this sequence is functional because it
corresponds to how readers will "see" the scene in their minds.

Good to Know: The Functional Tradition in Theories of
Grammar

The distribution of information and the discourse function of sentences
are the focus in various syntactic theories with a usage-related component, adding interesting aspects to the discussion of discourse syntax.
For example, the theory of Systemic Functional Grammar (e.g.,
Fontaine 2013) emphasizes the importance of the social function of
language, adding to the level of the proposition (called "experiential"
meaning) and the co-text ("textual" meaning) a third level that highlights the so-called "interpersonal" meaning of an utterance, that is, the
relation between the speaker and the addressee. The framework of
Functional Discourse Grammar (e.g., Keizer 2015) also emphasizes

the relevance of interpersonal relations but, in addition, contributes the idea that the social functions of discourse are expressed in specific components, in what is called "discourse acts" and "moves." For example, adverbials in initial position regularly occur within the move of opening a discourse, like in (12), or they continue a move, like in (13). By contrast, the same adverb will simply relate to the semantic level, that is, be a part of the proposition, when in non-initial position, as in (14).

(12) When he was warm and twenty-something, the Grey Star had been a garden of delights. *Then* responsibility fell on his shoulders. (COCA, Fiction, 2003)

(13) At least Blake's predecessors, the flamboyant Schnellenberger and the colorless Gary Gibbs, brought some solid credentials to the table. *Then again*, if high qualifications are any barometer of future success, it makes all the sense in the world that Oklahoma decided on Blake. (COCA, Magazine, 1996)

(14) [...] he became fascinated with death. He *then* became a medical doctor. (COCA, Spoken, 2015)

Cognitive Grammar argues that syntactic choices are often grounded in the structure of human perception. A cognitive view highlights that different sentence patterns direct the attention to different elements within the sentence (technically, this process is called "profiling"). For example, in the sentence in (15) the event, a trolley colliding with a car, is expressed as a change that also affects the trolley. In one reading of the sentence, the event could be that Herman Strodmann is driving the BMW; in another, he could be the initiator, acting upon the trolley (*he hit the brakes and smashed the trolley into the BMW*):

(15) Herman Strodmann hit the brakes just as the trolley smashed into the BMW and rode up over it. (COCA, Fiction, 2015).

Despite this ambiguity, the sentence in (15) is made possible by the argument structure of the verb *smash*, which allows the profiling of the theme as an instrument.

Having discussed that a functionalist view on syntax has quite a long and varied tradition, we now turn to reporting actual research in this area, looking at two fundamentally different approaches that integrate discourse into the analysis, and to the basic procedures for gathering usage-based data from a corpus.

We saw above that the distinction between "given" and "new" information can lead to different syntactic patterns. We will talk more about this in Chapter 3. For now, you should be able to handle exercises 4 and 5, which build on that contrast.

## 2.4  Gathering Data for the Study of Discourse Syntax

As the discussion so far has highlighted, evidence in the field of discourse syntax must be based on the actual use of sentences. One way of gathering usage-based data is to pull sentence attestations from linguistic corpora. Other methods of collecting data include conducting surveys or eliciting data experimentally, but we will focus on corpus data here. In principle, any collection of utterances from real language use is called a *corpus* (from the Latin word for "body") in linguistics. However, these days the term usually refers to a searchable electronic database of texts. Corpora (the Latin plural of the word "corpus") in this sense are collections of written texts and/or transcripts of spoken language in digital form, which can usually be searched by way of a specific interface. They can be collections of full texts, but more often they comprise text excerpts. Usually, corpora are pre-analyzed in some way. For example, in most linguistic corpora words are tagged as belonging to a specific part-of-speech category by running them through specific tagging software. A large and well-known group of corpora for English, which we also use for illustration throughout the book, is available at the online interface English-corpora.org (Davies 2004–). The website provides free access, for example, to the British National Corpus (BNC), the Corpus of Contemporary American English (COCA), or the Corpus of Historical American English (COHA). In this book, we mainly use examples from COCA (and sometimes from other corpora from that interface), but note that new corpora are constantly becoming available (for example, in 2020, when the world started fighting the novel coronavirus, a new corpus consisting of texts about the virus and COVID-19 was added to the corpus site at English-corpora.org).

Using a corpus or corpus interface, you can type in an individual word or a sequence of words, such as the highlighted sequence *think that*, illustrated in the screenshot in Figure 2.4. You can also expand each attestation to see the surrounding co-text. The interface will also tell you which year and register the example comes from (in Figure 2.4, all attestations are from blogs). As you can see right away, it is much easier to search for something that is present (the verb *think* followed by a clause beginning with the **complementizer** *that*) than for something that is absent (the verb *think* followed by a clause in which *that* has been omitted).

Most corpora also allow you to search for syntactic categories ("parts of speech", or POS, search), as well as specific lexical items. For example, you might be interested in checking the occurrence of *that* after any verb, not just after *think*. The POS search is also helpful in the case of homonyms, of which English has a lot. For example, you might wish to find out how often and in which registers *impact* is used as a verb (some people still argue that it cannot be used in that way – they would be surprised to see how often it is). A corpus like COCA allows you to add a part-of-speech tag to a search term, giving you the ability to look at occurrences of a word only when it is used as that part of speech. Instead of looking for *impact*, which is what led to the result list shown in Figure 2.5, you'd be searching for <impact_v*>, or, to include all forms of the verb *impact* (e.g., *impacts, impacted, impacting*) for <IMPACT_v*>. If this all seems technical and complicated, don't worry. Web-based corpora usually provide documentation on how to use them and there are also videos available on YouTube. For working with part-of-speech tags, see the toolbox at the end of this section.

In addition to giving you attestations, corpora also often provide you with quantitative data and charts. The image in Figure 2.6, for example, includes frequency information – both in raw numbers (second column) and in occurrences per 1 million words (fourth column and bar chart). You can see that *impact* as a verb occurs most frequently in web-based registers and in academic writing and that it is becoming more and more frequent.

However, you should always go through your attestations to see if there are any false positives. Usually some form of **data cleaning** is

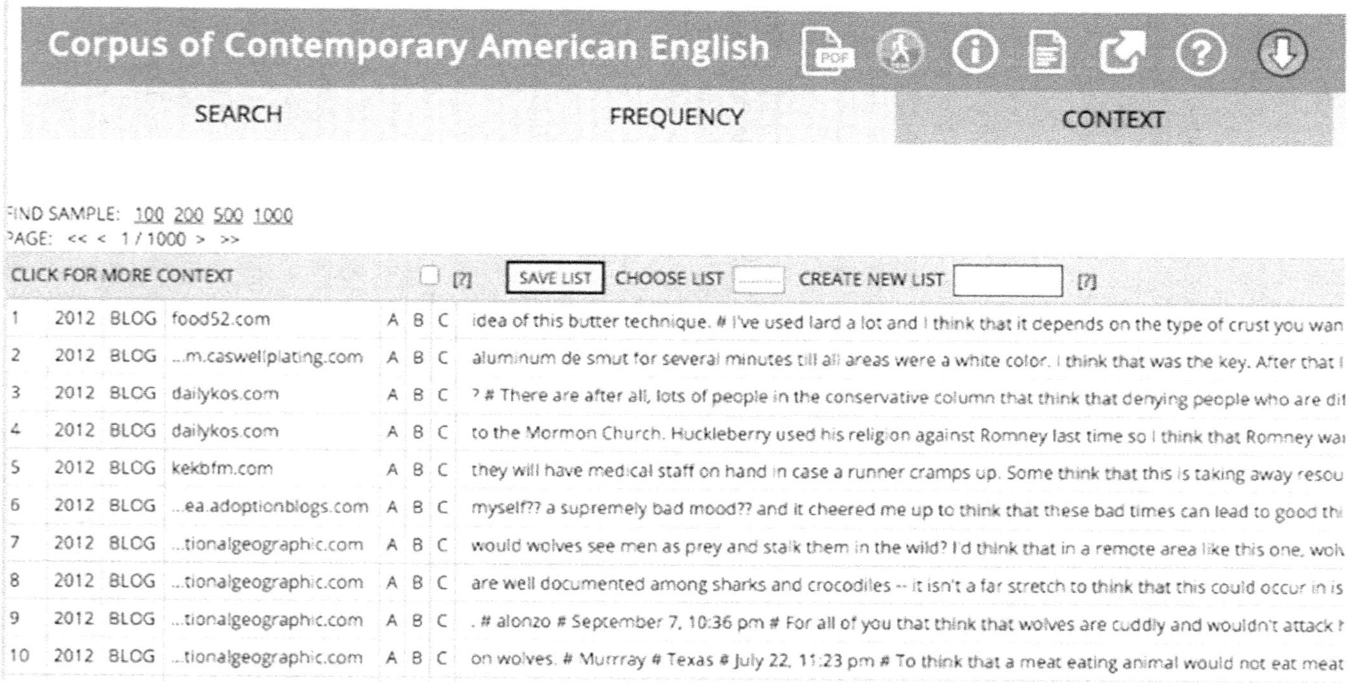

**Corpus of Contemporary American English**

SEARCH  FREQUENCY  CONTEXT

FIND SAMPLE: 100 200 500 1000
PAGE: << < 1 / 1000 > >>

CLICK FOR MORE CONTEXT

[ ] [?]   SAVE LIST   CHOOSE LIST [ ]   CREATE NEW LIST   [ ]

| # | Year | Source | Site | A B C | Context |
|---|------|--------|------|-------|---------|
| 1 | 2012 | BLOG | food52.com | A B C | idea of this butter technique. # I've used lard a lot; and I think that it depends on the type of crust you wan |
| 2 | 2012 | BLOG | ...m.caswellplating.com | A B C | aluminum de smut for several minutes till all areas were a white color. I think that was the key. After that I |
| 3 | 2012 | BLOG | dailykos.com | A B C | ? # There are after all, lots of people in the conservative column that think that denying people who are dif |
| 4 | 2012 | BLOG | dailykos.com | A B C | to the Mormon Church. Huckleberry used his religion against Romney last time so I think that Romney wa |
| 5 | 2012 | BLOG | kekbfm.com | A B C | they will have medical staff on hand in case a runner cramps up. Some think that this is taking away resou |
| 6 | 2012 | BLOG | ...ea.adoptionblogs.com | A B C | myself?? a supremely bad mood?? and it cheered me up to think that these bad times can lead to good thi |
| 7 | 2012 | BLOG | ...tionalgeographic.com | A B C | would wolves see men as prey and stalk them in the wild? I'd think that in a remote area like this one, wol |
| 8 | 2012 | BLOG | ...tionalgeographic.com | A B C | are well documented among sharks and crocodiles -- it isn't a far stretch to think that this could occur in is |
| 9 | 2012 | BLOG | ...tionalgeographic.com | A B C | . # alonzo # September 7, 10:36 pm # For all of you that think that wolves are cuddly and wouldn't attack k |
| 10 | 2012 | BLOG | ...tionalgeographic.com | A B C | on wolves. # Murrray # Texas # July 22, 11:23 pm # To think that a meat eating animal would not eat meat |

Figure 2.4 COCA screenshot highlighting search item

FIND SAMPLE: 100 200 500 1000

PAGE: << < 34 / 34 > >>

| | | | | | | | | |
|---|---|---|---|---|---|---|---|---|
| | | | ☐ [?] | SAVE LIST | | CHOOSE LIST ------- | CREATE NEW LIST | [?] |

| CLICK FOR MORE CONTEXT | | | | | | |
|---|---|---|---|---|---|---|
| 3301 | 1991 | SPOK | CNN_Crossfire | A | B | C throughout the country and when you try to put social issues into the military you impact readiness in this country |
| 3302 | 1991 | SPOK | PBS_Newshour | A | B | C everyone pay their fare share, and I think that's an issue that could impact the automotive industry quite positively |
| 3303 | 1991 | SPOK | PBS_Newshour | A | B | C conference were at a very delicate stage and the administration needed time to review what impact the loan guara |
| 3304 | 1991 | SPOK | PBS_Newshour | A | B | C : Speaking through interpreter Thank you. MS-WOODRUFF: Tomorrow, we will explore what impact the President's |
| 3305 | 1991 | SPOK | PBS_Newshour | A | B | C New York. What do you think this case is going to have, what impact this case is going to have in the work place, its |
| 3306 | 1991 | SPOK | CNN_NewsSat | A | B | C When we come back, I'd like to raise the question of what impact all this will have right here in Washington where |
| 3307 | 1991 | SPOK | ABC_Nightline | A | B | C to be a television critic. Comment for me for a moment now on what impact you think is being made by this extrac |
| 3308 | 1991 | SPOK | ABC_Nightline | A | B | C wants them to say KOPPEL Did you have any way of gauging at all what impact the bombing is having on morale? A |
| 3309 | 1991 | SPOK | ABC_Nightline | A | B | C of the end of the war, that means our surrender, you know what impact it gave on the women's lives in Japan, the |
| 3310 | 1991 | MAG | Smithsonian | A | B | C the letter explained. " Inappropriate behavior on the part of young children can negatively impact the experience. |

**Figure 2.5** COCA screenshot for the word *impact* (noun or verb)

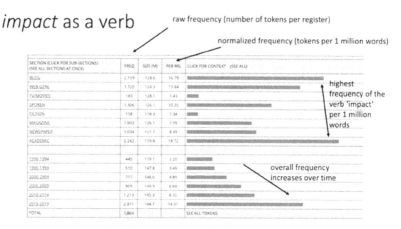

**Figure 2.6** Annotated COCA screenshot for *impact* as a verb

required. For example, some false hits found for the verb *smash* in COCA include a reference to the NBC series "Smash" or the use of the expression *SMASH!* in fiction. After deleting such cases from your set of attestations, the attested sentences from the corpus are ready for an analysis as attested utterances. For example, they could now be analyzed in terms of the distribution of information within them, something we did with the corpus attestations (10) and (11); as being specific discourse acts or moves, as we did with the sentences (12) to (14); or for the grammatical subject co-occurring with *smash*, which is what we looked at when discussing the use of *smash* in (15). Also problematic are mistakes in a corpus (which you will see in a few examples in later chapters). There may be spelling errors (for example, if someone misspells the word *occasion* as *occassion,* it won't come up in a search for *occasion*) and disfluencies, which can often be observed in corpora from spoken language. For example, a speaker might self-correct the choice of verb, resulting in a sentence like *He gave sent me the money*, which, in isolation, everybody would rate as ungrammatical. (You may be familiar with marking an ungrammatical sentence with a preceding asterisk and a semantically not well-formed sentence with a preceding question mark.) More information on the searches for specific constructions in a corpus and on analyzing the corresponding results will be provided in Section 2.5 and also later in the book.

## Part-of-speech Tagging in a Corpus

One major difference between data from linguistic corpora and data that you might compile yourself by just amassing text is that linguistic corpora are pre-analyzed. At a minimum, corpora are annotated for part-of-speech information by software referred to as a tagger. (The error rate is estimated at 1–3 percent.) There are different tagger applications and they all use different labels, but what they have in common is that they go well beyond the nine or twelve major part-of-speech classes you may be familiar with from an introductory syntax class (verbs, nouns, adjectives, modals, conjunctions, etc.). For example, the CLAWS tagger ("Constituent Likelihood Automatic Word-Tagging System"), versions of which were used to tag the British National Corpus (BNC) and the Corpus of Contemporary American English (COCA), has a set of about 60 different tags, which can be quite specific. The tagset used for COCA includes, for example, tags for singular common nouns (NN1), plural common nouns (NN2), singular proper nouns (NP1), singular weekday nouns (NPD1), and singular locative nouns (NNL1). There are tags for subordinating conjunctions in general (CS), as well as for particular conjunctions (CST for *that*, CSW for *whether*), and tags for different morphological forms of verbs, including VVG for the *-ing* participle, VVD for past tense verbs and VVN for the past participle. The tag label is not always intuitive (for example, the tag for *not* and *n't* is XX), which is why it is important that you look up the tag list for the corpus that you are working with. Some corpora, such as the current version of COCA or the BNC, will also allow you to select tags from a drop-down menu, which means that you don't have to memorize any tags, as illustrated below:

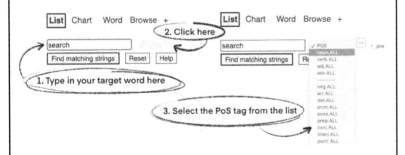

Lancaster University, where the CLAWS tagger was developed, provides free access to a web-based version of the tagger, which you can use for small portions of text (https://ucrel.lancs.ac.uk). A sentence like [*The bunny dreamt of eating the carrot*] tagged by CLAWS comes out as [The_AT0 bunny_NN1 dreamt_VVD of_PRF eating_VVG the_AT0 carrot_SENT ._PUN]. For larger portions of text, you would need a license – or you can rely on an existing corpus.

## 2.5 Two Approaches for Studying the Relationship of Syntax and Discourse

In the following section, we will explore two common approaches to examining the interaction of grammar and discourse. The main difference lies in the research goal and object of analysis. If one is mainly interested in syntax and in why one way of expressing things is chosen over another, the object of analysis will be a specific construction. For example, one might look at the discourse to figure out why speakers sometimes choose the **get-passive** over the *be*-passive in English. We will call this the **variationist approach**. Alternatively, one might be mostly interested in the syntactic properties of a specific discourse type or register. For example, one might ask how web-based news writing is different from traditional news writing. We will call this the **text-linguistic approach**. There are other labels one could use, but for the sake of consistency, we will stick with the terms variationist and text-linguistic in this book.

Depending on the research goal that is pursued, the research design and data analysis will be different. Let's illustrate this with an example. For a construction as illustrated in (16), you will find that the frequency of the construction varies a lot by discourse type.

(16)    "*This guy* he maybe come back and run this ranch?" said Madelaine. (COCA, Fiction, 2000)

Left-dislocation, the construction illustrated in (16), is a phenomenon that mostly occurs in spoken discourse. This observation is a result of looking at the occurrence of topicalization in different contexts –

employing a text-linguistic perspective. To see this, we have to compare the use of the same construction in different contexts. By contrast, other phenomena of word order are better understood by comparing their occurrences to those of a competing variant. For instance, the placement of the indirect object directly after a ditransitive verb is more plausibly studied by collecting data that includes both variants of the placement of the object, that is, comparing, for example, *give somebody money*, as in (17a), with the alternative placement, *giving money to somebody*, as shown by (17b).

(17)   a.   Why are you giving this guy money?
      b.   Why are you giving money to this guy who subsequently is arrested for killing your husband? (COCA, Spoken, 2002)

In all likelihood, the discourse will play a role in determining which placement is chosen. In (17b), the placement of *this guy* underlines the relevance of the indirect object for the following discourse. Indirect object movement is therefore likely to occur when the indirect object has greater importance in the discourse. To test this assumption in a project requires a research design in which the discourse is not the object of investigation, but potentially predicts a certain pattern of variation.

To reiterate: A project in which discourse has the role of predicting syntactic variation, but is not the proper object of the analysis itself, is a study of syntactic variation, also called a *variationist* research design. In research of this kind, the ultimate objects of investigation are two (or possibly more) syntactic variants: active and passive voice, *get*-passive and *be*-passive, subordinate clauses with and without *that*, the *of*-genitive and the *'s*-genitive, *because* followed by a clause and *because* followed by just a noun (there is more on this particular construction in Chapter 9). On the other hand, if the usage of grammar is studied as a characteristic set of features of a particular type of discourse, the primary objects of investigation are texts and a *text-linguistic* research design is applied.

Let us turn to a simple example to see how the research procedure will be different. It is well known that speakers of English often omit the complementizer *that* in informal speech, but tend to maintain it in more formal writing, such as in academic writing. Examples (18) and (19) show the two variants:

(18)    [...] he argued Park was not strong enough. (COCA, Spoken, 2014)

(19)    Ifenthaler, Eseryel, and Ge (2012) argued that learning in the twenty-
        first century must challenge students to become innovative [...].
        (COCA, Academic, 2015)

To test our assumption that there is an effect of the medium (**written vs.
spoken language**) and the formality of the discourse on the omission of
the complementizer, we need of course more usage-based data. In this
case, a variationist study (since our object of investigation is a particular syntactic construction, along with its competitor), our data set
should consist of sentences from both formal and more informal contexts. We want to figure out in which kind of discourse speakers or
writers are more likely to omit the complementizer *that* and in which
kinds they are likely to keep it. We thus need corpus-based findings
from at least two registers that differ in formality. Data like this can
come from a corpus that has data from different registers or, for
example, from a usage-based reference grammar, like the *GSWE*
(Biber et al. 2021). One such set of results, based on a sample of
3,000 *that*/Ø-clauses from the *GSWE* corpus, is shown in Table 2.1.

The data in Table 2.1 documents that the formality of the register is
indeed a reasonable predictor for the omission of *that* in different kinds
of discourse: Only 14 percent of the **complement clauses** in conversation contain a complementizer, compared to 73 percent in news writing
and 94 percent in academic discourse. Since we are interested in a
syntactic choice, that is, the variation of *that* vs. **that-omission**, we
should illustrate the outcome as *proportional frequencies*.
Proportions are already indicated as percentages in the table; the
corresponding chart should visualize the preference for one variant
over the other, with the difference in register being an independent
**variable**, or the predictor. In this kind of chart (also known as a
stacked column chart), the proportions are best given within a
single column for each register, which is what you see in Figure
2.7. In a proportional frequency chart, the numbers always add up
to 100 percent. The same kind of information could also be presented in three pie charts (data in a pie chart always adds up to
100 percent, which is characteristic of visual representations of
insights from a variationist study).

Table 2.1 *Data on complementizer omission in three types of discourse*

|  | Conversation | News discourse | Academic discourse |
| --- | --- | --- | --- |
| verb + *that* | 141 (14 %) | 733 (73 %) | 940 (94 %) |
| verb + Ø [no complementizer] | 859 (86 %) | 267 (27 %) | 60 (6 %) |
| Total | 1,000 (100 %) | 1,000 (100 %) | 1,000 (100 %) |

Source of data: Biber 2012.

Figure 2.7, with the three registers as independent variable on the horizontal (or *x*-) axis and the proportions of the two variants shown on the vertical (or *y*-) axis, illustrates the preference for the omission of a complementizer in conversation, and the much higher likelihood of its retention in the context of academic and news discourse.

With the registers being the predictor, the data in Table 2.1 and the chart in Figure 2.7 constitute a case of syntactic variation. What this research design does not look at is the actual pattern of usage in discourse, that is, the frequency of the variants in each kind of context. The reason for this is that the data set that is used is not one that can tell us in which register *that*-clauses, or *that*-less clauses, are overall more frequent. For example, based on other sources, but counter to what Table 2.1 suggests at first sight, the mere occurrence of complement clauses retaining *that* is more than twice as high in newspapers as it is in academic prose: 3,440 compared to 1,260 occurrences per million words in the corpus on which the *GSWE* is based (Biber 2012: 15). This difference is due to the overall higher frequency of complement clauses in the news register. Table 2.1 and Figure 2.7, following a variationist research design, therefore only highlight that once a *that*-clause occurs, the preference for *that*-retention will be stronger in academic discourse than in news. It would be wrong to conclude from Table 2.1 that academic discourse has more complement clauses introduced by *that* than the other registers.

The other approach to studying an interaction of syntactic form and discourse is to treat it as a case of text-linguistic variation. This type of

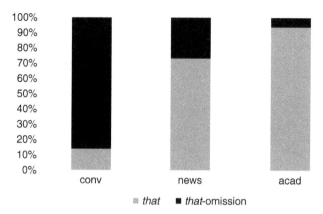

**Figure 2.7** Proportions of complementizer omission in three registers of English
Data is from Biber 2012.

research on syntactic usage has different varieties of discourse as its primary focus of interest and looks at the density, that is, frequency, of occurrence of certain grammatical features. The frequencies must be calculated as *rates* of occurrence, whereby the frequency of a given grammatical feature is determined relative to the length of a text or the size of a corpus. This process, known as normalization (see the Toolbox below) allows us to compare frequency rates rather than raw or proportional frequencies.

Calculating Normalized Rates of Occurrence

Text samples or sub-corpora often vary considerably in length. COCA, for example, is quite balanced at the highest level of register and contains roughly the same number of words from spoken language, fiction, newspaper, magazine, and academic writing, but within these registers the composition of sub-corpora may vary considerably. For example, in 2020, the sub-corpus for local news was about three times as large as the one for editorial writing. In order to compare frequencies across different registers, as one would do in a text-linguistic study, we have to "normalize" them, which means that we compute them at a rate per a certain number of words. In a large corpus, we often note the occurrence rate per one million words.

The general formula for this computation is the following:

(raw count ÷ total word count) × reference size in number of words

Example: If we look at the frequency of the conjunctive adverb *however* in different sub-corpora of news writing based on COCA, we find that there are 2,169 tokens in a sub-corpus of editorial writing (4.8 million words) and 3,498 tokens in a sub-corpus of local news (13.8 million words). In order to compare those numbers, we have to normalize them. Using the formula above, we calculate the rates of occurrence per 1 million words for both sub-corpora:

Editorial writing: (2169 ÷ 4,800,000) × 1,000,000 = 451.88

Local news: (3498 ÷ 13,800,000) × 1,000,000 = 253.48

We can now easily see that, relatively speaking, *however* occurs more frequently in editorial writing than in local news (which will not come as a surprise, considering that *however* is used to express a writer's stance).

With a smaller corpus size, it is common to normalize to a rate per one hundred or per one thousand words, accordingly:

(raw count ÷ total word count) × 100

or

(raw count ÷ total word count) × 1000

Note that you should never inflate the size of your corpus in calculating the frequency rate. If your corpus only has 1,000 words and your target construction occurs twice, it would be appropriate to say that the frequency rate is 2 per 1,000, but not that it is 2,000 per 1 million words, even though mathematically both express the same ratio.

Tip: If you use COCA, the "chart" view of your search results will compare the normalized rate (occurrences per 1 million words) for you, as you can see in the third column of the screen shot in Figure 2.8.

| SECTION | FREQ | SIZE (M) | PER MIL |
|---|---|---|---|
| NEWS:Misc | 8448 | 31.7 | 266.15 |
| NEWS:News_Intl | 1871 | 6.3 | 295.90 |
| NEWS:News_Natl | 2800 | 11.5 | 242.96 |
| NEWS:News_Local | 3498 | 13.8 | 253.03 |
| NEWS:Money | 2517 | 8.7 | 288.46 |
| NEWS:Life | 4320 | 20.3 | 213.28 |
| NEWS:Sports | 3605 | 19.2 | 188.21 |
| NEWS:Editorial | 2169 | 4.8 | 452.11 |

**Figure 2.8** COCA screenshot of chart view

Text-linguistic research is equally interested in the connection of syntax and discourse, and rates of occurrence are good evidence of the close connection between discourse and syntax as well. However, the focus is not on variation within the grammar, but on variation among different types of texts. Text-linguistic research examines which constructions are typical of which type of discourse and thus has properties of discourse as its ultimate object of investigation. For example, comparing conversation and academic prose, the *GSWE* describes higher rates of occurrence for passives or some other non-canonical constructions in academic texts while, for example, noun phrase tags (*They are alright, the kids?*) or *wh*-clefts (*What I need is some good news*) are typical features of conversations (Biber et al. 2021: 948).

The text-linguistic approach is also generally applied in studies of register. It is based on comparing the relative frequency of a feature in different types of discourse, with the aim of finding out in which register a feature is more "pervasive," in the sense that the feature under investigation occurs with some frequency throughout the text (following Biber & Conrad 2019). According to this approach, the texts are therefore the primary objects of our observations, which, with regard to most features, differ in typical distributions of an individual feature. Such an approach is necessary for anyone who works with corpora that are built from text excerpts. Only pervasive features are likely to be represented in text excerpts. For example, a salutation like *Dear Ms. Franklin* may be highly characteristic of letters, but it is not a pervasive feature of letters. In fact, it typically occurs only once per letter. A corpus constructed of letter excerpts is not necessarily likely to include many salutations. By contrast, second-person pronouns (*you, your*) will occur throughout a letter and may constitute a pervasive feature. However, while studying a register means looking at all features with a characteristic distribution, the focus of discourse syntax is somewhat more limited, being only about the occurrence of the syntactic phenomena under investigation. Nonetheless, findings about the textual variation of these phenomena contribute to the analysis of registers and genres (see Chapter 9 for more details on register-related effects).

Returning to the case of complementizer omission, there are also detailed results on the register distribution of *that*-clauses, based again on data from the *GSWE* corpus. The frequencies presented in Table 2.2 show, on the one hand, that complement clauses are overall more pervasive in news discourse and in conversation than in scholarly writing. On the other hand, you will note that there is a different picture for the respective occurrences of verb + *that*-clauses and verb + Ø-clauses in the three registers: for verb + *that*-clauses, conversation and academic discourse are closer, and for verb + Ø-clauses, news and academic texts are more similar. A corresponding chart must therefore highlight the difference among registers in total, but also separately for each construction, which is what you see in Figure 2.9.

Table 2.2 *Rates of occurrence\* of verb +* that-*clauses in three types of discourse*

|  | Conversation | News discourse | Academic discourse |
|---|---|---|---|
| verb + *that* | 890 | 3,440 | 1,260 |
| verb + Ø | 5,400 | 1,250 | 80 |
| Total | 6,290 | 4,690 | 1,349 |

\* Per 1 million words. Data is from Biber 2012.

The chart in Figure 2.9 – a comparative column chart – visualizes a case of text-linguistic variation, regarding both the occurrence of the feature of *that*-clauses in general (the columns in dark grey), and of *that*-retention and *that*-omission, in particular (columns in black and light grey). Each register thus constitutes a context which we analyze for the occurrence of complement clauses. With regard to the differences among texts, a striking difference is that, while complement clauses are overall most pervasive in conversation, complement clauses with *that*-retention are most pervasive in news.

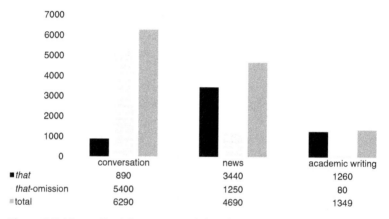

|  | conversation | news | academic writing |
|---|---|---|---|
| ■ *that* | 890 | 3440 | 1260 |
| *that*-omission | 5400 | 1250 | 80 |
| ▓ total | 6290 | 4690 | 1349 |

**Figure 2.9** Normalized frequencies of *that*-clauses in three registers Based on Table 2.2.

Taking both approaches together, the patterns that we found tell us something both about the construction, as predicted by the discourse context, and about the three kinds of discourse as an object of investigation by itself. Now that we have isolated patterns, the next task will be to find explanations for the patterns that we observed. These will again refer to properties both of the construction and of the discourse. For example, a relevant property of conversation is that the sentences are generally shorter. Therefore, we may not expect many complement clauses in the first place. On the other hand, we know that in conversations people often talk about their and other people's opinions, which means that we have a relatively high number of verbs like *think, say,* and *believe*, which are all typically followed by a complement clause. These verbs make the entire construction with a complement clause overall more predictable and *that*-omission in conversation therefore more likely. In news discourse and academic writing, complement clauses tend to occur together with longer sentences in an environment that does not favor shortness, a reasonable explanation for why the feature of complementizer retention is more pervasive than complementizer omission in most written discourse (for concrete numbers, see the *GSWE*, Biber et al. 2021: 673–4). Additionally, retaining *that* helps the reader parse the structure of long and complex sentences.

You may wonder if all discourse syntax phenomena can be studied from a variationist as well as a text-linguistic perspective. The answer is "sort of." Of the phenomena of discourse syntax that you will learn more about in this book, some constructions, such as cleft sentences, or pronouns and **ellipsis**, are typically explored by a study of text-linguistic variation, while others, for instance particle placement or indirect object movement, lend themselves more readily to a variationist approach. Throughout this book, we will ask you repeatedly to be cognizant of both types of research design.

> This is a good point to check out Exercise 6 as well as the Level 2 Exercises 7 and 8, which focus on research design and the difference between the two approaches we have just discussed.

## 2.6 Summary

In this chapter we have emphasized that sentences seen as utterances are discourse-driven in many ways. They are shaped by the discourse situation and package their information in accordance with what is given or new at the moment of the utterance. We have highlighted the difference between the surrounding co-text and the more comprehensive context of an utterance. Furthermore, we have been able to see that speakers and writers make their syntactic choices in accordance with the discourse type and the register.

With syntactic choices being rooted in the context of use, we took a brief look at the origins of the interest in usage-based, **functional linguistics** and at corpora as an important source for gathering usage-based data. (You will occasionally read about other sources of evidence, such as experiments, in other chapters in this book.) We then looked in some detail at two different research perspectives for the study of grammar and discourse. We first looked at the procedure for the study of syntactic variation, where the objects of analysis are variants of sentence structure, such as complement clauses with and without *that*. We then compared this research design to text-linguistic research, where texts and their grammatical properties are the primary object of investigation. We also dealt with the analysis and the presentation of data, which must be in accordance with the research question.

Together with Chapter 1, this chapter forms the foundation for much of what we present in the remainder of the book. Part II of this book (Chapters 3 to 5) deals with grammar *in* discourse, looking at how different sentence patterns are realized in specific discourse situations. The chapters in this part move from left to right in their organization: from non-canonical beginnings (such as topicalization) to variation in the **core clause** (for instance, passivization) to complex sentence endings (for example, a cleft construction). In Part III of this book (Chapters 6 to 8), you will learn about the elements of the grammar *of* discourse, which means grammatical devices that turn sentences into discourse, such as connectives or pronouns. The final chapter (Chapter 9) moves beyond the local discourse and discusses syntactic phenomena as conditioned by genre.

## 2.7 Exercises

### *Level 1: Classification and Application*

1. At the beginning of this chapter, we asked you to rearrange sentences so that they are in a sequence informed by your intuitive knowledge about elements of discourse syntax. Below is the answer to that question.

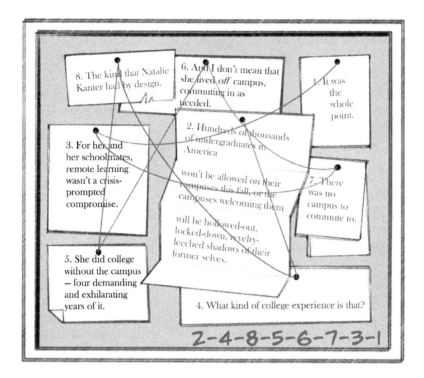

8. The kind that Natalie Kanter had by design.

6. And I don't mean that she lived *off* campus, commuting in as needed.

1. It was the whole point.

3. For her and her schoolmates, remote learning wasn't a crisis-prompted compromise.

2. Hundreds of thousands of undergraduates in America

won't be allowed on their campuses this fall, or the campuses welcoming them

7. There was no campus to commute to.

will be hollowed-out, locked-down, revelry-leeched shadows of their former selves.

5. She did college without the campus — four demanding and exhilarating years of it.

4. What kind of college experience is that?

2-4-8-5-6-7-3-1

Let's do the same activity again, and this time, let's pay even closer attention to the linguistic means that you rely on to make your decision, including the use of pronouns, determiners, and the flow from given to new information. The following sentences (again, arbitrarily numbered) are taken from the beginning of a *Washington Post* article on the funeral of civil rights leader John Lewis in July 2020.

1. *In it, he challenged the next generation to lay "down the heavy burdens of hate at last."*
2. *His words came as the country has been roiled by weeks of protests demanding a reckoning with institutionalized racism – and hours after President Donald Trump suggested delaying the November election, something he doesn't have the authority to do.*
3. *Hailed as a "founding father" of a fairer, better United States, John Lewis was eulogized Thursday by three former presidents*

> and others who urged Americans to continue the work of the civil rights icon in fighting injustice during a moment of racial reckoning.
>
> 4. The longtime member of Congress even issued his own call to action – in an essay written in his final days that he asked be published in The New York Times on the day of his funeral.
>
> 5. The nation's first Black president used the moment to issue a stark warning that the voting rights and equal opportunity Lewis championed were threatened by those "doing their darnedest to discourage people from voting" and to call for a renewal of the Voting Rights Act.
>
> 6. Former President Barack Obama called Lewis "a man of pure joy and unbreakable perseverance" during a fiery eulogy that was both deeply personal and political.
>
> 7. After nearly a week of observances that took Lewis' body from his birthplace in Alabama to the nation's capital to his final resting place in Atlanta, mourners in face masks to guard against the coronavirus spread out across pews Thursday at the city's landmark Ebenezer Baptist Church, once pastored by the Rev. Martin Luther King Jr.
>
> (Martin 2020)

2. In Section 2.2 we discussed the distinction between sentences and utterances. Consider the sentence *I told you this before* and imagine how it can be used as two (or more) different utterances. How do you imagine the discourse to which it belongs, and what might be the communicative purpose of the sentence in each case?

3. In Section 2.3 we highlighted that co-text, discourse type, and situational context are the three components of the discourse situation of an utterance. Discuss how the two utterances in italics shown below with some of their context are influenced by these factors: What is there in the co-text and the situational context that turns the same sentence into two very different utterances?

> (20)  Interviewer (CBS news): Would you say that the President is wrong to release that memo?
> Senator:   I would definitely say Mister President, *please don't do that*, that is wrong, it is absolutely wrong. (COCA, Spoken, 2018)
>
> (21)  When reading this article, some developers will think that it's a good idea to register their app for every possible file extension, because it will keep their app and logo in front of their users as often as possible. *PLEASE DON'T DO THAT*. That rule applies to App Contracts as well. Don't abuse them, especially if you aren't actually providing the functionality required. (COCA, Web, 2012)

4.  Describe the difference between (22a) and (22b), referring to the function of given and new information in a sentence, discussed in Section 2.3. Considering the role of the surrounding discourse, why do you think the sentence in (22a) was chosen as the original version?

> (22a)  This morning we'd dropped into a broad valley, then climbed steadily for 2,000 feet, until now we were traversing a cinder cone whose lower reaches must once have oozed pasty lava. *To the left rose a steep slope of volcanic cinders*; to the right the lava fell away in a jumble of jagged rock. (COCA, Fiction, 2004)
>
> (22b)  This morning we'd dropped into a broad valley, then climbed steadily for 2,000 feet, until now we were traversing a cinder cone whose lower reaches must once have oozed pasty lava. *To the left a steep slope of volcanic cinders rose*; to the right the lava fell away in a jumble of jagged rock.

5.  From the point of view of the English grammar system, as discussed in Chapter 1, the clauses in italics in (23)–(25) are all non-canonical, i.e., there are more basic versions for all of them. What would these canonical versions look like, and what kind of co-texts would be in line with them?

(23)   It is very true, we do owe our existence to LotRO [= Lord of the Rings Online] – I never would have, by chance (*if chance you call it*), join the same server [...]. (COCA, Blog, 2012)

(24)   Just outside the starting cave there's a little campfire blazing beneath a rock outcropping – the same one I scaled. *Sitting in front of the fire is an old man.* (COCA, Magazine, 2017)

(25)   [...] it's clear that Ohtani the hitter is as good as ever. *That much the Angels' designated hitter showed on Thursday night* [...]. (COCA, Magazine, 2019)

6. In Section 2.5, we discussed two kinds of research design for the study of discourse syntax. Below you find two excerpts from abstracts of articles published in a peer-reviewed linguistics journal. Which one represents a variationist research design, and which one uses a text-linguistic methodology?

A. In this paper we analyse variable presence of the complementizer *that*, i.e. *I think* that/Ø *this is interesting*, in a large archive of British dialects. Situating this feature within its historical development and synchronic patterning, we seek to understand the mechanism underlying the choice between *that* and *zero*. Our findings reveal that, in contrast to the diachronic record, the *zero* option is predominant – 91 percent overall. Statistical analyses of competing factors operating on this feature confirm that grammaticalization processes and grammatical complexity play a role. (Tagliamonte and Smith, 2005)

B. The so-called invariant tags, such as *eh*, *okay*, *right* and *yeah*, are extremely frequent in general English speech and have been studied extensively in recent years, especially in the spoken expression of teenagers, where they are a very common feature. In this article I focus on *innit*, as in *She love her chocolate innit?* and *It was good innit?* For this purpose, I analyse and discuss data extracted from two comparable corpora of teen speech [...]. Findings confirm that *innit* is typical of the language of London teenagers and has not gone out of use; on the contrary, its frequency has increased over the last few years. In contrast, the proportion of tokens found in the language of their adult counterparts is rather marginal. (Martínez 2015)

## Level 2: Interpretation and Research Design

7. According to the influential *Chicago Manual of Style*, the adjective *anxious* means "worried" and should not be used as a synonym for *eager*. Consequently, it should not be followed by an infinitive clause (*anxious to help, anxious to leave*), but by a prepositional phrase introduced by *about* (*anxious about a result*). The following table is adapted from a study based on data from COCA (Dant 2012).

|               | Spoken | Fiction | Magazine | Newspaper | Academic |
|---------------|--------|---------|----------|-----------|----------|
| *anxious about* | 13 % | 10 % | 25 % | 19 % | 26 % |
| *anxious to*    | 87 % | 90 % | 75 % | 81 % | 74 % |

   a. The study combines both syntactic and text-related categories. What type of approach does it exemplify?
   b. How would you visualize the results? What type of chart(s) would you choose?
   c. What does this table *not* tell you about the distribution of *anxious* in the five main registers in COCA?
   d. Are the results from the study expected, given the *Chicago Manual of Style*'s guidance?

8. In English, the complementizer *that* can often be left out, especially if it comes after a verb (like *say* or *believe*).

   a. Describe the design of both variationist and text-linguistic studies that look at the phenomenon of *that* omission from different angles.
   b. For the variationist study, pick three different verbs and retrieve a set of fifty attestations for each verb from a corpus (for

instance, from COCA). How do you ensure that your data includes different tenses? Are there any false positives you need to discard?

c. Based on this data set, carry out an analysis that treats complementizer omission as a case of syntactic variation and visualize your results. Produce a pie chart for each verb. What is the best way to present your results in a chart?

## Further Reading

- For an overview article that illuminates the distinction between a discourse analytic and discourse syntactic perspective on the relationship between grammar and discourse, see Bowie & Popova (2020). For a discussion of non-canonical syntax, see Ward & Birner (2006) or Lange & Rütten (2017).

- For the origins of functionalism and its development in the history of European and North American linguistics, see Newmeyer (2001). Newmeyer (2003) provides a thorough and well-argued reconciliation of form-based and usage-based linguistics. For a combined look at discourse and cognitive linguistics, see Tenbrink (2020). An accessible introduction to corpus linguistics can be found in McEnery & Hardie (2012) or, with emphasis on English, Lindquist & Levin (2018). On corpus data as an empirical method, including some description of statistical testing, see Stefanowitsch (2020).

- For a classic variationist approach that discusses a range of grammatical phenomena from this perspective, see the studies collected in Rohdenburg & Mondorf (2003); for studies of text-linguistic variation, see, for example, Schubert & Sanchez-Stockhammer (2016).

# PART II

# Grammar in Discourse

# 3 | *Non-canonical Beginnings*

## 3.1 Introduction

This chapter focuses on the beginning of sentences. In Chapter 2, we discussed how a non-canonical clause can be derived from a more basic pattern for reasons that often lie within discourse. We also saw that, against the background of rigid English word order, the position of the verb's arguments is generally fixed. When, for example, in a given utterance, an object occurs before the subject, this violates the basic Subject–Verb–Object order of English grammar and the pattern is considered non-canonical. We will also turn to adjuncts in this chapter, which do not have a single, canonical position. However, since adjuncts also occur at sentence beginnings, they are included in the discussion that follows.

Some elements that also typically occur sentence-initially are excluded for the time being. These are elements that are added to the clause to bracket or structure the discourse, usually in interactive, spoken discourse. They function, for instance, as so-called "prefaces" (like *well*) or "**comment clauses**" (like *I mean* or *you know*) and occur outside the core clause. Following the structure of our book, they belong to the grammar *of* discourse and will be discussed in Part III in Chapter 8 (on discourse markers).

The clausal patterns we turn to now all have an element of the core clause, which is not the grammatical subject, in their left periphery. This means the element is positioned in front of the subject. Let us illustrate the range of possible constructions by variation on a single example.

(1)     Most of what I found belonged to my father: chipped cuff link, an
         empty pack of cigarettes, black sock, toenail clippings. *These things* I

gathered in a pile by the door, to be thrown away later. (COCA, Fiction, 2015) (fronting)

(2)    *These things* I gathered *them* in a pile by the door. (left-dislocation)

(3)    *Among the things I gathered in a pile by the door* were an empty pack of cigarettes, black sock, and toenail clippings. (inversion)

(4)    *In a pile by the door* there were an empty pack of cigarettes, black sock, and toenail clippings. (sentence-initial adjunct)

In example (1), the grammatical object (*these things*) is in initial position, displaced from its canonical position behind the verb. This construction contrasts with examples (2) to (4) as follows: Example (2) shows the same position for the object, but differs from (1) in that the object is resumed later by an anaphoric pronoun (*them*). In example (3), the fronted constituent is not the grammatical object, but a verbal complement of the copula verb *be* (*among the things I gathered in a pile by the door . . .*). Since *be* is a so-considered "light" verb, which means it usually does not stand alone, the subject must move to the position behind the verb. Finally, example (4) also has a constituent other than the subject in initial position, but this time the constituent is an adjunct (*in a pile by the door*). Strictly speaking, this pattern is not non-canonical since adjuncts are not verbal arguments. However, an adjunct in front-position is also a starting-point for the sentence other than the grammatical subject.

You may have discussed these constructions in grammar classes, and perhaps you have been told different names for them. One name that is often used to refer to (1) through (3) is "topicalization," a term which emphasizes that matters of discourse, notably the topic under discussion, supersede the placement of the subject as the first element in the clause. However, the classification we will use in the following is form-based. We distinguish the mere *fronting* of a clausal element, as in (1), from **left-dislocation**, as in (2), where the fronted element does not leave a gap in the remaining clause but is resumed by a pronoun. (3) is an example of *inversion,* resulting from the fronting of a verbal complement, followed by the reversal of the position of the main verb and the subject. Finally, (4) is a sentence with a sentence-initial adjunct, to which we will turn first in order to take a general look at the role of sentence beginnings in discourse.

After reading this chapter, you will be able to:

- identify different types of non-canonical beginnings;
- describe the reasons why they are used with reference to the surrounding discourse;
- gather attested sentences with a non-canonical beginning from a text or corpus;
- develop a research method and choose a format for your results in line with the research question you want to pursue.

## Concepts, Constructions, and Keywords

*adjuncts in initial position, VP-/clause-oriented adjuncts, NP-fronting, left-dislocation, full inversion, locative and non-locative inversion, topic/ topicality, topic persistence, information-packaging*

Before continuing your reading, turn to Exercise 1 in order to practice distinguishing the four constructions introduced above.

## 3.2 Adjuncts in Front-Position

The beginning of a sentence has an important role in discourse. But what exactly does that mean? On the one hand, sentence beginnings serve our processing needs, in that it is easier to understand something beginning with, and thus connecting to, what we already know. As discussed in Chapter 2, this preference leads to a characteristic packaging of information within the sentence. Sentences tend to sequence given information before new information, whereby the end of the sentence becomes its main area of interest, its normal (or "unmarked") **focus** of attention (a more detailed definition of focus is given in Chapter 4). On the other hand, speakers or writers can also highlight an element by moving it to the initial position. Resulting from this movement, such an element gets some extra attention, becoming a *marked* focus.

The category of adjuncts is by definition more flexible with regard to their position. An adjunct can occur in initial position as well as in mid- and end-position of the clause and therefore does not cause any non-canonical pattern and special attention when occurring in front-position.

Which position is common for an adjunct depends to some extent on its semantics. Types of adjuncts that are characteristically sentence-initial are those referring to the speaker's attitude (*unfortunately*) or certainty (*surely*, *certainly*), or to the speech event as a whole (*honestly*); another obvious group are connective adjuncts, such as *next* or *moreover*. These adjuncts, which contribute a meaning that is more external to the core clause (they don't really tell us why or how something happened), are commonly referred to as "clause-oriented adjuncts" (Huddleston & Pullum 2002: 576). Other adjuncts, such as adjuncts of time or place, also occur in front-position, but they are characteristically *VP-oriented*, meaning they relate more closely to what is in fact asserted by the clause. A test showing this distinction is the so-called "lie test" (Erteschik & Lappin 1979): To test whether the information of the adjunct belongs to what is asserted by the clause, you deny the truth of the adjunct. For example, in response to the clause *Unfortunately, in 2018 we had a very hot summer*, you could answer *That's not true – that wasn't in 2018,* but not *\*That's not true, it wasn't unfortunate.* This test shows that *unfortunately* is more loosely related to the predication of the core clause than the temporal adjunct *in 2018*.

Grammars of English typically observe that the front-position is the one favored for a clause-oriented adjunct, while a VP-oriented adjunct is said to be favored in end-position. However, this is only a first generalization, because there is a lot of variation possible. For example, in (5) the temporal adjunct *one day* is placed at the end of the verb phrase (*stood before Merabor*), while in (6) it comes first.

(5)    The admiral stood before Merabor *one day* as the dragon sat and ate. (COCA, Fiction, 2009)

(6)    *One day*, she'd stop saying sure when she meant no. (COCA, Fiction, 2017)

Still, it makes a difference where a temporal adjunct ends up being placed. We can note that, due to the association of the front-position with clause-oriented adjuncts, the temporal adjunct in (6) has a wider range of meaning, setting the time frame for the entire clause, than in (5). This more general scope is often also expressed by a signal of detachment, such as a pause in spoken discourse or, as in Example (6), by a comma. A corresponding contrast can be found in two possible interpretations of adverbs like *hopefully* or *practically*, which may be verb phrase modifiers (*to work hopefully*, meaning, for example, full of energy) or clausal modifiers (meaning *it is to be hoped that*).

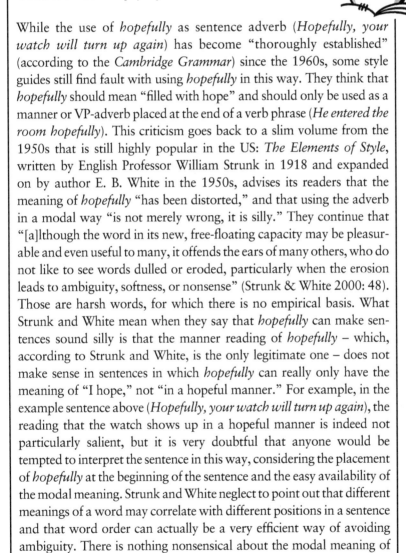

Good to Know: *Hopefully* as a Sentence Adverb

While the use of *hopefully* as sentence adverb (*Hopefully, your watch will turn up again*) has become "thoroughly established" (according to the *Cambridge Grammar*) since the 1960s, some style guides still find fault with using *hopefully* in this way. They think that *hopefully* should mean "filled with hope" and should only be used as a manner or VP-adverb placed at the end of a verb phrase (*He entered the room hopefully*). This criticism goes back to a slim volume from the 1950s that is still highly popular in the US: *The Elements of Style*, written by English Professor William Strunk in 1918 and expanded on by author E. B. White in the 1950s, advises its readers that the meaning of *hopefully* "has been distorted," and that using the adverb in a modal way "is not merely wrong, it is silly." They continue that "[a]lthough the word in its new, free-floating capacity may be pleasurable and even useful to many, it offends the ears of many others, who do not like to see words dulled or eroded, particularly when the erosion leads to ambiguity, softness, or nonsense" (Strunk & White 2000: 48). Those are harsh words, for which there is no empirical basis. What Strunk and White mean when they say that *hopefully* can make sentences sound silly is that the manner reading of *hopefully* – which, according to Strunk and White, is the only legitimate one – does not make sense in sentences in which *hopefully* can really only have the meaning of "I hope," not "in a hopeful manner." For example, in the example sentence above (*Hopefully, your watch will turn up again*), the reading that the watch shows up in a hopeful manner is indeed not particularly salient, but it is very doubtful that anyone would be tempted to interpret the sentence in this way, considering the placement of *hopefully* at the beginning of the sentence and the easy availability of the modal meaning. Strunk and White neglect to point out that different meanings of a word may correlate with different positions in a sentence and that word order can actually be a very efficient way of avoiding ambiguity. There is nothing nonsensical about the modal meaning of *hopefully* per se. If you do a simple lexical search in a corpus like COCA and scroll through the results, you will see that the great majority of tokens belongs in the sentence adverb class (especially sentence-initial *hopefully*) and that, thanks to its expanded meaning, the adverb is becoming more and more popular – not exactly an indicator of "erosion, softness, or nonsense."

In case you are wondering why *hopefully*, of all adverbs that have more than one meaning, is the one that gets picked on, you are in good company. The *American Heritage Dictionary* remarks in a usage note that it is not easy "to explain why people selected this word for disparagement" and concedes that "its widespread use reflects popular recognition of its usefulness." Merriam-Webster's Dictionary points out in another usage note that *hopefully* behaves like other adverbs in this regard (*thankfully, naturally, ideally*) and advises solomonically, "[y]ou can use it if you need it, or avoid it if you do not like it." More conservative style guides have also come around. In 2012, the editors of the *Associated Press Stylebook*, a reference publication for many journalists and newspapers, announced on Twitter that the Associated Press now supports "the modern usage." The tweet continues, "[h]opefully, you will appreciate this style update."

With their clause-orientation and wider scope reading, initially placed adjuncts commonly provide the frame for a longer stretch discourse, since they constitute the point of departure for everything that follows. Take, for example, the title of Leonard Cohen's song "First we take Manhattan, then we take Berlin," in which the adverbs *first* and *then* provide the temporal frame for the sequence of events as a whole. For this reason, you can't repeat *first* in the second sentence (*First we take Manhattan, first we take Berlin*). By contrast, in the excerpt in (7), which is taken from Barack Obama's speech following Donald Trump's election in 2016, the adverb *first* modifies several VPs in successive sentences. In this excerpt, each occurrence of *first* pertains to only one VP, not to the clause as a whole, which is why several statements can all be claimed to hold true *first*. The repeated use of the adjunct in (7) is acceptable because *first* does not express a succession in discourse. It modifies, after a pair of negated predicates, two positive statements without causing a contradiction.

(7)    Now, everybody is sad when their side loses an election, but the day after we have to remember that we're actually all on one team. This is an intramural scrimmage. We're not Democrats first. We're not Republicans first. We are Americans *first*. We're patriots *first*. (Garunay 2016)

In contrast to the use of *first*, note that *now* in Example (7), being sentence-initial, is an adjunct with a clause-oriented, wider scope function. *Now* does not add temporal information to the proposition here, but initiates a new discourse segment.

This discussion has highlighted that initially placed adjuncts, especially those with a locative or temporal meaning, provide something like a "signpost" for situating what comes next in the discourse (Virtanen 2004). Due to its discourse function, an initially placed temporal adjunct can initiate a new episode or set the temporal frame for an entire story. Take the excerpt in (8), in which Richard Maduku, a novelist and blogger for *The Guardian*, structures his life story by using different sentence-initial temporal adjuncts to mark the chronology. What you can see in the excerpt is that a more significant turn within the discourse is signaled by more material (*on my return ...*), while a more local turn, here the beginning of just an episode, is initiated by a shorter, less informative adjunct (*one day*).

(8)    *On my return to my hometown a couple of years later after the collapse of my restaurant venture in the North*, I designed a signpost for my residence to differentiate it from the others. Apart from my birth name that I decided to use on it, I also drew what I regarded as a house in the centre of the miniature signpost. It had a tailless arrow pointing to my house on each side. I became very proud of it whenever I heard neighbours using it to describe their houses to their would-be visitors on phone. But *one day* a boyhood friend who always faulted almost everything I did, visited me. He told me that the arrow of my signpost was pointing skyward and went on to ask mockingly if my house was in the sky! My explanation that what he called an arrow was in fact a stylistic representation of a house did not impress him! He dismissed my tailless arrows with a wave of his hand. Fearing that other visitors or even passers-by might have mistaken the house of my signpost for an arrow as my friend had done, I grudgingly removed it. (Maduku 2018)

Narrative and descriptive types of discourse, in particular, show a systematic correlation between the amount of information in the adjunct and major as opposed to minor turns in a text (Virtanen 2010, 2014). However, depending on the type of discourse or genre, an initial position

**Figure 3.1** Initial adjuncts as global vs. local signposts in Example (8)

for an adjunct does not always mean that its scope is beyond the single
sentence (Verstraete 2004, Crompton 2006). For example, in recipes or
other instructive texts, adjuncts function again more locally, typically
supporting the chain of actions that is presented.

Let us conclude that initially placed adjuncts are quite symptomatic
of the role the sentence-initial position has for the discourse. An initial
adjunct provides the point of departure for the upcoming text, which is
why it can support the structuring and processing of information.
However, initial adjuncts are not in a non-canonical position, which
is why the actual effect that is achieved is quite varied. In the remainder
of this chapter, we will focus on the fronting of verbal arguments,
which leads to a non-canonical construction.

Turn to Exercises 2 and 3 to test your understanding of
the distinction between VP-oriented and clause-oriented
adjuncts.

Corpus-based Analysis of the Use of Adjuncts

In order to find out if a particular adverb or phrase is characteristic-ally a VP-modifier or a clausal modifier, or whether it can in fact be both, we have to look at how it is attested in English usage. For gathering data on this, we could again work with a corpus of English, as described in Chapter 2. Type in an individual adverb (for instance, *recently*) or an adverb phrase (e.g., *just recently*) or use the word class tagging. In COCA, the string for retrieving adverbs, which is also listed in the POS (part of speech) menu, is <_r*>. Note that many other realizations for an adjunct (noun phrases, prepos-itional phrases, subordinate clauses) will be difficult to retrieve automatically, which is why it can be preferable to work with a given lexeme or phrase (we describe this as a general strategy of a "lexical shortcut" in Section 3.3). For example, we worked with the lexeme *first* and the phrase *one day* for retrieving the examples discussed in Section 3.2. For a small-scale project on the positioning of these two adjuncts, you could work with a random list of 100 hits, coding each occurrence for the property of having the adjunct being used clause-initially or -internally. This analysis enables you to calculate the proportion with which the adjunct is used in the left periphery, i.e., whether it serves as a point of departure in discourse. See Exercises 6 and 7 (Level 2) for more ideas about a project on adjunct placement and more on the corpus-based retrieval of con-structions with non-canonical beginnings in sections 3.3 and 3.4 below.

## 3.3 NP-Fronting and Left-Dislocation

We now turn to the two non-canonical constructions in which a noun phrase as verbal argument precedes the subject at the beginning of the sentence. Such an NP can either just be fronted, or occur as a left-dislocation, in which case an anaphoric pronoun fills the gap resulting from the movement of the NP. The difference between the two con-structions is illustrated here again by (9) and (10), repeated from above:

(9)     These things I gathered in a pile by the door, to be thrown away later.

(10)    These things I gathered them in a pile by the door, to be thrown away later.

While the two constructions are similar in their syntactic form, we will now investigate them more closely for the discourse conditions in which they occur. Left-dislocation is described in the literature as a syntactic mechanism for negotiating or clarifying a new topic for the discourse (Geluykens 1992), like in Example (11). We will therefore have to explore, not only the **information status** of the fronted NP and its relation to the preceding discourse, but also its relation to the subsequent discourse.

(11)    A:    These things ...
        B:    Yes ...
        A:    They are awful ...

We will first deal with each construction separately before contrasting them as syntactic variants.

---

Good to Know: Spoken Language Data

Note that spoken language data as contained in a corpus comes from transcripts, suggesting a fluency that in real life of course these utterances haven't had. Natural conversation is full of disfluencies like pauses, intonation, or repair. In linguistics, research on these phenomena is done much more thoroughly within Conversational Analysis, with its own system of notation and categories for phenomena of disfluency. However, you should be aware of these characteristics when referring to spoken data in research on discourse syntax.

---

### 3.3.1 The Discourse Function of Fronting

How can a fixed word order and SVO language such as English allow for the fronting of a non-subject NP? Fronting such an element is an obvious case where discourse needs supersede the rules of canonical grammar. More precisely speaking, fronting is acceptable when the fronted constituent is properly "linked" to the preceding discourse (Birner & Ward 1998: 32).

Look at the nature of this relation between a fronted NP and the discourse preceding it. Examples (12) and (13) are acceptable, while Example (14) appears not to be:

(12)  A:  He's gone because he was a coward?
      B:  *A coward I can tolerate*. But he said he loved you, and it proved he didn't understand love at all. (COCA, Fiction, 2015)

(13)  A:  He's gone because he was a liar?
      B:  *A coward I can tolerate*. But he said he loved you, and it proved he didn't understand love at all.

(14)  A:  He's gone because he wants to run his own business?
      B:  ?*A coward I can tolerate*. But he said he loved you, and it proved he didn't understand love at all.

In (12) and (13), we find that the fronted constituent contains information that is given, or at least inferable, from the previous discourse. In (12), the NP *a coward* is mentioned in the previous sentence while, in (13), its discourse familiarity is due to a potential set of roles or subtypes (*liar, coward, cheater, . . .*), which – in this context – is dealt with as belonging to the superordinate category of *a loving person*. This set membership creates a sufficient familiarity for the fronting to be acceptable. By contrast, in (14), the concept of being a coward comes completely out of context, which is why the fronting is not acceptable.

There are two effects which such a close link to a prior discourse, expressed by way of fronting, can produce. The first occurs with sentences that place an element which contains given information in front-position. In that case, the main focus of the utterance remains in its usual, sentence-final position. As a result, the sentence highlights two elements: the fronted constituent as well as what remains of the information in end-position. In speech, this type of NP-fronting will receive two sentence accents, like in Example (15), where the speaker discusses the works of a painter:

(15)  Whistler thought of it, characterized it in very different terms. *This* we have to *refine* [. . .]. (COCA, Spoken, 1995)

The other possible effect of fronting is that it can signal that the element in front-position is the most informative element. The link to the previous discourse then exists via an "open proposition" (Huddleston & Pullum 2002: 35), which means everything in the clause, except for the fronted element, is given or inferable. For example, in (16), the proposition "it costs some amount of money" is given information, because the act of ordering something implies that this costs money.

(16)    She orders an elevator seat for the stairs. *Almost ten thousand dollars it costs, installed.* (COCA, Fiction, 2016)

If the link to the previous discourse exists via an open proposition, the discourse function of fronting is to highlight the initial information in the first place. In speech, a clause like (16) would be likely to carry only one main accent.

Let's summarize: NP-fronting either moves the main focus of attention to the sentence beginning, or it keeps it in the usual end-position but adds the fronted NP as a secondary focus, expressing some kind of connection. We have seen that in both cases the fronting of a verbal argument depends on a close link to the preceding discourse.

### 3.3.2 Left-Dislocation as a Discourse Strategy

We have already described how left-dislocation formally differs from the mere fronting of a verbal argument. We now turn to the function of left-dislocation in discourse. Let's start with Example (17), which is from spoken discourse:

(17)    One of the guys you know on another network told me that we are lower in the last poll he had seen than pol – politicians. And that's not fair to you, but it's – but some of the people in that business are intrusive. They'll ha – they feel they have to get a story if there's a rumor out there. And so it makes it – it makes it – a lot of good people say, "Well, I'm not going to run," and that's one reason I'm so proud of our boys. And, yes, *this guy he*'s running against has gone negative on him, but – but his record is out there. (COCA, Spoken, 1998)

Example (17) shows the fronting of the NP *this guy*, which is resumed by the pronoun *he*. One might wonder why the pronoun is used here at all since the information status of *this guy* does not appear to be new in this context. However, what we find is that, with the left-dislocation, it is re-activated. The reason for this re-activation lies in the preceding discourse, where *this guy* has come to compete with other grammatical subjects, such as *they* and *I*. This temporary discussion of what other people think has turned the *guy* into a topic that can be less expected as a subject. The left-dislocation thus identifies a referent that is still new to the discourse in some way.

The discourse function of left-dislocation exemplified by (17) helps us to understand why the contextual requirements are different from those that we noted about fronting. In a left-dislocation construction, the givenness of the initially placed constituent can stem from a more distant part of the text, or it may even be due to knowledge from outside the discourse. You find this situational givenness in an example like (18), in which the referent of the NP *this guy* is not mentioned in the prior discourse at all. Speaker B in this dialog can nonetheless expect a FedEx agent to be part of the narrative, which means its givenness is to some extent inferable.

(18)   A:   By the way, FedEx – here's what happened.
       B:   They found –
       A:   The tree had been delivered. It was delivered to the wrong address.
       B:   Right.
       C:   Okay.
       A:   Treetopia did deliver it.
       B:   And FedEx saved the day.
       A:   FedEx tracked it down.
       B:   So here I am walking around my neighborhood with this little wanted poster with my tree on it asking anyone, had they seen my tree. Out of nowhere like a vision, *this guy, he starts floats towards me.* (COCA, Spoken, 2016)

In sum, the discourse function of a dislocated NP is to remind the reader or listener of a referent which is simply not given or expected enough at a given point of discourse to be talked about without previous (re-)identification. In contrast to fronting, which requires a referent to be given or inferable in the immediately preceding discourse (see Figure 3.2), left-dislocation arises out of more variable connections to the previous discourse.

As the discussion in this section has shown, left-dislocation is a discourse strategy that simplifies referent identification. Considering the variable connections which the dislocated constituent has in relation to the previous discourse, we have also seen that there is a clear

**Figure 3.2** Information status of fronted NP without resumptive pronoun

difference between left-dislocation and NP-fronting in their relation to the previous discourse. As our next step, we turn to the relation of both constructions to the subsequent discourse.

To check whether you are now in the position to tell the two constructions and their requirements of discourse apart, go to Exercise 4.

### 3.3.3 Topicality in Discourse: Fronting vs. Left-Dislocation

So far, we have focused on the roles of fronting and left-dislocation in relation to the preceding discourse. We have seen that, with the mere fronting of a verbal argument, the connection between prior discourse and the clause is relatively local and more restricted, while the discourse function of left-dislocation is a more general one of identifying referents from a ground of shared knowledge. Rather than depending on discourse familiarity, left-dislocation is used when the dislocated NP deserves referential reinforcement. But do we know when and why a referent truly deserves this?

This question is related to the concept of *topicality*. In the linguistic literature, attempts for a definition of "topic" typically center on the idea of "aboutness" (Dalrymple & Nikolaeva 2011: 48, Leuckert 2019). Being the topic means, broadly speaking, being the focus of interest at a given point in discourse. For example, in (18) above, *FedEx* is the discourse topic, that is, the company and its services is what the discourse is about. *Fedex* is also the topic of several utterances in the sense that it is what these utterances are about (*FedEx saved the day, FedEx tracked it down*). The NP *FedEx* thus possesses topicality because it is for a while the focus of interest in the discourse. Based on this definition, we will see now whether there is a difference between NP-fronting and left-dislocation with respect to how they deal with topics in discourse. More concretely, we want to find out in which case the initially placed NP is more topical in the corresponding context of discourse. However, to answer this question empirically, one first needs to find a precise way of operationalizing topicality.

One way in which topicality shows itself in a text is topic persistence, or topic continuity. In practice, this means you count the number of times the referent of an NP (including a pronoun or a synonym) recurs in subsequent clauses. This method has been applied to the study of fronting and left-dislocation (Gregory & Michaelis 2001). The researchers gathered all instances of NP-fronting and left-dislocation from a corpus of telephone speech (44 cases of fronting and 187 instances of left-dislocation) and coded these occurrences for their topic persistence. Following their methodological decisions, a persistent topic meant that the referent of the pre-clausal NP recurred within five subsequent sentences. Their analysis further took note of whether the recurrence had the form of a fully repeated NP or a pronoun. The results are the counts as shown in Table 3.1.

Table 3.1 *Rates of occurrence\* for topic persistence of pre-clausal NPs*

|  | No persistence | Repeated NP | At least one pronominal use |
|---|---|---|---|
| NP-fronting | 32 | 2 | 10 |
| left-dislocation | 66 | 11 | 110 |

\* Absolute frequencies. There were 44 attestations of fronting and 187 of left-dislocation. Data is based on Gregory & Michaelis 2001.

The results can also be presented in a bar chart like Figure 3.3. The graph shows the three discourse conditions both for NP-fronting and left-dislocation on the *x*-axis and their frequency as the dependent variable on the *y*-axis.

Figure 3.3 highlights that there are indeed differences between the two constructions and that left-dislocation is higher in topic persistence

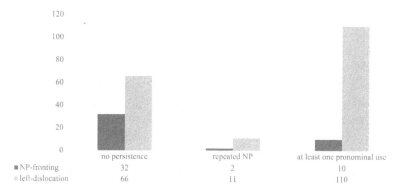

**Figure 3.3** Topic persistence of pre-clausal NPs in fronting and left-dislocation
Rates of occurrence (absolute frequencies) for topic persistence of pre-clausal
NPs in 44 attestations of fronting and 187 of left-dislocation. Data is based on
Gregory & Michaelis 2001.

than NP-fronting. However, an obvious problem with interpreting this
chart is that the overall frequencies of NP-fronting and left-dislocation
differ considerably. For example, the chart shows a higher frequency of
pre-clausal NPs with no persistence for left-dislocation, but does
not make it obvious that this is still low, compared to the persistence
of pronominal recurrence for left-dislocation. By contrast, for NP-
fronting the graph has a comparatively low column for NPs without
persistence, although 32 hits is in fact the highest score in that category.
It is therefore more advisable to transform Figure 3.3 into a diagram
based on percentages, as shown by Figure 3.4.

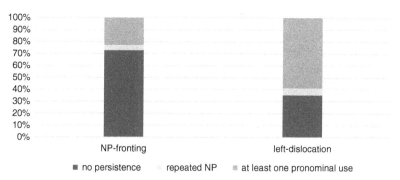

**Figure 3.4** Topic persistence of fronting and left-dislocation (proportions)
Based on Table 3.1 and Figure 3.3.

Figure 3.4 is apt to illustrate that, in our data set, in the majority of cases of NP-fronting (73 percent), the NP did not persist as a topic in the subsequent discourse. By contrast, in the majority of cases of left-dislocation, the dislocated NP re-occurred as a topic. We learn from this outcome that left-dislocation and fronting, despite resulting from non-canonical sentence beginnings that are formally similar, have different functions relating to the topic structure in discourse.

How to Develop a Research Design

As the case study in Section 3.3.3 highlights, any kind of research design process involves multiple steps and decisions. The point of departure is usually a theoretical assumption that has led you to your research question. The first step toward answering this question is to come up with a hypothesis, which is basically a statement that could be true or false. The second step is to find a way of testing your hypothesis by operationalizing it, which requires you to think about choosing your method. The method consists, first, of the category of analysis that you are going to investigate and, second, of the choice of the source of data. In line with the hypothesis, you then come up with a prediction about the way your category will behave in the given source of data. When evaluating your results, you check whether the data matches this prediction (this is commonly done by falsifying the null hypothesis, which means you check whether you can *exclude* that there is *no* effect).

The results discussed in Section 3.3.3 were based on the hypothesis that left-dislocation differs from NP-fronting in the function it has for the subsequent discourse, notably in its topic persistence. The prediction was that the topic persistence for left-dislocation would be higher. As categories, three degrees of topic persistence were defined. The finding was that the majority of NPs in left-dislocation (more than 50 percent) persisted as topic in the data, whereas more than 50 percent of the fronted NPs did not. This finding was in line with the initial prediction. To substantiate this outcome, you could now continue by applying statistical analyses (which are not dealt with in this book, but see our suggestions for further reading at the end of this chapter) before interpreting and evaluating your results in the context of existing research.

It is important that your research question can be transformed into a testable prediction. For example, the assumption that left-dislocation is used when the NP requires clarification could not be directly addressed in a meaningful way. It is equally important that the format in which you present your results fits your prediction. The results about topic persistence in Table 3.1 could not confirm the assumption that when an NP has no topic persistence it commonly undergoes fronting. Despite the fact that the category of "no persistence" is the largest proportion within the category of NP-fronting, this reverse assumption is certainly not true.

Exercises 8 and 9 (Level 2) deal with the interpretation of data and collecting data for a research project on the difference between fronting and left-dislocation.

### 3.3.4 Text-Linguistic Variation of Fronting and Left-Dislocation

We now turn to the occurrence of fronting and left-dislocation in different types of discourse, that is, we will look at them using the text-linguistic approach (see Chapter 2). Due to the limited possibilities of corpus methodology in this area (see the toolbox below), this kind of evidence will be based on relatively small amounts of text.

In line with what we said above about left-dislocation as an interactive strategy, most research on this construction is limited to conversation, that is, to unplanned and informal speech. However, when looking at data from both spoken and written English, it turns out to be not entirely true that left-dislocation occurs exclusively in speech. There is some research that also attests occurrences in written English, like the data shown in Table 3.2. These results were collected manually and are based on a small, historical corpus (Tizón-Couto 2012). Since the size of the texts in the corpus sections varied, the frequencies in parentheses had to be normalized to a **rate of occurrence** per 10,000 words (see Chapter 2 on how normalized rates are calculated).

Table 3.2 *Frequency of left-dislocation in some discourse types*

| Drama | Fiction | Journals | Sermons | Letters | Science | News |
|-------|---------|----------|---------|---------|---------|------|
| 177 | 55 | 13 | 13 | 10 | 8 | 9 |
| (2.05) | (0.63) | (0.15) | (0.15) | (0.11) | (0.09) | (0.1) |

The figures show absolute numbers and normalized frequency per 10,000 words. Data is from Tizón-Couto 2012.

You will note that all the frequencies in Table 3.2 are really low, which is also why these results cannot reasonably be turned into a chart. In a bar chart, fiction, for example, would have a bar four to five times as high as the categories of journals and letters, but emphasizing this as a difference would hide the fact that *all* numbers are very low. Still, the numbers in Table 3.2 inform us that left-dislocation is relatively more frequent in discourse that simulates or contains speech (drama and fiction), or in discourse that is written to be spoken (sermons). A study of fronting showed similar results. Based on the British component of the *International Corpus of English,* the rates of occurrence of fronting in speech – notably in conversation, phone calls, and classroom speech – ranged from 1.92 to 2.96 per 10,000 words (Leuckert 2019). We are thus safe to conclude that, from the point of view of text-linguistic variation, both constructions are a grammatical characteristic of unplanned spoken rather than planned written discourse.

Keep in mind that corpus results like these have other limitations. They will not tell you whether or not the use of fronting or left-dislocation is overshadowed by other non-canonical syntactic patterns (for instance, agentless passives, to be discussed in Chapter 4, or inversion, to be discussed in Section 3.4 below). Nor do the rates of occurrence per discourse type relate to the contrast between a sentence with and one without left-dislocation, nor to the choice between left-dislocation and fronting. Remember that, when dealing with text-linguistic variation, discourse types or individual texts are the object of investigation, not the syntactic variants as such (see Chapter 2). In addition, there is the general problem of retrieval, which overall limits the data that is available. For projects on the use of left-dislocation or fronting, we therefore suggest a methodological shortcut; follow the instructions in the toolbox below and in Exercise 9.

Lexical Shortcut for Retrieving Constructions in a Corpus

It is almost impossible to search reliably for left-dislocation and NP-fronting in an unparsed corpus. There are two reasons for this problem.

First, a possible search string for an initially placed non-subject NP is generally identical to the one for an NP with a relative clause and an omitted relative pronoun. For example, the sequence of words in the sentence *This is a coward I can't tolerate* is the same as in Example (12) above. Second, it is not possible to predict the range of intervening material between the fronted NP and the resuming pronoun. As Example (19) illustrates, a dislocated NP (*this woman*) may occur in close proximity to the pronoun (*she*), or, as in the case of (20), the syntactic distance can be more substantial. Since this distance is altogether variable, there is no obvious single search string available for safely extracting all instances of left-dislocation or fronting from a corpus.

(19)    Yes, I've played so many mothers in my career, but *this woman she* kind of turns the idea of motherhood on its head. (COCA, Magazine, 2018)

(20)    *This guy*, which we have talked about on this show, unlike all the other insane dictators globally, *he* is an extra brand of crazy. (COCA, Spoken, 2017)

In cases like these, as a methodological shortcut, you can extract a set of occurrences based on a lemma search, that is, on a fixed lexeme or phrase. With the set of attestations that you thereby receive, you can then carry out a limited quantitative data analysis, or a qualitative analysis, that is, you analyze the discourse function of individual occurrences. For example, similar to the data analysis in Section 3.3.3, you could look at proportions of topic persistence or givenness values within the data set, or carry out an in-depth analysis of the surrounding discourse, making detailed observations about NP-fronting or left-dislocation as a communicative strategy.

## 3.4 Reversed Argument Order: Inversion of Subject and Verb

### 3.4.1 Basic Form and Function

We will now turn to inversion, which is another construction that is marked by the initial placement of a non-subject argument. We start with its formal characteristics; for these, take a look at Example (21) from a piece of fiction:

(21)    "Who comes?" the questioner repeated, and *into the room came* a studious-looking man who was five feet six inches tall in Space and thirty-nine years long in Time. (COCA, Fiction, 2001)

What you find in this example and what we refer to as inversion here is the positioning of the entire verb phrase in front of the subject. This is what defines, more precisely speaking, a "full" inversion, which contrasts with subject–auxiliary inversion, such as in interrogatives or after a clause-initial negative element (*Where did the studious-looking man come from? Never had I seen such a man before*). In full inversion, the grammatical subject is placed behind the entire verb phrase and thus in clause-final position.

Let us next look at inversion from the point of view of the elements that occur at the sentence beginning. These elements typically function as predicative complement within the verb phrase, while inversion is not possible with other verbal arguments. For example, in (22a), *some ice cream* is the direct object of the verb *offer,* whereas in (23a) *among his favorite flavors* is a predicative complement. You probably know that verbs taking an object are classified as transitive verbs, while those with a predicative complement (like *be*) are called copular verbs. (We will look in greater detail at the notion of **transitivity** when we discuss the passive in Chapter 4.) What characterizes the distinction between the object of a transitive verb and a predicative complement on the level of meaning is that the former refers to a participant (animate or inanimate) in an event, while a predicative complement expresses a property (usually of the subject). Some verbs also take complements which are neither participant nor property but, as illustrated by (24a), instead refer to local or temporal circumstances (*into his life*):

(22)    a.    George offers Harold some ice cream.

(23)    a.    Lemon and vanilla are among his favorite flavors.

(24)    a.    Then a new taste came into his life, the love for chocolate chip.

This distinction of verb classes is relevant because inversion only occurs with intransitive and copular verbs but cannot follow the object of a transitive verb. If we take the examples from above, you see that only *be* and *come* are grammatical with inversion, while (22b), which includes the verb *offer*, is ungrammatical. This is because with a transitive verb one automatically parses the sentence as Subject–Verb–Object, which means that *ice cream* would be constructed as subject rather than a fronted constituent and *offer* as the verb in its regular position. The reading would be that it is the ice cream that is doing the offering (which is hard to imagine outside a cartoon world).

(22)  b.  *Some ice cream offers George to Harold.

(23)  b.  Among his favorite flavors are lemon and vanilla.

(24)  b.  Into his life came a new taste, the love for chocolate chip.

Sometimes, but quite rarely, the fronted element followed by an inversion is a verbal modifier, that is, an adjunct, occurring with an intransitive verb. In such a case, as in (25a) and (25b), the initial placement of the adjunct is grammatical both with and without inversion, that is, the inversion is optional.

(25)  a.  […] it was a mystery how Iranians would react to Khomeini's sermons. Neither the ayatollah nor the shah could know it, so the CIA couldn't know it either. *A decade later* came the startling collapse of the Soviet Union. (COCA, Spoken, 2002)
      b.  A decade later the startling collapse of the Soviet Union came …

Apart from the verb type and the corresponding restrictions on the fronted element, there are several subtypes of inversion depending on the phrase type occurring in initial position. This sub-classification establishes inversion with fronted PP, NP, AdjP, VP, or AdvP. The typology correlates, to a certain extent, with two larger semantic classes of inversion, which also play a role in its function in discourse: If the phrase expresses a spatial or temporal location or direction, the inversion is a *locative* type of inversion. This type is typically associated with the formal types of AdvP- and PP-inversion and is illustrated by examples (26) and (27):

(26)  So, *now* is the time for the international community, in all its dimensions, to come together. (COCA, Spoken, 2017) (AdvP-inversion, locative)

(27)   *Near the front door* is a collection of the couple's cowboy hats. (COCA, News, 1999) (PP-inversion, locative)

By contrast, the class of non-locative inversion types is typically realized by a fronted AdjP or a predicative NP, as in (28) and (29):

(28)   *Most disturbing* is the 50% increase in the risk of death for women with depression between 1992 and 2011. (COCA, Magazine, 2017) (AdjP-inversion, non-locative)

(29)   *An exception to this* is the Test of Narrative Language. (COCA, Academic, 2017) (NP-inversion, non-locative)

The correlation of semantic type and phrasal realization is not a perfect one, which is what Figure 3.5 illustrates. On the one hand, inversion following a fronted participle, which is a VP-type of inversion, is commonly also a locative inversion, because the fronted participle is more often than not combined with a locative prepositional phrase. As a result, the initial constituent contains locative and non-locative meaning, as in (30):

(30)   *Peering over the fence* was the new boy who had just moved with his family into the house behind ours (COCA, Fiction, 2009) (VP-inversion, locative and non-locative type combined)

On the other hand, there are also prepositional phrases followed by inversion which do not express locative meaning, as can be seen in (31):

(31)   *Of greater concern* is the loss to the nation of the enormous leadership potential that this returning cohort represents. (COCA, Academic, 2007) (PP-inversion, non-locative type)

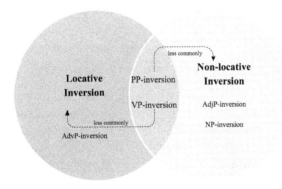

**Figure 3.5** Phrasal and semantic types of inversion

Having distinguished the formal and semantic types of inversion, let us finally turn to its function in the discourse. One aspect of this function is very basic. As you have seen, all types of inversion have in common the fact that they use a property of the subject as the point of departure for the clause. The subject is in this way located within the discourse, which is why the locative type is often also considered as something like a "prototype" of inversion. Resulting from a property of the subject as the point of departure for the clause, followed only by the verb *be*, the focus of the clause is on the subject, and the predication is mainly one of "appearance" into the discourse. This is why the basic function of inversion is *presentative*, meaning that the subject is introduced into the discourse by locating it via a locative or non-locative property. Examples (32)–(36) illustrate this function, which applies to all types of inversion, including those that use a property, rather than a proper location, as their point of departure:

(32)   *Here* is an interesting book. (AdvP-inversion)

(33)   *Next to the candle* was an interesting book. (PP-inversion)

(34)   *Lying next to the candle* was a book that raised our interest.
       (VP-inversion)

(35)   *More important than the book* was the picture next to it.
       (AdjP-inversion)

(36)   *Another interesting object on the table* was a strange-looking picture.
       (NP-inversion)

The presentative function results from placing the subject, which would be in preverbal position in a canonical sentence, in the position of end-focus. A second important function of inversion is information packaging, to which we turn now.

## 3.4.2 *The Information-Packaging Function of Inversion*

We have already pointed out that, in discourse, known information tends to precede new information and that this is the main cause for changing the word order in a sentence. Accordingly, it can reasonably be hypothesized with respect to inversion that the initially placed constituent contains information that is more given than the information expressed by the subject.

Evidence from work on inversion confirms this assumption. For example, a study of about 700 attestations of inversion found that by far the most common distribution of information in inversion is the one where the fronted constituent represents information that is recoverable from the previous discourse, while the postposed subject contains information that is new (Birner 1994). An example of this pattern of **information packaging** is given in Example (37).

(37)　Hefty and expensive, Abraham Lincoln: A History sold only 7,000 copies, but for every person who bought the collection, 50 others read extensive excerpts in its serial run. *More important than sales was the book's intellectual reach*. (COCA, Magazine, 2014)

In (37), the NP *sales* is evoked by the verb *sell*, which was a predicate in the sentence previous to the inversion. By contrast, the grammatical subject *the book's intellectual reach* has the status of new information in the discourse.

Apart from this highly typical information structure in inversion, it is also possible that both the fronted constituent and the postposed subject contain elements that are given from the previous discourse. This may be the case when the postposed subject contains some information that has already been mentioned. An example is (38a), in which the coordinate NP, referring to two characters from fantasy fiction, contains one element that is given and one that is new:

(38)　a.　"No, we will not break it, Bone! We will fulfill it too well." A storm frothed against King Rainjoy's palace, and the hall of mists felt like a ship deck at foggy dawn. Salt, Mist, and Scald stepped toward the ivory throne, knelt beside the swan pool. *Behind the Pale Council stood Persimmon Gaunt and Imago Bone*. (COCA, Fiction, 2002)

We do not have to understand an example like (38a) as counterevidence against the general information-packaging assumption about inversion. But we should modify the exact wording of the hypothesis. Perhaps it is not always the case that new information follows given information in an inversion. But one hypothesis, which does not seem to have been falsified to date, is that there is no inversion in which the information of the fronted complement is less familiar than the information of the postposed subject. Working with examples like (38a) shows how tricky it can get to investigate the conditions of information structure empirically. We return to the question of investigating information structure and the corresponding methodological decisions in the next toolbox and in the exercises below.

There is an interesting difference between locative and non-locative inversion in their information-packaging function. In comparison to the locative type, non-locative inversion does not only underlie the pragmatic constraint of relative givenness, as just described, but it requires that the entire sentence contains an open proposition. In Section 3.3.1, we already defined an open proposition as having the full clausal content derivable from the preceding text except for one component of the clause. In the case of inversion, this component is the postposed subject. This means that, in the non-locative type of inversion, the entire proposition, except for the postposed subject, must be given information. For instance, (39a) presents (39b) as contextually derivable, and only the NP *the promise to give up altogether* is signaled to be new:

(39)  a.  [...] whiskey advertisements also are to be discouraged. *More significant* is the promise to give up altogether [...]. (COHA Corpus, Magazine, 1910)
      b.  That whiskey advertisements are to be discouraged is significant.

In sum, we can conclude that inversion is a construction whose primary function is clearly in line with the principle of placing given before new information in the clause. For distinguishing the formal types and for a closer look at how inversion is used in different texts, turn to Exercise 5. We will also turn to the use of inversion in different types of discourse in the next section.

Toolbox

Inversion in Corpora

Based on what you learned in Chapter 2, you will have noted that we did not deal with inversion here as a case of syntactic variation. Remember that, in order to do so, one would need to contrast its occurrence with all the clausal patterns that could potentially be inverted. This is an almost impossible task since the word order constraints of Modern English are strong and favor various other options. Rather than choosing between inversion and its canonical variant, speakers or writers of English resort to other sentence patterns, for instance, using an existential *there*-construction or choosing a different kind of verb. For example, an order of constituents similar to the one in Example (38a) is easily achieved by the sentences in (38b) and (38c):

(38)  b.  Behind the Pale Council there stood Persimmon Gaunt and Imago Bone.
      c.  Behind the Pale Council one could see Persimmon Gaunt and Imago Bone.

Studying inversion as a real syntactic variant, with discourse being the predictor, is therefore not an option, at least not when using corpus-based data (you could more easily set up an experiment on this). This limitation is why most studies of inversion work with a fixed set of attestations and are not based on the entire usage in a corpus.

For the challenge of retrieving a set of attestations automatically, you can again use a shortcut based on selected lexemes. This means you first limit your study to one particular type of inversion, such as PP-inversion. You then search by individual lexemes: for example, you search for occurrences of inversion following the preposition *among*. Using the POS information and the tagging within the corpus, you set up, for example, the search string starting with *among*, followed by a determiner, possibly an adjective, and a noun, followed by a verb. If you further limit this search to sentence beginnings (by adding punctuation and capitalizing the preposition), this search string with a common, locative preposition like *among* is likely to provide you with a considerable set of attestations (of the type *Among the numerous examples are some nice ones*). From the overall number of hits for this string, you select a randomized set of items, which you can use in your analysis. For example, based on a set of attested inversions together with their expanded contexts, you can investigate the information structure of inversion. See Exercise 10 (Level 2) for a related project.

### 3.4.3  Text-Linguistic Variation of Inversion

In this section, we explore the text-linguistic variation of inversion, despite the limits of its automatic retrieval. The evidence we discuss covers both the occurrence of the construction as a whole and the usage of the different subtypes, following the form-based classification that we introduced in Section 3.4.1.

Let us first take a look at the occurrence of inversion in general. Table 3.3 contains the rates of occurrence of inversion in three different kinds of non-fiction texts. Note that these results do not include NP-inversion since, with its NP-*be*-NP sequence, the decision over whether a clause is an inversion or not is usually difficult to make.

As you can see, the average rates of occurrence of inversion vary only slightly across the three discourse types. The frequency is a bit higher in biographical texts and lower in newspaper editorials, with reportages being somewhat in the middle. The presentative function of inversion that we noted above gives us a plausible explanation for this pattern of variation: Since a presentative function means something like "appearance on the scene," it makes sense that texts dealing with life accounts or news stories are likely to contain more settings or scenes to describe. Even though non-locative inversion can have a related function of appearance into the discourse (see text C in Exercise 5, *Adding to the problem is . . .*), such shifts of attention are likely to be less numerous in an editorial.

Our next step in dealing with the text-linguistic variation of inversion is to look at its different subtypes. Table 3.4 presents results from a corpus study of inversion (based on the British National Corpus), which took into account two types of texts: fiction and academic discourse. Given that the numbers of attestations per text category varied, the chart in Figure 3.6 is an appropriate visualization, showing us the proportional shares of the different subtypes of inversion as the dependent variable on the *y*-axis.

Table 3.3 *Frequency of inversion in three types of non-fiction discourse*

| Text category (number of text samples) | Biography (68) | Reportage (68) | Editorial (54) | Total Texts (190) |
|---|---|---|---|---|
| mean frequency | 1.3 | 1.0 | 0.8 | 1.1 |
| (absolute frequency) | (91) | (71) | (42) | (204) |

Data is from Dorgeloh 2006. There were 190 text samples = 380,000 words.

**Table 3.4** *Frequency of inversion types in fiction and academic writing*

| Inversion type | Fiction | Academic writing |
|---|---|---|
| AdjP-inversion | 8 | 156 |
| AdvP-inversion | 21 | 16 |
| PP-inversion | 194 | 160 |
| Part-/VP-inversion | 41 | 60 |

Data is from Kreyer 2006.

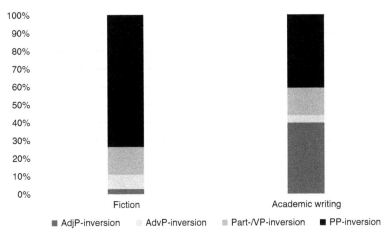

**Figure 3.6** Proportions of formal types of inversion in two types of discourse Based on Table 3.4.

Figure 3.6 shows a clear discourse-related difference. We see that PP-inversion, though in absolute numbers the most frequent realization of inversion in both types of texts, is dominant only in fiction, whereas in academic texts there is an almost equal proportion of inversion following a fronted PP or AdjP. This pattern of variation suggests that there are two different contexts for the usage of inversion. On the one hand, there are texts which mainly make use of the locative types of inversion, often because they aim at producing the illusion of the visual perception of a scene (in Ex. (33), for instance, you first imagine the candle and then the book). This effect can be described as an "eyewitness perspective" or "immediate-observer effect" (Dorgeloh 1997; Kreyer 2006), and it is achieved mainly by PP-inversion and AdvP-inversion. The results in

Figure 3.6 plausibly show that this function of inversion applies, in particular, to fictional discourse. By contrast, inversion in academic writing is not predominantly locative since academic texts are less likely to evoke scenes from real or fictional worlds. Instead, we find a considerably larger proportion of non-locative inversion, notably AdjP-inversion, in this discourse, which, as you see in Example (40), often combines an evaluative and a connective element in the fronted element. Such non-locative constituents followed by inversion are typically associated with academic argumentation. Their purpose is to build connections and to structure the discourse (Dorgeloh & Kunter 2015).

(40)    No doubt, there is something vaguely troubling about routinely
        aestheticizing one's feeling. But *even more troubling* is the habit of
        aestheticizing feelings that play a central role in our moral lives.
        (Example from Prado-Alonso & Acuña-Fariña 2010: 539)

In conclusion, we can note that the pattern of variation observed for the usage of inversion matches its semantic and formal types as discussed above (Figure 3.5). Even though the correspondences are not perfect, there is a higher likelihood of locative inversion, that is, of PP-, AdvP- and VP-inversion, to be used in texts that often contain descriptions of real-life or fictional scenes. In discourse dealing with more abstract topics, both locative and non-locative inversion types are more likely to serve the discourse structure. In sum, we have seen that both the information status of the preposed and postposed constituent in inversion as well as its text-linguistic variation are triggered by the discourse.

## 3.5 Summary

In this chapter, we have discussed sentence beginnings and, in particular, the non-canonical positioning of a core element to the left of the grammatical subject of the clause. We have seen that the filling of this position has the general purpose that the information contained in the clause is packaged differently. We also discussed more specific effects achieved by the different constructions, such as choosing a specific point of departure, serving topicality in discourse, and creating the illusion of a more immediate perception.

We looked at the positioning of adjuncts, fronting, left-dislocation, and inversion and discussed both their syntactic form and their text-linguistic variation. We saw that adjuncts as sentence beginnings are signposts for what is to follow. For fronting and left-dislocation, we showed that, even though the two constructions are formally similar, they occur under different conditions of discourse regarding information status and topic persistence. Finally, we split the phenomenon of inversion into a presentative locative type and a more abstract, non-locative type, which enabled us to explain how the use of inversion is associated with different discourse types.

We also highlighted in this chapter how, and to what extent, evidence on the use of these constructions can be produced when using a corpus, and we discussed the development of a research design and different formats for presenting corpus-based results. The research outcomes we discussed relate to the concepts of information status, topicality, and information packaging in discourse.

## 3.6 Exercises

### *Level 1: Classification and Application*

1. Imagine a text that opens as follows: *There are plenty of dishes that satisfy every member of the family.* Here are several versions of how the discourse could continue:

   - Only, pea soup, no one can stand it.
   - Only, on Saturdays, when there is always pea soup for lunch, no one is happy.
   - But among the dishes that no one can stand is pea soup.
   - Only, pea soup no one can stand.

   Underline the fronted non-subject constituent in each sentence and name the type of construction (adjunct in initial position, fronting, left-dislocation, inversion).

2. Underline all adjuncts in the following excerpt from the fairy tale *The Frog Prince*. Which ones are sentence-initial, clause-oriented adjuncts, and which ones are VP-oriented adjuncts? Why do you think the information in the adjuncts used at sentence beginnings is a suitable point of departure for the subsequent discourse?

---

A. One fine evening a young princess put on her bonnet and clogs, and
went out to take a walk by herself in a wood; and when she came to a
cool spring of water, that rose in the midst of it, she sat herself down
to rest a while. Now she had a golden ball in her hand, which was her
favourite plaything; and she was always tossing it up into the air, and
catching it again as it fell. After a time she threw it up so high that she
missed catching it as it fell; and the ball bounded away, and rolled
along upon the ground, till at last it fell down into the spring. The
princess looked into the spring after her ball, but it was very deep, so
deep that she could not see the bottom of it. Then she began to bewail
her loss, and said, "Alas! if I could only get my ball again, I would
give all my fine clothes and jewels, and everything that I have in the
world." ("The Frog Prince" from Grimms' *Fairy Tales*, 2001)

---

3. Some (manner) adverbs that often occur sentence-initially are *suddenly, happily, quickly, stupidly, slowly, skil(l)fully,* and *gradually*. Choose two (or a set) of these adverbs and carry out a search for them in a corpus like COCA or COHA. Based on a set of 50 attestations for each adverb, calculate the proportional frequency of its usage as clausal modifier. Which one(s) is/are particularly likely to occur as the point of departure for a sentence?
4. As explained in Section 3.3, there is no single search string that yields a reliable set of attestations for NP-fronting or left-dislocation. The following occurrences were found using the search string *these things I* (as in *These things I enjoy and look forward to*). As expected, they require subsequent manual cleaning of the data set. Decide which attestations are instances of NP-fronting and which ones have to be discarded as false positives.

---

1. *I was trying to call because I've – I've got all these things I have to do before moving.* (COCA, Spoken, 2016)
2. *My best baby shower present was a complete basket of all these things I didn't know I was going to need.* (COCA, Spoken, 2016)
3. *I got to the point where I was trying all these things I read online, and it never really worked.* (COCA, Spoken, 2015)
4. *All these things I've talked about doing, my opponent is against those.* (COCA, Spoken, 2010)
5. *But each one of these things I've risen, I've risen from. I've grown better.* (COCA, Spoken, 2007)

6. *You know, some of these things I've dug. I've dug being the baddest guy in the party.* (COCA, Spoken, 2004)
7. *Beyond these things I've missed you most when late at night I dream of you, the little things, your face, your eyes and walking in the market, too, but even in my dreams you rise.* (COCA, Spoken, 2002)
8. *But here – you know, some of these things I'd have in my restaurant, [...]* (COCA, Spoken, 1999)
9. *[...] but some of these things I would have at home or I'd send them to people for gifts.* (COCA, Spoken, 1999)

5. For the cases of inversion marked in the passages below, identify the type of inversion, referring to the formal category of the fronted constituent (AdvP, PP, VP, or AdjP) as well as to the difference between locative and non-locative inversion. Describe the function of inversion as presenting given and new information and as either presenting a scene or structuring the discourse. Do you think these functions can apply simultaneously?

---

B. Built by Empress Maria Theresa, who wanted it to dwarf Venice's famous plaza, the piazza faces the sea and is the only main square in Italy without a cathedral. It was renovated in 1999 and is marred only by Fontana dei Quattro, called "the ugliest fountain in Europe," a rock pile with a group of statues. *At the back of the piazza is the Town Hall* topped by a clock tower with two bronze figures – Mikeze and Jakeze – which clang the hours. *Behind the central square is a warren of narrow streets* winding through rows of centuries-old buildings. These lanes become alive at night with Triestinos enjoying apertivos after work and hearty dinners after 9 p.m. (COCA, News, 2014)
C. But all those pieces will need to fit together." *Adding to the problem* is size of the overall product and the sheer number of players involved. (COCA, Academic, 2007)

---

6. In her section "Evidence from Corpora" concerning sentence adverbs, Virtanen (2008) presents some of her results as follows:

a. In the BNC *carefully* shows frequencies above the average for imaginative prose and, secondly, informative writing labelled "leisure", [...]. (p. 288)

b. *Carefully* occurs at the beginning of a clause or sentence in 7% of the hits (443 out of 6476), [...] but above the average also in informative writing. (p. 289)

Which of these statements is an observation made from the point of view of syntactic variation, and which one is about the textual variation of *carefully* as an adjunct?

## Level 2: Interpretation and Research Design

7. In Section 3.2 we saw that some temporal and locative adverbs in sentence-initial position are typical signposts for the upcoming discourse. In a study on manner adverbs (such as *quickly*, *carefully*, or *gradually*), Virtanen (2008) notes that sentence-initial adverbials of manner are quite characteristic of instructive discourse. One of her findings is about the use of adverbials in recipes (for example, *gradually add the sugar* ...) and instructions for bodily exercise (such as in *slowly bend your right knee* ...). She observes that uses like the sequence "adverbial of manner" + "imperative form of a dynamic verb" are a highly characteristic sentence pattern. In the light of what you have learned in this chapter about the discourse function of sentence beginnings, can you explain the close association of this sentence pattern and instructive discourse?

8. Take the results shown in the chart below. Which of the statements below are supported by the chart?

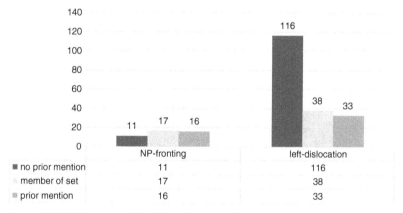

| | NP-fronting | left-dislocation |
|---|---|---|
| ■ no prior mention | 11 | 116 |
| member of set | 17 | 38 |
| ■ prior mention | 16 | 33 |

**Figure 3.7** NP-fronting/left-dislocation and givenness
Data is based on Gregory & Michaelis 2001.

    a. The majority of NPs in NP-fronting are either previously mentioned or members of a previously mentioned set.

    b. NPs belonging to a previously mentioned set are more frequently used with NP-fronting.

    c. The proportion of NPs that are either previously mentioned or members of a previously mentioned set is higher in the category of NP-fronting than in left-dislocation.

    d. In left-dislocation, the majority of NPs have no prior mention.

    e. The results confirm the hypothesis that the conditions of givenness for NP-fronting differ from those for left-dislocation.

9. We saw that the majority of NPs in left-dislocation, but not in fronting, persist as a topic in discourse. For a project on fronting and left-dislocation, you could test this assumption based on your own set of attestations. To create a corresponding data set, combine the lexical shortcut described in Exercise 4 (Level 1), i.e., using the lexical string for a fronted NP *these things*, with part-of-speech (POS) information available in a corpus. Use the POS tag for pronouns in COCA, which will give you hits for more sentences, i.e., with *you, we, he, they, it,* and *she* as subject pronoun (sentences starting with *yourself, himself, herself* and *his* have to be discarded). After cleaning the data, choose a fixed number of instances for NP-fronting and left-dislocation and decide for each sentence: Which degree of topic persistence (no persistence, repeated as NP, at least one pronominal use) does the NP in initial position have? (You will have to add a certain stretch of the subsequent discourse to each attestation.) Do your results confirm the difference between the two constructions as described in the chapter?

10. (a) In Section 3.4, we presented the general assumption about the information structure of sentences with inversion, namely that the initially placed constituent contains information that is more recoverable from the previous discourse than the information expressed by the subject. You should now test this hypothesis by retrieving your own set of inversions from a corpus. Retrieve attestations based on a selected lexeme, say, a single preposition. For example, using the lexical tagging of your corpus and the lexeme *among*, you set up the search string *among* + determiner + adjective + noun + verb at sentence

beginnings (i.e., preceded by a full stop or colon). Working on a set of only ten attestations – which is enough since you also have to look at their expanded contexts – decide for each sentence whether the information in the fronted PP and in the postposed subject NP is given (explicitly mentioned within previous discourse), is inferable (known from the context, though not mentioned before), or constitutes altogether new information. Does your result support the information-packaging hypothesis concerning inversion?

(b)  Now let's say that, in addition to the information-packaging function of inversion, you want to come up with a research project relating to topicality (the discourse function discussed in the chapter as applying to left-dislocation). Which of the two constituents re-ordered by the inversion do you expect to be the more topical? Formulate a testable hypothesis on this and come up with a reasonable prediction about the structure of the data set that would confirm it. Test this hypothesis using the corpus of sentences with inversion as gained for (a) above. Similar to the method described in Section 3.3.3 for the difference between left-dislocation and fronting, adopt the topic persistence values of "no persistence," "repeated NP," and "at least one pronominal use" to an analysis of your ten cases of inversion and their subsequent discourse. Do the results match your prediction?

## Further Reading

- For an overview of non-canonical word order focusing on information structure, see Ward & Birner (2006) and the chapter on information packaging in the *Cambridge Grammar* (Huddleston & Pullum 2002: Ch. 16).
- On the different motivations that contribute to the position of an adjunct in the sentence, namely, complexity, semantic type and type of discourse, see Diessel (2005). On the scope of adjuncts over subsequent discourse, see Crompton (2006). For more work on the discourse functions of adjuncts/adverbials, see Sarda et al. (2014) and Keizer (2018).

- Classic work about fronting and inversion is Prince (1981), Birner (1994), Birner & Ward (1998), and Ward & Birner (2006). For the method of gathering and analyzing data on fronting and left-dislocation, see Gregory and Michaelis (2001: 1680–90). See Kreyer (2006: 105–19) for the automatic retrieval of inversion in a corpus. See Leuckert (2019) on fronting in spoken genres from different varieties of English.
- A detailed description of the development of a research design and dealing with quantitative data can be found, for example, in Rasinger (2013). A comprehensive and state-of-the-art introduction to dealing with corpus data statistically is Brezina (2018).

# 4 | *Variation in the Middle*

## 4.1 Introduction

Chapter 3 dealt with variation patterns at the left periphery of the sentence, that is, constructions that target the area preceding the subject position. We saw that adjuncts (PPs, AdvPs) in the sentence-initial position give structure to the discourse by setting the stage for what is to come, while fronted complements (NPs), for example, in a left-dislocation construction, reintroduce a previously mentioned referent. In this chapter, we will discuss "variation in the middle," which we take to mean syntactic processes that involve the core clause and, in particular, syntactic choices regarding the subject and object position. These positions are usually filled with the verb's arguments – syntactic phrases, often NPs, that are needed to fully express a verb's meaning in syntax. For example, a verb like *drink* usually takes two arguments: the entity that drinks (often referred to as "agent"), realized as the subject, and the liquid that is ingested (often referred to as "**theme**"), realized as the object.

There are different theories discussing the mapping of semantic arguments to syntactic positions and they all have to account for the fact that, unlike with adjuncts, there isn't really all that much flexibility when it comes to the realization of subject and object arguments. The number of arguments a verb takes is driven by the verb's meaning. In order for an event to qualify as "drinking," somebody (the agent) has to ingest something liquid (the theme), which, syntactically, translates to *drink* being a transitive verb. Intransitive verbs (like *sleep* or *jump*) take only one argument (typically realized as subject), and ditransitive verbs (like *give*) take three (one subject and two objects). That is as high as the number of arguments goes. There are also verbs with no arguments at all: the so-called "weather verbs" (like *rain* or *snow*), which only occur with a non-referential dummy subject (*It is raining*), due to the requirement in English that the subject position be filled (see Chapter 1).

In this chapter, we will discuss two syntactic constructions that allow for the non-canonical realization of arguments. In English, as outlined in Chapter 1, in a canonical sentence, the agent argument typically precedes the verb and corresponds to the subject of the sentence and the theme argument follows the verb and corresponds to the direct object. Unlike in languages that mark the function of subject and object with

morphological case, such as Latin or Polish, one cannot simply switch the verb's arguments around in Modern English. A sentence like *The horse kicked the cow* can only mean that the horse is doing the kicking and that the cow is at the receiving end of the kicks.

However, there are processes that allow for a different pattern of argument realization in the core clause as well as processes that change the number of arguments of a verb (*They opened the door/The door opened*), raising the question of whether the verb under observation is still the same verb. In this chapter, we will discuss two of these patterns in detail: the passive construction (*The cow was kicked by the horse*), in which the semantic object of the verb ends up in the subject position, and the **verb-particle construction** (*He looked the information up*), in which the direct object can be realized in a verb-adjacent position or in a position after the particle. As a reminder, we use the term "construction" to indicate that the verb is only one structural piece in these sentences and that other factors, including discourse-related ones, are in play.

Psycholinguistic studies have shown that using a non-canonical argument realization pattern is costly in terms of sentence processing. If it is harder to process a sentence in which the verb's arguments are not realized in their canonical positions (agent as subject, **patient** as object), there must be a benefit associated with this pattern. We will show that the non-canonical realization of the verb's arguments within the core sentence is often motivated, and sometimes fully determined, by factors beyond the structure of the sentence, such as the choice of discourse topic or the focus of attention, but also by genre conventions.

After reading this chapter, you will be able to:

- detect marked and unmarked patterns of argument realization;
- identify discourse motivations for choosing non-canonical argument positions, especially in passive and particle verb constructions;
- understand limitations that exist for retrieving argument alternation patterns from electronic corpora;
- interpret research findings presented in different types of charts;
- formulate research questions that test hypotheses for discourse-based research questions on argument alternation patterns.

## Concepts, Constructions, and Keywords

*agent, animacy, argument realization,* get-*passive, information status, particle shift, passive construction, preposition stranding, Principle of End-Weight, syntactic complexity, theme/patient, Theory of Minimizing Domains, topic position, transitivity, verb-particle construction*

## 4.2 Canonical and Non-canonical Argument Realization

Let us return to the rigidity of English word order (Chapter 1) and the mapping of the agent role to the subject position. As outlined above, in a passive-voice sentence, the arguments of the verb are not realized in the canonical way. Crucially, the subject of the sentence is not an agent. Most often, it is the "theme" (sometimes also referred to as the "patient") of the action described by the verb: an entity that participates in or undergoes the action expressed by the verb and that may or may not be animate. If the agent is realized at all – in most passive construction it isn't, as in (1) below – it shows up as part of a postverbal *by*-phrase, as in (2). Passives with a *by*-phrase are usually referred to as *long passives*. The verb itself occurs as a past participle, which means that, in a finite clause, an auxiliary (usually a form of *be*) is needed to support tense and agreement.

(1)    Owen said the pipeline *was shut down* immediately after the leak *was discovered*. (COCA, Magazine, 2016)

(2)    Last December, a Maryland couple *was investigated by Montgomery County officials* for child neglect. (COCA, Magazine, 2015)

The "against the grain," or non-canonical, realization pattern of arguments, which is typical of passive constructions, is "marked" in two senses of the word: It is associated with a particular morpho-syntactic environment (typically through the combination of a participle and a form of *be*) and it is less frequent than the active-voice construction. The *GSWE* (Biber et al. 2021: 475) reports that only 2 percent of all finite verbs in conversations occur in the passive voice: a number that is higher in other registers (up to 25 percent in academic writing), but still considerably under 50 percent.

---

Good to Know: A Note on Passives and Preposition Stranding

The subject of a passive construction does not always correspond to the direct object of the passivized verb. It can be an underlying indirect object (*My sister was given a merit scholarship*), a dummy subject (*It is known that exercising regularly has many benefits*), or the subject of a lower clause (*My sister is expected to get into Harvard*).

In a sentence like *Precision was called for* the subject originates as the object of the preposition *for*. Such a construction – a sentence in which the object of a preposition is shifted to a position in which it doesn't follow the preposition anymore – is referred to as "**preposition stranding.**" Preposition stranding is a classic topic in prescriptive accounts of English. Some people feel that a preposition should not be separated from its object at all (because, after all, the morphology of the word *preposition* itself indicates that a preposition should be placed "pre," i.e. before, their object), others think preposition stranding is just not elegant and should be restricted to informal speech. Seventeenth-century writer and editor John Dryden even went so far as to edit out instances of preposition stranding found in Shakespeare's plays. From a linguistic viewpoint, however, there is nothing wrong with moving an object to another position in the sentence and, if anything, preposition stranding is simply one of many constructions in English that allow the displacement of a syntactic phrase. In fact, preposition stranding has a long history in English, in spoken as well as written language. Ingrid

Tieken-Boon van Ostade (2014) has shown that Jane Austen, a writer celebrated for her precision and clarity, used preposition stranding freely in both her letters and novels. If you are interested in learning more about the origins of the myth that preposition stranding is somehow ungrammatical or unnatural, see Yáñez-Bouza (2015).

The markedness of argument realization in the passive is also illustrated through the way in which children interpret passive constructions. Studies of the acquisition of the passive voice by young children have shown that children tend to interpret the subject of a sentence as the agent, especially in so-called "reversible" passives as in (3). Parsed correctly, that is, as a passive construction, sentence (3) means that the horse is the kicker and the cow is at the receiving end of the kicks (Figure 4.2), but young children, when asked to select a picture that matches the meaning of the sentence, tend to pick a picture in which the cow kicks the horse, as in Figure 4.1, thereby showing that they link the subject position to an agent interpretation (Turner & Rommetveit 1967, Borer & Wexler 1987) when this interpretation seems possible.

(3)    The cow was kicked by the horse.

(4)    The apple was eaten by the boy.

By contrast, for non-reversible passives, like sentence (4), children may select the correct picture (Figure 4.3) – but not necessarily because they parse the sentence as a passive construction and compute its meaning as

**Figure 4.1** Horse kicked by cow          **Figure 4.2** Cow kicked by horse

"A boy ate the apple," but because the "subject = agent" interpretation does not match their experience of the world (boys eat apples, but apples don't eat boys), so only Figure 4.3 matches their experience of the world.

**Figure 4.3** Apple eaten by boy     **Figure 4.4** Boy eaten by apple

Some linguists (Borer & Wexler 1992) have taken this behavior to mean that children under five have not mastered the syntax of the passive yet, while others (Pinker et al. 1987, O'Grady 1997) have pointed out that young children are very well able to understand passive constructions, even those produced on the basis of novel verbs, that is, verbs that they have never encountered before. To test if children would understand and correctly produce passives placed in a proper discourse environment, researchers carried out an experiment in which they introduced four-year-olds to one-syllable nonce-verbs like *to pell* or *to kale* with meanings like "jump on top of and then over" and then asked children to act out a scene with two toys ("Can you make it so that the doggy is being kaled by the elephant?"). They found that the comprehension rate was close to 100 percent (Pinker et al. 1987).

Overall, it seems safe to generalize that young children have a preference for interpreting subjects as agents, but that they are able to parse sentences as passives when the use of the passive is discourse-appropriate: for example, when an animate patient is the topic of the discourse. The researchers were also interested in seeing if children would *produce*, rather than just understand, passive constructions. To elicit such passives, they created a specific discourse environment that would be conducive to using a passive construction. The children were presented with a situation where the object of a transitive verb (the theme or patient) was also the topic of the discourse or prior focus of attention. For example, the researchers might first talk about cats and their habits and then introduce a context in which a specific cat was present as the target of another animal's actions, say, a dog chasing the cat. They then asked the child to describe what happened to the cat, thereby making the cat (the non-agent) the topic of the discourse. And indeed, young children did use the passive voice to answer such questions. In other words, when the discourse conditions favor the use of a passive construction, young children will not only *understand* the passive, they will also *produce* it, even with nonce-verbs that they have only just learned. This shows that young children understand that under appropriate discourse conditions the marked pattern of argument realization can be the preferred one.

Let us now shift to a construction with a more subtle way of rearranging the verb's arguments: the verb-particle construction. Particle verbs, also known as phrasal verbs, are verbs that are followed by – and often form a semantic unit with – a particle (*give up, put off, look up, switch on*). The semantics of the verb-particle combination can be more or less transparent. If you know the meaning of *switch* and *off*, it's not too hard to figure out the meaning of *switch off*, but knowing the meaning of *run* and *up* will not really set you up for figuring out the meaning of *run up* as in *running up a tab* at a restaurant. Some particle verbs are also part of idiomatic expressions, that is, they can only be followed by one particular noun phrase, as in *giving up the ghost* (said of a machine that stops working).

Particle verbs also come in different syntactic varieties: Intransitive particle verbs like *sleep in* don't take any kind of object, transitive particle verbs require a direct object (*look up the information, put off a meeting*), and prepositional particle verbs are followed by a prepositional phrase (*put up with the situation, give up on something*). We will focus on transitive particle verbs here, for reasons outlined below.

So how are particle verbs special? Syntactically, at first glance, the particle looks just like a preposition, but it can be demonstrated quite easily that particles have syntactic properties that set them apart from prepositions. Unlike transitive prepositions (*up* in *up the hill,* as in (6)), particles (like *up* in *looking up the recruiting page,* see (5)) do not seem to form a constituent with the NP that follows them: The particle and the NP cannot be fronted together (see the contrast between (6) and (7)), nor can they be coordinated with another phrase, as shown in (8), or foregrounded as a constituent in a cleft sentence, as shown in (9). The particle seems to go with the verb that precedes it rather than with the NP that follows it.

(5)    He looked up the US Army recruiting page. (COCA, Fiction, 2016)

(6)    Back at the stable, Red turned Jake around, and up the hill they went. (COCA, Magazine, 1995)

(7)    *Up the US Army recruiting page he looked online.

(8)    *He looked up the US Army recruiting page and up the requirements for serving in the Army Reserve.

(9)    *It was up the US Army recruiting page that he looked online.

What the particle *can* do is shift from its position between verb and NP and into the position after the NP, a phenomenon often referred to as "particle shift." (We will use the term "particle shift" here even though some syntacticians have suggested that the element that changes its position is actually the NP.) In the example below, the particle *up* is separated from the verb *look* by a rather long noun phrase, *the US Army recruiting page.*

(10)    He *looked* the US Army recruiting page *up* online.

We will focus on transitive particle verbs here because they are the ones that allow for these two patterns of argument realization: the continuous form (V-Prt-NP) and the discontinuous form, in which the particle has shifted to the position following the direct object (V-NP-Prt), as illustrated in (10). The whole construction – a transitive verb followed by a particle that can shift, followed by a noun phrase – is commonly referred to as "verb-particle construction" (Dehé 2002, Gries 2003, Diessel & Tomasello 2005). Alas, not all linguists use the label "particle" as a part-of-speech category. For example, the *Cambridge Grammar* refers to particles as "intransitive prepositions." We will stick with the term "particle" here.

Which of the two patterns – V-Prt-NP or V-NP-Prt – should be considered the unmarked argument realization pattern? Generally, the consensus is that on some level the particle forms a unit with the verb that precedes it (known as the "single verb hypothesis") and that the discontinuous word order (the one in which the particle is not adjacent to the verb) is marked and has to be motivated and derived somehow. This approach aligns with the non-compositional semantics of many particle verbs: *up* in *look up* or *give up* does not really indicate movement from a lower to a higher point, nor does *give* in *give up* have a lot to do with the core meaning of *give*, which may be paraphrased as passing an object from A to B. Semantically, the verb *give* and the particle *up* seem to form a unit, much like a compound. On the other hand, with regard to inflection, particle verbs like *look up* do not really behave like a compound verb. If they did, we would expect that the past tense affix would attach at the end of the compound verb, but the past tense of *look up* is *looked up*, not *look upped*. Still, even if the verb and the particle do not form a single word, they seem to form some kind of unit and we would expect that this unit stays together in the sentence and precedes the direct object, as in (11). It is not immediately clear why one would break up that unit and place the direct object between verb and particle, but that's exactly what happens in sentences (10), (12), and (13).

(11)    Verizon customer service *looked up* the number on my receipt and told me to ignore the Bill. (COCA, Magazine, 2009)

(12)    She ... went to the telephone and *looked the number up* and called the school. (COCA, Magazine, 1992)

(13)    I said, look, you know, I need a franchise document. He goes, I know nothing about that. So, you know, he *looked it up*. (COCA, Spoken, 2017)

While at first sight it looks as if the continuous (or "joined") and the discontinuous (or "split") word order are merely stylistic variations of the particle-verb construction, the behavior of pronouns indicates that something else is at play. If a transitive particle verb is followed by an unstressed pronoun, the discontinuous word order becomes obligatory, as illustrated by the contrast between (13) – *looked it up* – and (14) – *\*looked up it*.

(14)    *The customer service agent *looked up it* on my receipt.

There's something about the pronoun that makes the discontinuous word order necessary, and it is not just the fact that the pronoun is short. Example (15) below illustrates that particle shift is not required if the particle verb is followed by a one-syllable object that is not a pronoun (*Tom*). The crucial difference between a pronoun (*it, him, them*) and a short NP (*Tom*) is that the pronoun typically expresses known information, while a noun phrase can introduce new information.

(15)    If you're going to call up Tom, you better do it now. (COCA, Fiction, 2006)

Evidence from psycholinguistic studies confirms that speakers don't treat the two placement patterns as equivalent to each other and that under specific discourse conditions the discontinuous pattern, which would normally be perceived as the marked pattern, becomes the preferred pattern (Dehé 2002), just as under specific discourse conditions the passive construction is preferred to the active construction. We will discuss insights from such studies below.

> Before you move on, you should look at Exercise 1 to make sure that you can detect and correctly classify the target constructions that we will discuss.

## 4.3 Argument Realization in the Passive

Let us return to the passive construction. Before we examine reasons for choosing the passive over the active, we will briefly explore the various syntactic forms the passive can take. While the passive in itself is a non-canonical sentence structure in that the agent argument is not mapped onto the subject position of the sentence, there are also canonical and non-canonical passives. The *Cambridge Grammar* gives the following sentences as a representative pair of the canonical passive (Huddleston & Pullum 2002: 1427):

(16)    Pat stole my surfboard.

(17)    My surfboard was stolen by Pat.

The subject of the active, an agent (the NP *Pat*), appears in a non-obligatory *by*-phrase, the object of the active (the NP *my surfboard*) appears as the subject, the verb (*steal*) appears in its past participle form (*stolen*) and is preceded by a finite form of the auxiliary verb *be* (*was*). The passive can easily be mixed up with sentences in which *be* is actually a copular verb followed by an adjective that is homophonous with a participle, such as *disappointed* in (18).

(18)     The woman shook her head. She looked at me as if she was disappointed, and I looked away. (COCA, Fiction, 2013)

How do we know if a word that ends in *-ed*, such as *disappointed* or *surprised*, is an adjective or a participle? There are sentences that are simply ambiguous, but one way to make the decision is to imagine the degree adverb *very* in front of the word ending in *-ed* or to ask yourself if the *-ed* word can be replaced by a word that is clearly an adjective (such as *happy* or *sad*). If that switch sounds acceptable, you are most likely dealing with an adjective and the verb phrase it is part of expresses a state rather than an event. For example, in (18), we could easily replace *disappointed* with *sad* and we could also insert a degree adverb like *very* in front of *disappointed* without changing the meaning of the sentence too much. Therefore, the example should not be counted as a passive construction. Obviously, such ambiguities present problems when working with a large corpus.

You should now be able to take on Exercise 2, which asks you to distinguish between passive and adjectival readings.

Pairing an active and a passive sentence like those in (16) and (17) may suggest that passive sentences typically include a *by*-phrase, but that is not the case. One of the hallmarks of the passive construction is that the agent need not be overtly realized, and, indeed, in most occurrences of the passive, it is not. Corpus-based findings (e.g., Biber et al. 2021) show that, in all registers, so-called "short passives" (passives without a *by*-phrase) by far exceed "long passives" (passives that include a *by*-phrase). Biber et al. (2021: 934) therefore conclude that the short passive is "basic" and that the choice of a long passive has to be motivated in a particular way. We will address this issue below.

In addition to the canonical *be*-passive, there are also non-canonical passives, that is, passives that are not formed like the one in (17). One candidate in English is the *get*-passive, illustrated in (19).

(19)    Yeah, he *got fired*, because you're not allowed to put up a nanny cam in the office. (COCA, Spoken, 2016)

On the surface, the *get*-passive seems to be just like the *be*-passive, with the only difference being that the construction is formed with *get* instead of *be*. However, the differences between the two constructions run deeper. While *got* in (19) could easily be replaced with *was,* the syntax of the *get*-passive and the *be*-passive is not the same. Unlike *be, get* does not behave like an auxiliary verb, as shown below in (20) and (21). In question and negation contexts, it requires *do*-support just like a lexical verb. A syntactic analysis of a *get*-passive construction will therefore have to be biclausal (see Haegeman 1985 for an example).

(20)    No, he was not/*got not/did not get fired for putting up a nanny cam in the office.

(21)    Was he/*Got he/Did he get fired for putting up a nanny cam in the office?

The differences between the *be*-passive and the *get*-passive go beyond the syntax of the construction. While the *be*-passive is a marker of formal writing, accounting for about 25 percent of all finite verb phrases in academic prose, the *get*-passive occurs mostly in conversation and even there accounts for only 0.1 percent of all verbs (Biber et al. 2021: 476). This distribution has consequences for the kind of verbs that occur in both constructions. Verbs typically found in the *be*-passive include verbs often used in academic writing, such as *be applied, be calculated,* or *be suggested*, while verbs that occur with some frequency in the *get*-passive (at least five times per one million words) do not include verbs that express mental activities. There is also a peculiar layering of agency in the *get*-passive. Unlike the subject of the *be*-passive, the subject of the *get*-passive is often constructed as somehow responsible for the event ("secondary agent reading"). In (22), for example, the person who *got fired* is not portrayed as an innocent victim, but rather as someone who brought the event upon themselves, similar to the subject in (21). This secondary agent reading may explain why the subject in the *get*-passive is typically animate, which is not the case in the *be*-passive.

(22)    Combat, that's what they called him, *got fired* for stealing two cases of bags. (COCA, Fiction, 2015)

Another non-canonical passive, referred to by the *Cambridge Grammar* as "bare passive," is a passive that occurs in participial constructions. Participial clauses only occur in subordinate positions and crucially do not require an auxiliary to support tense and agreement features. In other words, they do not require the presence of *be*. The example in (23) below includes a participial passive-voice relative clause that modifies the noun *items*. With this being a subordinate clause, no finite verb or auxiliary is needed. If we expand the relative clause to a finite clause, as in (24), a form of *be* needs to be inserted.

(23)    I ordered two items suggested by my waitress. (COCA, News, 2017)

(24)    I ordered two items that were suggested by my waitress.

---

Good to Know: A Note on Passives in Corpora

   In corpus studies of the passive, non-canonical passives, particularly bare passives, are often omitted for practical reasons. They are even harder to search for in an electronic corpus than the *be*-passive because they occur without a form of *be* or *get*. It has been estimated (Wanner 2009) that in scientific writing around 20 percent of all passives fall into the category of bare passives, a factor to consider when you extract passives for your own research project.

---

In the remainder of this chapter, we will focus on the canonical *be*-passive and discuss why speakers pick this marked argument realization pattern over the unmarked agent-becomes-subject pattern.

### 4.3.1 Short vs. Long Passives

One might be tempted to think that short and long passives are essentially the same construction. Syntactically, they mostly are – the *by*-phrase is an optional constituent, very much like adjunct PPs, such as *in the morning* or *with great difficulty*. However, unlike those PPs, the *by*-phrase in the passive corresponds to an argument of the verb. Not expressing the agent overtly does not completely remove it from the meaning of the sentence. We will not be concerned with the syntactic representation of the invisible agent in short passives here, suffice it to say that even in short passives, the existence of an agent is linguistically implied, as illustrated by the contrast in (25) vs. (26) below. In the passive construction in (25), the agent-oriented adverb *deliberately* can be added, indicating that the sentence includes an implicit agent (the person who kept someone else out of the loop deliberately). However, in the intransitive use of the normally transitive verb *open* in (26), there is no implication that somebody opened the door, which is why the agent-oriented adverb *deliberately* cannot be added. While a short passive may imply the *existence* of an agent, the *identity* of the agent is not expressed, and this turns out to be one of the main motivations for using a short passive construction.

(25)   I was kept deliberately out of the loop. (COCA, Spoken, 1992)

(26)   The door opened *deliberately.

Most passive constructions make use of the option of not expressing the agent. As indicated above, corpus-based analyses of the passive, for example Biber et al. (2021), report that short passives by far exceed the number of long passives. Let us look at their findings in more detail. In calculating the frequency of the passive construction, it is common to count the number of passives per a certain number of words, i.e. as rates of occurrence (see Chapter 2). In Figure 4.5, adapted from Biber et al. (2021), the frequency of the passive across genres is represented through black squares that themselves correspond to 500 occurrences of the passive per one million words. (The *GSWE* does not provide exact numbers.) Unfilled squares correspond to fewer than 250 occurrences per one million words. The table only covers passives in finite sentences; the numbers for non-finite passives are lower across the board and we will neglect them here.

|                | Conversation | Fiction    | News       | Academic   |
|----------------|--------------|------------|------------|------------|
| Short passives | ■■■■         | ■■■■■■<br>■ | ■■■■■■<br>■■■■■■ | ■■■■■■<br>■■■■■■<br>■■■■■■<br>■■■■■ |
| Long passives  | ☐            | ■          | ■■■        | ■■■        |

**Figure 4.5** Distribution of long and short passives in different registers
Adapted from Biber et al. 2021.

As we can see in Figure 4.5, long passives are almost non-existent in spoken language and make up about one eighth of all passives in academic writing, a register that is comparatively rich in passives overall. Obviously, the function of a long passive cannot be to suppress an agent. In Section 4.3.2, we will therefore examine more closely the second main function of the passive: aligning a non-agent with the subject position, typically the position associated with the informational status of the topic.

Before we move on, let us return to the two different linguistic perspectives one might take when looking at the impact of usage-related factors on syntactic form, introduced in Chapter 2: The syntactic *variationist* view is focused on the linguistic variable (here: voice) and on the factors that lead to choosing one variant over another. The *text-linguistic* perspective is focused on a specific text type, or genre, and on which syntactic variants can be considered characteristic of which genres. Figure 4.5 is clearly concerned mostly with the text-linguistic perspective. The table tells us that there are, comparatively speaking, more passives in academic writing than in conversation, but that does not necessarily mean that most verbs in academic discourse occur in the passive voice. In fact, measuring the number of passives per a set number of words (here: per one million words) may not be the best way of giving a sense of how pervasive the passive is in a given register. Compare the following two excerpts, one from a (scripted) conversation (taken from the show *Gilmore Girls*, which is praised for its lively dialog and its rapid turn-taking, a hallmark of naturally occurring conversation) and the other from an article in the academic journal *Political Research Quarterly*.

(27)   Lorelei (looking at a picture): Who's that? Rory: That's me with April. Lorelei: When _did_ you meet April? Rory: When I _went_ to Philadelphia for Jess' open house. Lorelei: Jess? Philadelphia? What _am_ I missing here? Rory: Nothing. Jess' work _had_ an open house, I _was invited_ and I _went._ And Luke _showed_ up there with April. It _was_ a total fluke. (52 words) (The TV Corpus, Gilmore Girls, 2006)

(28)   His conception of coordination challenges _incorporates_ such post-positivist sensitivity, while, it _is argued_ here, offering a suitable focus for engaging with evaluative questions about contemporary governance. This focus _concerns_ the epistemological challenges for policy makers of discovering and acquiring knowledge about potential decision impacts in the context of complexity (49 words) (COCA, Academic Prose, 2016)

Both texts are roughly of the same length (52 and 49 words), both include exactly one passive construction (marked in italics). However, the syntactic make-up of these passages is actually very different. In particular, if we look at how many verbs are used in these passages and how many of those occur in the passive, the two texts are not similar at all. The first text has eleven (finite) verb phrases (all finite verbs are underlined), that is, eleven theoretical opportunities for the passive, but only one of those verb phrases actually occurs in passive voice (<10 percent). The second text has only three (finite) verb phrases (there are fewer verbs because the text has longer, more complex NPs, a point we will address in greater detail in Chapter 9) and one of them is a passive (33 percent). We could therefore say that, from the viewpoint of syntactic variation, in the second text the passive is chosen more often, relatively speaking.

   Two studies that look at the passive construction from a variationist viewpoint are Seoane (2006), discussed below (Exercise 8), and Hundt et al. (2018). The latter is concerned with predicting voice alternation based on factors like **animacy** of subject, givenness of subject, complexity of VP, and length of _by_-phrase in different international varieties of academic English. Some of these factors will also be addressed in this chapter, albeit not from a comparative perspective.

You should now be able to attempt Exercise 3, which deals with long and short passives.

## 4.3.2  *The Role of Previous Discourse: Topic and Weight*

We briefly discussed above that the verb's arguments are mapped onto syntactic positions in a systematic way. The exact nature of these mapping principles has been the subject of many different proposals, suffice it to say here that the argument that is semantically interpreted as "agent" is usually mapped onto the subject position of a clause. Due to this realization principle, the functional role of topic (the entity the utterance is about) and the semantic role of agent (if the verb has such an argument) typically align in the structural position of the subject in a canonical clause. The passive construction is a way of breaking up that alignment. Short passives are used to demote the agent of the verb (from explicit specification to implicit realization) and to promote another argument of the verb, usually the direct object (semantically a theme), to the position of the subject, that is, the position normally associated with the topic of the sentence (the entity the utterance is about). Therefore, the short passive is most fortuitous when both detachment from a specific agent and topic-status for a non-agent are sought.

Let us illustrate how these two functions come together by expanding the context for sentence (25), see (29). The given sentence is excerpted from a TV interview with Caspar Weinberger, who served as US Secretary of Defense under President Reagan from 1981 to 1987. Five years after he resigned from his position, he was indicted on charges of perjury and obstruction of justice in connection with what has come to be known as the Iran-Contra Affair. The Reagan administration had used proceeds from illegal weapon sales to Iran to fund a rebel group, the Contras, in Nicaragua, allegedly to facilitate the rescue of American hostages. In the interview with ABC journalist Sam Donaldson, Weinberger talks about his experience as advisor to President Reagan and about whether or not Vice President Bush knew of the arms-selling scheme.

(29)    President Reagan ultimately accepted the proposal against my strong recommendation and George Shultz's strong recommendation. But I don't think that the details of the operation were necessarily disclosed to Vice President Bush, because they certainly weren't to me. You know, I had to get a great deal of my information about this whole affair from foreign sources, not from our own government, because *I was kept deliberately out of the loop*. (COCA, Spoken, 1992, from ABC interview on Dec. 27, 1992)

If we look at the underlined arguments in subject position, we see a gradual topic shift from President Reagan's decision-making to Weinberger's role in the process. Weinberger is the agent and topic in the sentence preceding the excerpted sentence (*I had to get a great deal of my information [...] from foreign sources*) and then Weinberger is still the topic, but, crucially, not the agent, in the italicized passive construction (*I was kept deliberately out of the loop.*). Essentially, he portrays himself as victim. Using the short passive here serves two functions: topic continuance (*I*) and the suppression of a specific agent. The presence of the adverb *deliberately* makes it abundantly clear that Weinberger thinks *someone* kept him out of the loop, but the identity of that person is not elaborated on, because the sentence is about Weinberger, not about the people who did not keep him informed. An active-voice sentence would have to realize the agent – the people who kept him out of the loop – as subject and the sentence would then not be about Weinberger and his (perceived) role as victim. The passive construction with its non-canonical mapping of arguments is needed to put a non-agent (Weinberger) in the position canonically associated with topic status. In the discourse situation of the interview, it is not advisable for Weinberger to name names, so the agent is left implicit, that is, a short passive is chosen. (Weinberger was pardoned by President George H. W. Bush before it came to a trial.)

Other reasons for not expressing the agent explicitly are illustrated by the examples below. The identity of the agent may simply not be known, as in (30), it may be common knowledge, as in (31), or it can be constructed from the text, as in (32). The subject of the passive in (32), *they*, refers back to the NP *participants*, which is introduced in the preceding adverbial clause. This being an excerpt from a scholarly article that reports experimental work, the identity of the agent of the passivized verb (*asked*) is clear from the context: The agent here is the group of researchers that carried out the study.

(30)   A Chick-fil-A manager in Chino Hills, Calif., *was robbed* of some cash – and maybe a little dignity – on Thursday of last week. (COCA, Magazine, 2017)

(31)   After 12 long years of Ronald Reagan and George H. W. Bush, Bill Clinton *was elected* president with Democrats in charge of both houses of Congress. (COCA, Magazine, 2016)

(32)    To keep participants reading with attention, they *were asked* to
        respond yes/no to comprehension questions after 25% of sentences.
        (COCA, Academic Prose, 2013)

We have just seen that the short passive usually combines two effects:
promoting a non-agent to subject/topic and demoting an agent to
adjunct status. However, these two functions of the passive do not
always align. In (33), the passivized verb, *argue*, is followed by an
object clause and the subject position is filled with *it*, a non-referential
"dummy subject." As a non-referential element, *it* cannot serve as a
topic. One might ask why one would choose a passive in such instances.
We will take up this question in Chapter 9, when we discuss the role of
genre conventions (for example, the tradition of minimizing the visibility of the researcher in scientific writing) in choosing non-canonical
sentences.

(33)    Nevertheless, in this article it will *be argued* that by creating an
        appropriate framework for the inclusion of causal responsibility into
        the equity principle, it may be possible to integrate proportionality,
        equality and need into a single principle. (COCA, Academic Prose,
        1994)

The reverse scenario, topic promotion but no agent suppression, is
exemplified by the long passive, that is, passives that include a *by*-
phrase. Obviously, the long passive does not leave the agent of
the event implicit. What, then, is the motivation for using a
long passive, that is, a construction that puts the agent in a non-
canonical position, namely the end of the clause? In many cases
two motivations come together. The first factor is topic status of
the non-agent, just as in the short passive. Corpus-based studies of
the long passive confirm that, in the majority of long passives, the
subject has a higher level of givenness than the agent. Biber et al.
(2021: 932) report that about 90 percent of agent phrases in long
passives express new information, and that in the majority of these
cases the subject expresses given information, as seen in Figure 4.6.
By contrast, the combination of a subject expressing new information and a *by*-phrase expressing given information is exceedingly
rare (it is represented by one hollow square in the second row of
the table).

|                          | *by*-phrase given information | *by*-phrase new information |
|--------------------------|-------------------------------|------------------------------|
| Subject given information | ■ | ■■■■■■ ■■■ |
| Subject new information   | □ | ■■■■ |

**Figure 4.6** Givenness of subject vs. agent phrase in long passives
Adapted from Biber et al. 2021. Each full square represents about 5%, and a hollow square represents a number lower than 2.5%.

In Example (34) we see that the topic shifts from *the federal probe* in the first sentence to the person who started that probe in the second sentence. *White* is the subject of the sentence-initial adverbial clause (note that the sentence refers to her by just her last name because her full name, *Mary Jo White*, has already been established), and the pronoun *she* continues this topic as the non-agent subject of the main clause. The *by*-phrase introduces a new entity (*James Comey*), which is elaborated on in a long and complex apposition.

(34)   *The federal probe* started under then-U.S. Attorney Mary Jo White, who now heads the Security and Exchange Commission for the Obama administration. When *White* left office in 2003, *she* was replaced by James Comey, the FBI director now under fire for notifying Congress last week about his agency's decision to review emails to and from Clinton aide Huma Abedin. (COCA, News, 2016)

The *Cambridge Grammar* generalizes that the "felicity of a long passive requires that the subject not represent information that is newer in the discourse than the NP governed by the word *by*" (Huddleston & Pullum 2002: 1444). The second, not completely unrelated, factor has to do with phrase length. Syntactically, higher topical status is often reflected in shorter length: A previously introduced subject can be realized as a one-syllable pronoun, while a newly introduced agent is typically longer. Another syntactic marker of givenness is the choice of a definite article or the use of a proper name. Since givenness is not a syntactic category per se, one needs some kind of workaround to classify corpus data automatically. Linguists typically work with syntactic correspondences, which can be quantified automatically. For example, Hundt et al. (2018), while recognizing that givenness is a

**Figure 4.7** The Principle of End-Weight

complex concept with no simple 1:1 syntactic correspondence, decide to code subjects as "given" when they are pronominal or definite and as "not given" when they are indefinite noun phrases.

In the sentence we just discussed, the subject NP consists of one word (*she*), while the *by*-phrase includes a lengthy modifier in the form of a relative clause (the modifier alone comprises more than twenty words). There is a tendency to place shorter phrases before longer phrases, not only with regard to the choice of argument realization patterns, but also in other situations where two different word order patterns express the same meaning, for example in the realization of possessor and possessed in the genitive construction. The longer a possessor, the more likely it is that the *of*-genitive will be chosen over the *'s*-genitive. If a possessor is short (*the teacher*), it is typically realized before the noun that is possessed, but if the possessor is long (say, *the new substitute teacher from Germany*), the preference shifts to realizing the possessor after the noun that is possessed. Hence, chances are that one would say *the teacher's car* (instead of *the car of the teacher*), but one would prefer *the car of the new substitute teacher from Germany* over *the new substitute teacher from Germany's car* (see Rosenbach 2014). This preference for presenting short phrases before long phrases is commonly referred to as the "**Principle of End-Weight.**"

In recent years, there has been a strong tendency to explain these weight effects in terms of syntactic parsing and processing (following Hawkins 1994 and 2004). Hawkins and others have argued that the reason behind the Principle of End-Weight is that longer, more complex phrases are more taxing on our short-term memory and take longer to process and integrate into the existing discourse.

Good to Know: The Principle of End-Weight
in Linguistic Theory

While the exploration into the psycholinguistic foundation of the
Principle of End-Weight is a fairly recent focus of linguistic research,
the principle itself – the observation that, where possible, shorter
constituents tend to precede longer constituents – has a long tradition
in linguistic theory. Historical German linguist Otto Behaghel
referred to it as the "Law of Growing Constituents" (1909).
Another name, "Panini's Law," links it to the work of the ancient
Sanskrit philologist Panini (Cooper & Ross 1975). In English grammar this Principle of End-Weight can be observed in many different
constructions not discussed in detail here, including the double object
construction and word order choices in the genitive (*my sister's
house/the house of my sister*).

You may wonder how exactly one calculates the "weight" of a phrase.
There are different factors to consider, including length (measured by
number of words or number of stressed syllables), syntactic density
(measured by number of syntactic nodes in a tree diagram), and information status (new information has more weight than old information). While there is no simple overall formula, it is important to point
out that all factors that are typically considered align in the case of the
long passive: The *by*-phrase at the end of the clause is usually "weightier" (longer, newer, syntactically more complex) than the non-agent in
subject position.

How to Measure Syntactic Complexity

There are different ways to measure **syntactic complexity**. Factors
that matter include the length and depth of a phrase. A simple way
to measure length would be just to count the number of words per
phrase. A simple way to measure depth would be to count the
number of "non-terminal branching nodes" inside the syntactic

representation of a phrase. In the diagrams below, terminal nodes are marked as such. They are the nodes that dominate a word. All other nodes are non-terminal nodes. We see that the diagram on the left has only one non-terminal node, the NP node at the top. The diagram on the left has no intermediate levels at all, while the diagram on the right has at least one intermediate level in the noun phrase (in generative grammar, this intermediate level is typically referred to as X′ pronounced "X-bar," in this case N′ or "N-bar"). Therefore, the diagram on the right has greater depth (the NP is also longer).

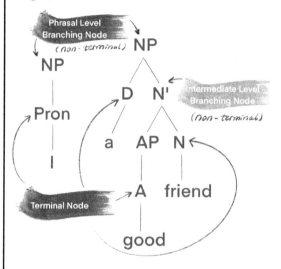

There are many studies on the concept of syntactic complexity and its role in language variation and change, as well as in first- and second-language acquisition. A lot of the recent work on syntactic complexity and constituent order was inspired by John Hawkins's work on order and constituency (Hawkins 1994). We will touch on his theory in our discussion of particle verbs below (Section 4.4.2) and will return to the concept of syntactic complexity, including a different approach to measuring it, in Chapter 9.

The following two examples illustrate this pattern: In (35), the choice of the passive allows for topic continuity (*note*), and the *by*-phrase (*by a Georgia family*) is clearly longer and syntactically more complex than the two-word subject. The topic of a *note* is first established as an indefinite noun phrase in the object position. The second sentence picks up on that topic, now no longer a new topic, realizing it as a definite noun phrase (*the note*) in the subject position of a passive construction. The agent of the passivized verb is realized as a *by*-phrase (*by a Georgia family*). The *by*-phrase is longer and more complex than the subject (*The note*) and it is also informationally weightier because it introduces new information. We can see that both reasons for using a long passive come together: Realizing the topic as subject and realizing a weighty agent argument at the end of the sentence, in line with the Principle of End-Weight.

(35)    This undated photo shows a note written by a young boy to his deceased father. The note was found *by a Georgia family* in their backyard. (COCA, News, 2016)

The next excerpt illustrates the same pattern: The first-person pronoun, *I*, in the passive construction in the second sentence (*was asked*) is the topic of the previous discourse. The passive construction here achieves topic continuity from the first to the second sentence. The agent of the verb is realized inside a *by*-phrase (*by a good friend*), which is weightier (longer, more complex, and informationally new, indicated by the indefinite article) than the subject (the pronoun *I*).

(36)    I'm nonreligious but very tolerant of other people's beliefs (i.e. I don't go around expounding on my atheism and mostly keep it to myself). Recently, I was asked *by a good friend* to serve as a godparent to his child. (COCA, Magazine, 2017)

The realization of arguments in these sentences may be non-canonical from a semantics/syntax-mapping viewpoint, but it is perfectly in line with linking syntactic positions to the ongoing discourse. As with other constructions, we find confirmed that "[i]n general, semantic role is the determining factor in the choice of subject in canonical clauses, while presentational status determines the choice between canonical and non-canonical constructions" (Huddleston & Pullum 2002: 235).

This would be a good time to check out Exercises 4 and 5, which deal with the interpretation of short and long passives.

## 4.4  Argument Realization in the Verb-Particle Construction

Like the passive construction, the verb-particle construction allows for two different argument realization patterns. We will refer to the pattern in (37) as V-Prt-NP or as the continuous pattern and the one in (38) as V-NP-Prt or the discontinuous (or "split") pattern.

(37)    Until that moment, we had not known that Flint himself was a writer. The next morning, I *looked up his name* in the periodicals index at the library. (COCA, Fiction, 2000)

(38)    Marshall has a rare ability, Norris says, to connect one on one. "You could be one of 100,000 people and feel he's speaking to you," she says. "He's very genuine. Very humble. You know, I *looked his name up* once. Joseph. It means to be a giver." (COCA, News, 1992)

In the particle-verb construction we are dealing with two realization patterns completely inside the verb phrase – the subject position is not affected, which indicates that, unlike with the passive, the notion of topic is not going to be an important factor here. Another difference between the verb-particle construction and the passive construction is that in the verb-particle construction, both realization patterns have the same number and types of arguments. This means that the other main function of the passive – backgrounding of an agent – is also not an issue. However, we will see that some of the concepts we introduced in the discussion of the passive are relevant in understanding the verb-particle construction as well. Before we discuss the role of the surrounding discourse in selecting a non-canonical pattern of argument realization, let us briefly reflect on which of the two realization patterns should be considered basic and which should be considered marked. Since none of the two orders is associated with a specific verb form, the answer to this question is not as obvious as in the case of the passive.

### 4.4.1  *Which Pattern is Basic?*

With the passive construction, it was fairly easy to say that the word order that gives us a non-agent subject and an optional agent in a *by*-phrase is a marked way to realize the arguments of the verb. Things are different in the verb-particle construction. Unless one assumes that the verb-particle combination is essentially one lexical item (a proposition that is challenged by the discontinuous pattern), it is not immediately obvious which word order should be considered unmarked, and, indeed, the literature on the subject includes proposals for either pattern as the basic one. Should the canonical argument realization be the one that occurs more often? The one that is easier to process? The one that is acquired earlier? Ideally, different criteria align, but what if they don't?

With the passive we saw that children acquire the passive – that is, the non-canonical realization of arguments – later than the active construction. Can we use a similar argument for the verb-particle construction? Unlike with the passive, we cannot rely on formal markedness – there is no particular affix or auxiliary associated with either word order in the verb-particle construction. So perhaps a look at acquisitional data will help us determine which word order should be considered basic and which should be marked.

Based on observational data from the CHILDES corpus (a database of spontaneous utterances by children), researchers found that children as young as two years old freely produce verb-particle constructions (Diessel & Tomasello 2005). The vast majority of these (93.5 percent of 572 tokens) shows the discontinuous order. Looking at these numbers, one might be tempted to think that the discontinuous word order must be basic, but a more in-depth look at the data shows that almost all of the attested examples included short noun phrases (up to two words: a pronoun, a bare noun, or a noun with a determiner) as the direct object that splits the particle from the verb. What we see, then, might be that when children acquire particle verbs they also acquire adult-like sensitivity to the length of the object. Corpus studies confirm that the longer the object, the less likely it is that the discontinuous word order will be chosen. Gries (2003) found that for NPs consisting of one to three words, the continuous word order is preferred, a result replicated in a study by Wasow & Arnold (2003). We will return to these findings below.

To control for factors like object length and idiomaticity of V-Prt meaning, Dehé (2002) constructed an experiment in which adult native speakers (n = 28) could choose the word order they preferred for completing a sentence. For a sentence that began with *she*, participants could select verb phrases, like *showed off her car*, *showed her car off*, as well as ungrammatical completions, such as *off showed her car*, as the continuation of the sentence. Dehé found that, for all particle verbs, whether semantically compositional or opaque, the continuous pattern (V-Prt) was the preferred one. Corpus data aligns with this finding, especially in idiomatic expressions, in which the NP that follows the particle is completely predictable. It has been argued that the more idiomatic the verb-particle combination is, as measured through criteria like the degree of semantic compositionality, the less likely it is that the discontinuous pattern will be chosen. For example, when doing a lemma search (as explained in the toolbox on lexical shortcuts in Chapter 3) of the idiomatic expression "[give] up the ghost" (said about a machine that has stopped working), COCA only gives results in the continuous word order, including the one in (39). By contrast, if *give up* means "yield control or possession," the choice of object is not predictable (one can give up a lot – a hobby, a privilege, an object) and one can find instances of both word orders, as illustrated in (40) and (41). In (40), the direct object is a noun phrase that is informationally new and the continuous word order is chosen, while in (41), the object has been introduced before and, just as with pronouns, the discontinuous word order is chosen.

(39)    These ironworks were long-lived. They only *gave up the ghost* in the 1970s (COCA, News, 1999)

(40)    After Daddy died, even when all the old neighbors had moved away, Mother wouldn't *give up the house on 41st Street*. (COCA, Fiction, 1994)

(41)    "William Jennings Bryan stayed in this house! ... The interior moldings and the woodwork are mahogany, the library pands – "You're real attached, I know." I was too attached to *give the house up* – it was true. (COCA, Fiction, 2006)

In the following, we will assume that the continuous word order (V-Prt-NP) is basic and that the choice of the non-continuous word order has to be motivated. As indicated above, factors that come into play include the length of the direct object (the longer the object, measured in words or syllables, the less likely it is that the discontinuous word order will be chosen), the degree of idiomaticity (the less predictable the meaning of the verb phrase is, the less likely it is that the discontinuous pattern will be chosen), and the semantics of the NP (abstract NPs occur more often in the V-Prt-NP order than in the V-NP-Prt order). In the next section, we will therefore focus on *discourse-related* factors. How does the surrounding discourse contribute to making the decision to choose a non-canonical over a canonical realization of arguments?

## 4.4.2 The Role of Previous Discourse: Information Status and Weight

We have already seen that unstressed pronouns typically only occur in the discontinuous pattern (V-Pronoun-Prt) and that this restriction is not simply a function of the pronoun being short, as illustrated by Example (15), now modified as (42).

(42)    If you're going to call up Tom/*him, you better do it now. (COCA, Fiction, 2006)

The main difference between the two noun phrases *Tom* and *him* is not one of length, but one of information status. *Tom* is a referential expression and introduces new information; *him* is a pronoun and as such referentially dependent, which means that it expresses previously introduced information (more on this in Chapter 6). Similarly, in idiomatic expressions the V-NP-Prt order is more common because the NP does not introduce information that is referentially new. Note that in idiomatic expressions the placement of the particle is not so much a matter of preference, it may actually be quite fixed. One can *cry one's eyes out*, but one can't *cry out one's eyes*. A machine can *give up the ghost*, but it doesn't *give the ghost up*. This pattern confirms that the discontinuous word order is associated with the direct object not introducing new information. Note that in (41) above, but not in (40), the direct object NP (*the house*) refers to an object previously introduced in the discourse.

> This would be a good time to look at Exercise 6, which asks you to apply what you have just learned about the choice of the continuous vs. the discontinuous pattern to selected corpus data.

If the object of a transitive particle verb is long, there is a preference for the continuous word order (V-Prt-NP), which is to be expected, because a noun phrase that is long is typically a noun phrase that contains modifiers, and modifiers bring in new information. This preference also aligns with the Principle of End-Weight (discussed in Section 4.3.2), which states that, given a choice, speakers tend to place long constituents after short constituents. In the example below, the head of the direct object (*chair*) is modified by a relative clause (*that he knocked over ...*), which itself includes an adverbial clause (*as he strode ...*), resulting in a long and complex postverbal NP. This is also the first and only mentioning of a chair in the discourse, which means that both weight (a long noun phrase) and information status (new information) align. A noun phrase that is both complex and new is typically placed in the postverbal position.

(43)    Greg Bennet did not bother to pick up the chair that he knocked over as he strode from the cafeteria. (COCA, Fiction, 1992)

Returning to the examples given above, we see that in (40) the NP that follows the verb-particle combination, despite not being completely new to the discourse (there has been talk about a neighborhood and people moving away), contains new and specific information in the form of a modifier. The object is not just *the house*, but *the house on 41st street*. By contrast, in (41), the object contains no new information, resulting in the choice of the discontinuous word order.

Let us look at a chart from a corpus-based study that illustrates the relationship between weight and information status on a larger scale. Figure 4.8 is adapted from an article by Lohse et al. (2004). The authors extracted 1,684 examples of verb-particle constructions from four different corpora, including data from American and British English, both written and spoken. They looked at the length of the direct object and counted how often each pattern (V-NP-Prt and V-Prt-NP) occurred. (They only included VPs that did indeed allow both patterns, so no VPs in which the NP was a pronoun or part of a fixed idiom.) The graph in Figure 4.8 shows the percentage of examples in the discontinuous word order (V-NP-Prt) – referred to as "split" in this paper – as the dependent variable on the *y*-axis.

We see in Figure 4.8 that the discontinuous word order is not the dominant word order in any scenario. (Bear in mind that sentences in which the NP is a pronoun are excluded from the corpus, as they do not typically allow both word order patterns.) It is chosen most often in the case of a one-word NP (such as proper nouns or mass nouns), at a rate of 47 percent, and still quite often in the case of two-word NPs. As the NP becomes longer, the discontinuous pattern becomes less frequent, with a steep decline between the two-word and the three-word NPs, a result that mirrors the findings by Gries (2003), a study based on a different corpus. What makes two-word NPs so different from three-word NPs? The difference is not just one of length, but also of

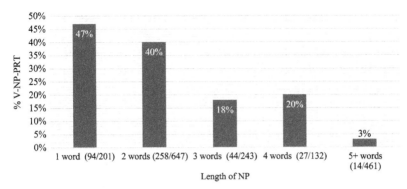

**Figure 4.8** Relationship between length of object and word order choice
Adapted from Lohse et al. 2004.

information richness. Two-word NPs are often NPs that consist of a noun and a determiner. If the determiner is a definite article, the NP does not really bring in new information (*look the number up*). By contrast, three-word NPs are more likely to include a modifier, for example an adjective (*look up someone's new address*).

> Exercise 7 introduces another chart from the same study and asks you to consider the findings in the light of the idea that processing cost is a factor in choosing one syntactic pattern over the other.

It is often assumed that the reason behind the pattern just described (the longer the NP, the less likely the V-NP-Prt order) lies in the way in which sentences are processed. Hawkins's theory of "minimizing domains" for syntactic processing claims that "[t]he human processor prefers to minimize the connected sequences of linguistic forms [. . .] in which relations of combination and dependency are processed" (2004: 31). Put simply, if we assume that in the particle-verb construction a VP branches into three immediate constituents (V, NP, Prt), we would ask how much lexical material has to be processed by the listener or reader before this structure – and thus the meaning of the phrase – can be figured out.

(44)  a.  They looked up the deadline for the registration.
      b.  They looked the deadline for the registration up.

In (44a), the verb *look up* is immediately followed by an NP that begins with a determiner (*the*), which means that the structure of the VP can be determined after the first three words in that VP (*looked up the*), while in (44b) the sequence *looked the deadline for the registration* (six words) has to be processed before we get to the particle *up*, which means that processing the syntactic structure of (44b) requires a longer hold on cognitive resources than processing (44a). From this perspective, then, (44a) is a more efficient arrangement of the verb phrase than (44b). The diagrams below illustrate that in the V-Prt-NP word order, the three-branch structure is determined after the third word, *the*. In the V-NP-Prt word order, the overall structure of the VP (three components, the verb *look*, the NP, and the particle *up*) is not determined until the third branch is introduced, which, in the given example (with the NP taking up words #2–5), would not be until we get to word #6:

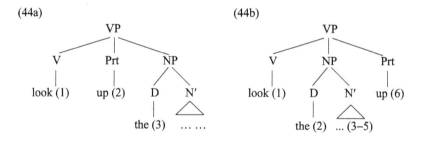

(44a)
(44b)

However, we have seen that efficiency can be trumped by information status: If the NP is an unstressed pronoun, the V-Prt-NP word order is not an option, even though, from a "minimal domain" viewpoint, both word orders would be equally efficient. Therefore, we will take a deeper dive into the role of the surrounding discourse next.

(45)   a.   They looked it up.
       b.   *They looked up it.

The role of the surrounding discourse is not only important to determine if the direct object is new or given information. Work based on spoken data has shown that the two alternative patterns differ with regard to the placement of stress and that one needs to consider which phrase the speaker wants to emphasize or, to use a more technical term, focus. The focused part of an utterance is the part that is highlighted by the speaker, usually through a combination of phonological (stress), syntactic (word order), and lexical choices (a discussion of the expression of focus through sentence-final positioning or *it*-**clefting** will follow in Chapter 5). For example, in the famous line from Shakespeare's *Romeo and Juliet* in (46), the *it*-cleft construction would be accompanied by stressing the focused phrase *the nightingale*. (The context here is that Juliet, who is secretly spending the night with Romeo, wants to assure him that the night is not over yet. He thinks he has heard a lark announce the morning, but she asserts that what he heard was the song of a nightingale instead.)

(46)    It was the nightingale, and not the lark, that pierced the fearful
        hollow of thine ear. (Shakespeare, *Romeo and Juliet*, 2003 [1597]:
        III.v.2)

The focused part of an utterance cannot be taken for granted or inferred from the discourse, which is not quite the same as saying that a focused phrase cannot be a phrase previously mentioned. The role of focus becomes clearest in situations in which the NP is stressed to emphasize a contrast or unexpectedness, as in the example above. Wulff & Gries (2019: 878) point out that "contrastive stress is the only variable that can overrule the otherwise very strong preference of pronominal objects preceding the particle." They provide the sentence in (47) (not taken from a corpus and not contextualized further), where capitalization indicates contrastive stress.

(47)    He picked up HIM, not her.

All NPs in (47) are pronouns and presumably refer back to persons previously introduced. In that sense, they all constitute known or given information. However, the addition of *not her* makes it clear that the sentence is produced in response to an expectation that the object of the verb would be the **referent** of the object pronoun (*her*). With regard to this expectation, the choice of the object *him* is informationally new. It is marked with contrastive stress and is placed after the verb-particle combination, the position generally associated with new information. We see that contrastive stress on *him* syntactically aligns with the continuous pattern, which is not normally found with pronouns. And indeed, unstressed pronouns do not occur in the continuous pattern.

In an empirical study, Dehé (2002) asked ten native speakers of English to read out brief prepared discourse passages that included sentences with verb-particle constructions in neutral (non-contrastive) focus situations. She recorded these readings and analyzed them for pitch and accent placement. She found that "the placement of the accent depends on the speaker's intention and on the focus structure of the sentence" (2002: 175). Interestingly, there was no statistical difference between semantically compositional and non-compositional verb-particle constructions. Accent placement was on the noun in the continuous pattern and on the particle in the discontinuous pattern, regardless of whether or not the particle carried independent meaning.

## 4.5 Summary

In this chapter, we have discussed word order variation patterns "in the middle" (i.e., inside the core sentence) that affect the realization of the arguments of the verb. Drawing on arguments from linguistic theory, corpus findings, language acquisition, and language processing, we have introduced ways of determining which pattern is the basic pattern and discussed motivations for choosing an alternative argument realization pattern, focusing on motivations that are tied to the surrounding discourse.

For the passive construction, we saw that one of the main motivations for using the passive construction is to align a non-agent topic (which is normally realized as an object) with the canonical topic position, that is, the subject position. For the particle-verb construction, we showed that the position after the verb-particle combination is associated with new or relevant information.

On the way, we touched on general principles of word order organization, such as the Principle of End-Weight and the Theory of Minimizing Domains. Throughout this chapter, we have highlighted insights from corpus- and experiment-based research and presented data in context.

Now, it is time for you to engage with the Level 2 exercises and/or turn to the original research articles cited in this chapter to learn more about how linguists operationalize their research questions before you design your own research project.

You should now be able to take on Exercises 7–10 and be
prepared to design your own corpus-based research
project. What is a concept that you would like to get
a deeper understanding of? What is a question that you
would like to delve into? The list of further readings at the
end of this chapter will help you explore selected topics further.

## 4.6 Exercises

*Level 1: Classification and Application*

1. Classify the sentences below as (a) passives, (b) particle-verb constructions, (c) both, or (d) neither. Which criteria do you use to
   make your decision?

   a. An icy shiver ran up her spine. (COCA, Fiction, 2017)
   b. Adherence was sampled across classrooms. (COCA, Academic
      Prose, 2015)
   c. The first thing she did was run down to the family room.
      (COCA, Fiction, 2002)
   d. Agnes ran up the plastic stairs. In an instant, she was at the
      window. (COCA, Fiction, 2017)
   e. This is not a small thing: to have a place where the bartender lets
      you run up a tab that you will never pay. (COCA, Fiction, 2013)
   f. While you were busy Snapchatting with your girlfriend just now,
      you nearly got run down. (COCA, Fiction, 2017)

2. We saw that *be*-sentences may be ambiguous between a copular
   (stative) and a passive (event) reading. A sentence like *The shop was
   closed* could mean that somebody is talking about a shop that is not
   open (stative reading with *be* functioning as copula or linking verb)
   or about an event in which someone closed the shop (eventive
   reading with *be* functioning as auxiliary). Often, however, there
   will be clues in the sentence or the surrounding discourse as to
   which reading is intended. In the screenshot on the next page, for
   the sequence *was closed* in COCA, determine which of the tokens

| # | Year | Reg | Source | | | Context |
|---|---|---|---|---|---|---|
| 1 | 2017 | SPOK | NBC: Today Show | A | B C | very apparent when somebody doesn't want an advance to happen. My body was closed I was frozen. I looked |
| 2 | 2017 | SPOK | PBS: PBS Newshour | A | B C | as a transit shelter two years ago. But since the migrant trail north was closed down in the Balkans, it has effec |
| 3 | 2017 | SPOK | PBS: PBS Newshour | A | B C | they would close to new entrants. There was a pool in Florida that was closed for decades. SREENIVASAN: Lisa |
| 4 | 2017 | SPOK | PBS: PBS Newshour | A | B C | 's largest refugee settlement with 300,000 residents, about the size of Pittsburgh, was closed to new arrivals in |
| 5 | 2017 | SPOK | NPR: How I Built This | A | B C | to close the stores for training. At 12:00, every store in America was closed for retraining. GUY RAZ# How much |
| 6 | 2017 | SPOK | NPR: How I Built This | A | B C | I needed something and I couldn't get to the shop and it was closed. All of the shops are closed. So we started |
| 7 | 2017 | SPOK | Fox: Tucker Carlson Tonight | A | B C | entire city is basically on lockdown, most of the evening, the subway was closed, the Central Station was on loc |
| 8 | 2017 | SPOK | Fox: Tucker Carlson Tonight | A | B C | terrible restaurant! One restaurant was a seafood place in Suburban Tech Avenue which was closed for health |
| 9 | 2017 | SPOK | CBS: 48 Hours | A | B C | Two days after Cory's death, her body was cremated and the case closed. A thirty-eight-year-old woman w |
| 10 | 2017 | SPOK | CBS: 48 Hours | A | B C | nobody found sufficient evidence, correct? ADAM GIBSON (in-co#) I read that it was closed. Yes. (ANNOUNCER) |
| 11 | 2017 | SPOK | ABC: Nightline | A | B C | , at that time, the compassion line was closed. B-ROW-PITTS# (Voiceover) Told from many, |
| 12 | 2017 | FIC | BkFourthHorseman | A | B C | the blazer said. His voice was slurred. # As soon as the door was closed the Mercedes took off toward the main |
| 13 | 2017 | FIC | BkBakerStreetJurors | A | B C | back to work as a solicitor in the bargain. # His office door was closed at the moment, and the blinds were shut |
| 14 | 2017 | FIC | BkKeeperStars | A | B C | off all but the security lights that softly illumined the building whenever the library was closed. Then she went c |
| 15 | 2017 | FIC | BkThousandFallingCrows | A | B C | , thought he saw a sign to his left warning that the road ahead was closed, under construction, that the bridge |
| 16 | 2017 | FIC | BkTransgalactic | A | B C | alien machine. If using it had ever been a possibility, that door was closed. That the process was a one-way trip |
| 17 | 2017 | FIC | BkArkwright | A | B C | bouquets that every florist in town had probably been cleaned out. Its lid was closed, for which Kate was quiet |
| 18 | 2017 | FIC | BkConfuciusJane | A | B C | having an affair with a clerk. The gold-buyer's store two blocks away was closed while police investigated allega |
| 19 | 2017 | FIC | BkLibrariansLostLamp | A | B C | stood watching. It was well after three in the morning and the brewery was closed, but that didn't matter to Fy |
| 20 | 2017 | FIC | BkFoggedInn | A | B C | for this year. # But by the middle of October, the clambake was closed down for the season and I was at a cros |

you consider true passives (eventive reading) and which are adjectival. Which criteria – linguistic or otherwise – do you base your decision on? Note that because this is just a screenshot, you cannot expand the context of the example, unless you did the search yourself in COCA. For which examples would you like to expand the context?

3.  a. In the passage below, taken from an article published in 2000 in the biochemistry journal *Cell*, go over all verb phrases, highlight the passive constructions, and classify them as long or short passives. If some verb phrases are hard to classify, note which ones, and why.
    b. Because the subject of the passive is never an agent, it is often not animate. By contrast, the subject in an active-voice sentence is an agent more often than not and therefore an animate entity. Is this true for the text sample below? If not, why not?

---

A. Typical of DNA bacteriophages and herpesviruses, HK97 assembles in two stages: polymerization and maturation. First, capsid protein polymerizes into closed shells; then, these precursors mature into larger, stabler particles. Maturation is initiated by proteolysis, producing a metastable particle primed for expansion – the major structural transition. We induced expansion in vitro by acidic pH and monitored the resulting changes by time-resolved X-ray diffraction and cryo-electron microscopy. The transition, which is not synchronized over the population, proceeds in a series of stochastically triggered subtransitions. Three distinct intermediates were identified, which are comparable to transitional states in protein folding. The intermediates' structures reveal the molecular events occurring during expansion. Integrated into a movie (see Dynamic Visualization below), they show capsid maturation as a dynamic process. (Lata et al. 2000)

---

4. Compare Figure 4.9 to Figure 4.6 above. Both are adapted from the *GSWE* (Biber et al. 2021). Each full square represents 5% of the corpus data, a hollow square represents less than 2.5%. How are the two charts related, how are they different? Is there anything unexpected in this chart?

|  | Agent in *by*-phrase length 1 word | Agent in *by*-phrase length 2–3 words | Agent in *by*-phrase length > 3 words |
|---|---|---|---|
| Subject length 1 word | ▪ | ▪▪▪ | ▪▪▪▪ |
| Subject length 2–3 words | ☐ | ▪ | ▪▪▪ |
| Subject length > 3 words | ▪ | ▪ | ▪▪▪▪ |

**Figure 4.9** Length of subject and agent phrase in long passives
Adapted from Biber et al. 2021.

5. In the passage B. below, an excerpt from the online news website *Huffington Post*, identify the short and long passives. For both, check whether or not the subject of the passive has topic status. What are your criteria for determining topic status? For the long passive, additionally check if the *by*-phrase is "weightier" than the subject. Again, what are your criteria? Lastly, discuss the choice of short passive over long passive (and vice versa).

> B. Ever since the release of the first iPhone, the iPhone Photography Awards have honored the true masters of mobile photography. Now in its 11th year, we're seeing just what some photographers can do with a camera they probably carry around all the time. While this competition is limited to those who use iPhones, there is a competition for mobile phone users as well, if you're interested.
> This year's winners were selected from thousands of entries and from photographers in 140 countries. The winning image, taken by Jashish Salam of Bangladesh and titled "Displaced," shows a crowded refugee camp with Rohingya children watching a film about sanitation. Other awards included prizes for photographer of the year and 18 other categories like Nature, Children and Travel.

6. In the sentences below, identify those that include a particle verb. Note whether the sentence makes use of the continuous or the discontinuous word order. Also take note of the discourse status of the object of the

particle verb. Is it known or new information? Which criteria do you apply to make that decision? If the discontinuous order is chosen, how many words separate the particle from the verb? Are the results in line with the findings presented in Figure 4.8 above?

---

a. Mr. Comey, however, was not in Washington to receive it. He was speaking to F.B.I. employees in Los Angeles when he looked up at a television screen in the back of the room and saw a breaking news alert that he had been fired. (COCA, News, 2017)

b. Before, when everyone had to review the necessary drawings and product samples for a project (that means windows, light fixtures, and the like), each individual would look the materials over and then mail them to the next person. With the new system, people just had to look the information up in the knowledge base and make their comments. (COCA, Magazine, 1996)

c. As officers rushed to break up three fights among the crowd, a woman dropped to the ground and used a detective's car as a shield. Officers put up more crime tape to keep the crowd farther away. An officer yelled she was arresting the next person who started a fight. (COCA, News, 2017)

d. Miners who work in the mine carry individual air purifying systems that would give them up to seven hours of clean air, said Tim McGee (COCA, News, 2006).

e. The Maryland State Police had called off their hunt for Jay when it became clear his disappearance was voluntary. Unwilling to give up the search, Nancy hired a private detective. (COCA, News, 1999)

f. Myers sat in the sun in a lawn chair out back and looked up the valley toward the peaks. Once he saw an eagle soaring down the valley, and on another occasion he saw a deer picking its way along the riverbank. (COCA, Fiction, 1999)

---

7. a. We saw that to some extent the placement of particles may be motivated by the need to minimize processing costs. If that is the case, would you expect to see differences in the placement of particles in spoken vs. written language?

b. Figure 4.10 is from the Lohse et al. (2004) study we discussed in Section 4.4.2. In this chart the authors present data from written samples and from spoken samples. What are the main differences in the graphs? Is the distribution what you thought it would be? Additionally, comment on the use of the line diagram vs. a bar chart, as in Figure 4.8. Which type of chart do you consider more appropriate, and why?

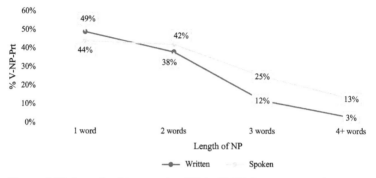

**Figure 4.10** Length of intervening NP in V-NP-Part constructions in spoken and written English
Data is from Lohse et al. (2004): 258.

## Level 2: Interpretation and Research Design

8. We saw above that Biber et al. (2021) represent their frequency data from a text-linguistic perspective. A different method to measure the frequency of the passive construction is employed by Seoane (2006) in her comparison of the use of the passive voice in British and American scientific writing (her data comes from two parallelly structured corpora). Unlike Biber et al., she measures the frequency of the passive as the percentage of transitive verbs that occur in passive voice in the corpus (100 percent would mean that all transitive verbs in the corpus occur in passive voice). The results, which are based on corpus data from the 1990s, can be seen below. What kind of insight do you gain from the chart in Figure 4.11? What is something that these charts do *not* tell you? What are the pros and cons of Seoane's and Biber's methodologies? Think of a research scenario in which you would employ the method applied by Biber et al. and one for which you would use Seoane's method of representing the number of passives.

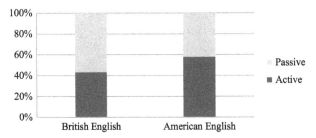

**Figure 4.11** Distribution of active and passive voice in transitive verbs in scientific writing

Adapted from Seoane 2006.

9. Convert the chart in Figure 4.5 into (approximate) numbers and compare the numbers for the short passive to the distribution of the passive in the same registers in American English (based on COCA). In order to do this, you will have to retrieve passive constructions in COCA. By now, you are familiar with ways of combining part-of-speech searches in COCA in order to find syntactic constructions. What search will you enter in order to identify passive constructions? (Note of caution: You will not find all passive constructions using this method, but a considerable subset.) Explain your decision and present your findings in a chart. You will have to make sure that the numbers you compare are on the same scale as the ones in Figure 4.5. How do you do that? What are your main findings?

10. In Chapter 2, we stressed the difference between a syntactic and a text-linguistic perspective on word order variation. The same distinction can be made at the lexical level. If we look at the passive from a *lexical variationist* perspective, we are interested in verbs that mostly occur in passive voice, even though they may not occur very often overall or in a particular register. At the other end of the lexical spectrum are verbs that, regardless of register, topic distribution, and length of agent phrase, mostly occur in active voice. According to Biber et al. (2021: 480) the list of these mostly active verbs includes *watch, hate, try, thank*, and *want*, all verbs that typically have human subjects. From a *text-linguistic* viewpoint, we know that passive constructions with high frequency in academic prose include *be expressed, be measured,* and *be performed*

(Biber et al. 2021: 476). That does not automatically mean, however, that the verbs *express, measure*, and *perform* typically occur in passive voice. They could be associated with academic prose as a register. Use corpus data from COCA to find out if these are mostly verbs that are register-specific or mostly verbs that are passive-specific.

11. a. It is now your turn to retrieve verb-particle constructions from a corpus. One thing to note is that COCA does not provide a "particle" tag, which means that you cannot just search for particles in the same manner you would search for nouns or verbs. Why do you think that is and how would you bypass this problem? Do a couple of searches and check if they bring up any false positives.

    b. We saw that unstressed pronouns and definite NPs, especially short ones, tend to occur in the V-NP-Prt pattern, while stressed pronouns and indefinite NPs, as well as longer NPs, tend to occur in the V-Prt-NP pattern. Let's see if you can replicate these generalizations with data from COCA for particular verb-particle combinations. Now that you have figured out a way of finding verb-particle constructions, select ten continuous and discontinuous orders each for three different verb-particle combinations and check the informational status and the weight of the NP that functions as the direct object. Do you see the generalizations that we discussed confirmed? (Note that if you need to see more context, you can expand your search results. Check out the Toolbox in Chapter 8 for instructions on how to do this.)

## Further Reading

- The *GSWE* (Biber et al. 2021: ch. 11) provides a good descriptive overview of quantitative facts about the English passive, based on data from four major registers (conversation, fiction, news, and academic writing).
- For a book that focuses on the role of the agent in the passive construction, including an analysis of the role of the passive in academic writing, see Wanner (2009).

- For an article that discusses various hypotheses for the decrease of passives in scientific writing in American English (as opposed to British English), see Seoane (2006).
- For a corpus-based article that contrasts the form and function of the *get-* and the *be-*passive in English, see Xiao et al. (2006). (The second half of the article discusses the form and function of different types of passives in Chinese.)
- For an overview of factors that have been considered in particle verb variation, see the corpus-based study by Gries (2003). Gries proposes that all factors that are statistically significant can be subsumed under the "Processing Hypothesis," essentially the assumption that minimizing processing cost is the main factor behind the placement of particles.
- For a corpus-linguistic study of the acquisition of particle placement in second-language acquisition, see Wulff & Gries (2019). One of their main findings is that L2 learners use the continuous word order (verb-particle-NP) more often than native speakers, regardless of context. The continuous word order has a lower cognitive load for the speakers because they do not have to keep the particle in mind while processing a potentially long noun. In a context where speakers have more time (such as in written language), L2 speakers' placement of particles is more native-like.

# 5 | *Special Endings*

## 5.1 Introduction

So far, we have dealt with patterns of the use of syntax at the beginning and in the middle of the sentence. In Chapters 3 and 4 we discussed how clausal organization tends to follow a general information-packaging principle, whereby given information typically comes first and new information appears later in the sentence. We saw that the reason for this principle is intuitively straightforward, namely that new information is usually more noteworthy and drives the discourse forward. Placing an element in sentence-final position is one way of highlighting this newsworthiness and importance. Coming back to a term we introduced in Chapter 4, the final position in the clause is a way of signaling its *focus*, which is why it can also be described as the end-focus position.

We have also seen in previous chapters that English has little word-order flexibility and that the subject is usually the first constituent in a canonical clause. However, the information that goes into a grammatical subject is not necessarily less noteworthy than the rest of the clause. One possibility of placing a subject later in the clause is to use *there* as a so-considered "dummy" subject, allowing us to re-position the original subject. This is the case, for example, in the sentence in (1), illustrated in Figure 5.1.

(1)   There once was *a woman who was very fond of a wild dog*. She would go every day and feed the dog until it finally became tame. She was very close to that dog. (COCA, Academic, 2016)

The sentence in (1) illustrates the so-called **existential construction,** which allows the information in the clause to be packaged differently. In (1) the identity of the woman is not known to the addressee, as signaled by the indefinite determiner (*a woman*), and the NP referring

**Figure 5.1** The existential construction

to the woman is therefore more naturally placed behind the verb. With the subject in preverbal position (?*A woman was very fond of a wild dog*), the sentence is not, strictly speaking, ungrammatical but sounds a bit odd (as indicated by the question mark in front of it). Sometimes stories or fairy tales begin like that, as in Example (2), but more often their beginnings look like the sentence in (3), that is, they begin with an existential construction.

(2)   Once upon a time, a beautiful young woman married a handsome young man. (COCA, Fiction, 2012)

(3)   Once upon a time, there lived a handsome prince, who was about to marry a beautiful maiden. (COCA, TV, 2001)

The existential construction expresses the existence or occurrence of the person or thing referred to by the subject (technically called the "referent;" see Chapter 7). This function of the construction is reflected, on the one hand, by its limitation to the verb *be* and some other verbs that express existence or appearance (such as *live* in Ex. (3)) and, on the other hand, by the fact that the subject noun phrase tends to be indefinite (*a handsome prince*). An indefinite noun phrase indicates that its referent is not yet identifiable to the reader or listener. The correlation of existential clauses and indefinite NPs as subjects is not absolute, as Example (4) illustrates, but studies have shown that by far the majority (around 90 percent) of existential clauses contain an indefinite rather than definite subject NP (Johansson 1997). If the NP is not identifiable, this also means that the information it carries is new to the reader or listener, which is why the correlation also reflects the principle of placing given before new information in the clause.

(4)    In the eighth century, there was the first synodal decree that marriages
       between nobles and lay commoners were to be contracted publicly.
       (COCA, Academic, 2009)

The existential construction is one type of construction resulting from
the function of clausal endings to carry the sentence focus. Other
constructions with a focus-related function are *it*-extraposition and
*it*-clefting, which we will explore more closely in this chapter. You
will learn to:

- describe the syntactic characteristics of *it*-extraposition and *it*-clefting;
- detect and distinguish extraposition and clefting occurring in texts;
- apply syntactic and discourse-related predictors to the study of their occurrence in discourse;
- discuss and visualize corresponding outcomes.


## Concepts, Constructions, and Keywords

*clefting, contrastive focus, end-focus, existential construction, extraposed
subject clause, focus, focus-marking, foregrounding,* it-*extraposition,*
it-*clefting, non-extraposition, presupposition*


## 5.2 *It*-Extraposition

*It*-extraposition is a construction that moves a clause, not just a phrase,
to the sentence-final position. As you probably know, a subordinate
clause can also function as the grammatical subject, as you see in
Example (5). Since such a subject clause tends to be more complex
than just an NP subject, it often makes sense for the speaker or writer to
shift this clause to the end of the sentence, as in Example (6).

(5)    That you won't be able to come to my party is too bad.

(6)    It is too bad that you won't be able to come to my party.

As you can see in (6), the placement of the subject clause at the end of
the sentence is made possible because the position of the subject is filled
by the pronoun *it*. The original subject clause becomes a so-called
extraposed subject, which is, technically speaking, no longer a proper
subject, but an element foreshadowed by the "dummy subject" *it*

(Huddleston & Pullum 2002: 1403). Let us look at a few corpus-based attestations of this type of construction, shown as examples (7a)–(9a). Examples (7b)–(9b) give the non-extraposed variants. The examples also illustrate that an extraposed subject clause can be either finite (*is, welcomes*) or non-finite (*to have*).

(7)   a.   It is bad enough that L.A. is almost 4 million with continued high density, intolerable traffic and parking problems, unaffordable housing and all while undergoing a continued drought. (COCA, News, 2016)

(8)   a.   It is bad to have such sharply diverging classes. (COCA, News, 2012)

(9)   a.   It is apparent how evil welcomes evil. (COCA, Fiction, 1991)

(7)   b.   That L.A. is almost 4 million with continued high density, intolerable traffic and parking problems, unaffordable housing and all while undergoing a continued drought is bad enough.

(8)   b.   To have such sharply diverging classes is bad.

(9)   b.   How evil welcomes evil is apparent.

As you see in (7a) through (9a), the extraposed clauses are relatively long and informative compared to the main clause. We have already seen that speakers tend to place long constituents after short constituents when we discussed the verb-particle construction in Chapter 4. This correspondence of the end-focus position and complexity or length was discussed in Section 4.3.2 as the end-weight principle. This principle now also explains why speakers and writers often prefer to position a subject clause in clause-final position. According to one corpus-based study, the occurrence of extraposition outnumbered non-extraposition (where the subject clause remains in its original position, like in Ex. (5)) by a ratio of 8:1 in favor of the extraposed variant (Kaltenböck 2000). Note, however, that there are also lexical constraints strengthening this preference, as, with some verbs, there is no canonical equivalent. For instance, with the verb *appear*, which is semantically similar to *be apparent*, occurring with and without extraposition in examples (9a) and (9b), extraposition becomes mandatory (*It appears that evil welcomes evil* is grammatical, but *\*That evil welcomes evil appears* is not).

Despite weight being a strong motivating factor for extraposing a subject clause, non-extraposition is sometimes equally acceptable. For a better understanding of the actual choice between extraposition and non-extraposition, to which we will turn in more detail in Section 5.2.2, let's first look at one more aspect of the extraposition construction. A crucial syntactic property is the realization of the subject clause. As we could see in the examples in (7a) – (9a) above, extraposition is possible with different types of subject clauses: finite *that-* or *wh-*clauses, as in (7a) and (9a), *to-*infinitives, like in (8a), as well as *ing-*participial clauses (*It's great seeing you again*). Sometimes, the predicate in the main clause requires a specific type of subject clause, while others allow for more syntactic variation. For example, the **matrix clause** predicate *be fun* in COCA only occurs with the *to-*infinitive and the *ing-*participle, as shown by examples (10) and (11), while the predicate *be possible* occurs both with non-finite and finite sub-clauses, as you can see in (12) and (13):

(10)    It is fun to watch this kind of crime. (COCA, Spoken, 2017)

(11)    It is fun watching the different trends and things that come full circle throughout the lives of the first ladies. (COCA, Spoken, 2015)

(12)    Ikeda is certain it is possible to be fat and fit. (COCA, News, 2003)

(13)    It is possible that I am a freak of nature. (COCA, Fiction, 1998)

In view of this range of syntactic variation, we could ask if all of these subtypes in fact show the same preference for an extraposition of the subject clause. To answer this question, let us look at some corpus-based results. Figure 5.2 is based on the occurrence of extraposition and non-extraposition in the ICE-GB corpus, which is the British part of the *International Corpus of English* (Kaltenböck 2004). The findings, given here in absolute frequencies as the dependent variable on the *y*-axis, include all of the syntactic categories we have just mentioned: the *to-*infinitive, the *ing-*participle, finite *that-*clauses (and, in addition, the category of "other" finite clauses, which included *if-* and *wh-*clauses).

The results in Figure 5.2 show that there is an effect of the formal realization of the subject clause: *ing-*clauses as subjects occur more often without than with extraposition. By contrast, the other types clearly favor extraposition over non-extraposition. This outcome

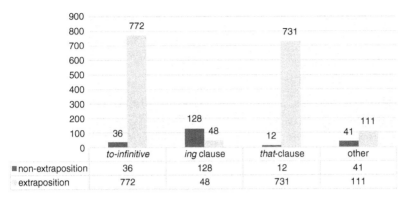

**Figure 5.2** Non-extraposition vs. *it*-extraposition with different subject clauses Data is from Kaltenböck 2004.

informs us that the syntactic realization of the subject clause is indeed a relevant factor for the choice of *it*-extraposition or non-extraposition. In the next two sections, we will see that the choice of construction also varies by discourse-related factors, notably by its information structure (5.2.1) and the type of discourse in which it occurs (5.2.2).

## 5.2.1 The Information-Packaging Function of It-Extraposition

Following the general principle of information-packaging (as described in Chapters 2 and 3) as well as what we have just discussed as the role of end-focus and end-weight, a subject clause in clause-final position is likely to be associated with new information. By implication, it is equally plausible to assume that non-extraposition is more likely to occur if the content of the subject clause constitutes information that is not new, that is, when the information is given or inferable from the discourse context.

Let us substantiate this claim by a quick ad hoc corpus search. We can search in a corpus, for example, for all sentences containing the string *to do so* in subject position, a clausal subject that almost certainly contains given information (due to the pro-form *do so*). Carried out in COCA, the search for *do so* followed by a verb provided us with more than 1,000 hits (note that a corpus like COCA is continuously growing), which all contained a subject clause like that in Example (14). We thus easily find instances of subject clauses with given information, showing us that non-extraposition is not altogether uncommon.

(14)   "[...] I can not accept it," he continued. "*To do so would be hypo-critical.*" (COCA, News, 2017)

However, subject clauses with given information also occur in sentence-final, that is, extraposed position. For instance, there is nothing weird about the extraposed version of (14) (*It would be hypocritical to do so*). Since both variants are, grammatically speaking, acceptable, the claim about the information-packaging function of *it*-extraposition raises an empirical question: Is it true that *it*-extraposition as a construction favors new information over given information in the subject clause?

To test this claim as a hypothesis, let us look at data which is available from the same corpus as the data we discussed above (Kaltenböck 2005). For interpreting the results, we first need to know how given and new information was exactly defined when dealing with the data. Kaltenböck (2005: 127) operationalized givenness by making use of the concept of **retrievability** in discourse. Information in the subject clause is understood as retrievable if it is either mentioned in the preceding discourse or inferable from the discourse situation. Examples of subject clauses with retrievable information are given in (15) and (16), while the extraposed subject clause in (17) is new information.

(15)   He became a lawyer and is now mayor of our hometown. If Mr. Murray is right, however, the next generation of educated profes-sionals will consist almost entirely of the sons and daughters of other educated professionals. Members of the upper class send their chil-dren to better schools, coach them in ways of success, and know how to game college admissions. Members of the lower class have little access to such advantages. Although critics have faulted details of Murray's argument, it is hard to deny his larger point: *It is bad to have such sharply diverging classes.* (COCA, News, 2012)

(16)   It was my first day of class, and I was 21, and the students came in saying, "Where is the instructor?" I said I was the instructor and they said, "You. *It is not bad enough that they gave us a lady* but you have on heels." (COCA, Academic, 2008)

(17)   We're back with our panel. Juan Williams, during the break, passed
        on a useful health tip. He noted that authorities are now informing us
        that *it is bad to use drugs* [...]. (COCA, Spoken, 2001)

In (15), the information contained in the subject clause is present from
the preceding text (*upper class, lower class*), while in (16) *they gave us a
lady* can be understood from the previous discourse (the speaker presenting as female), that is, the information is inferable. By contrast, a
sentence like the one in italics in (17) is new information because *to use
drugs* is not retrievable information. Note that, for the data we discuss
below, being retrievable from the preceding text was limited to a stretch
of discourse comprising nine preceding clauses (or similar units, if there
happened to be no complete sentences).

Let us now look at the corresponding outcome concerning the information status of extraposed subject clauses. Table 5.1 is based on a
collection of 1,701 instances of *it*-extraposition from the ICE-GB corpus and shows the absolute frequency as well as the percentage of
subject clauses with irretrievable (i.e., new) and retrievable (i.e.,
given) information.

Table 5.1 *Information status of subject clause in* it-*extraposition*

|  | Total number (in %) |
|---|---|
| Irretrievable (new) information | 1,217 (71.5 %) |
| Retrievable (given) information | 484 (28.5 %) |
| Total | 1,701 (100 %) |

Data is from Kaltenböck 2005.

In line with a prediction that follows the principle of information
packaging, the majority of the occurrences of extraposition in Table
5.1 contain a subject clause with irretrievable information. This finding
confirms our hypothesis, and it supports the end-focus function of the
construction. In other words, the non-canonical placement of a subject
clause clearly has to do with the subject containing new, and hence,
more important, information.

Having verified the discourse function of *it*-extraposition empirically, we may also ask if and how the information structure interacts
with the syntactic variable we discussed above. Does the syntactic form

Table 5.2 *Information status of different types of subject clauses in* it-*extraposition*

|  | Given information | New information | Total |
|---|---|---|---|
| *to*-infinitive | 286 | 486 | 772 |
| *ing*-clause | 21 | 27 | 48 |
| *that*-clause | 104 | 627 | 731 |
| other | 34 | 77 | 111 |
| Total | 445 | 1,217 | 1,662 |

Data is from Kaltenböck 2005.

of the subject clause affect the likelihood of given or new information being contained in the subject clause? The corpus study we are using here also has an answer to this question, which is what is seen in Table 5.2.

As you can see in Table 5.2, there is a considerable difference between finite (*that-*) clauses and non-finite (*to-* and *ing-*) clauses in the extent to which they contain given or new information when in extraposed, that is, sentence-final, position. Finite *that*-clauses have the clearest preference for shifting new information into the end-focus position whereas, for the infinitival and participial subject clauses, the difference between extraposed subject clauses with given information and those containing new information is less pronounced.

For visualizing this outcome in a graph, we again need to ensure that the choice of the diagram matches our research aim (see our discussion on charts in Chapter 3). Figure 5.3 thus derives from two decisions: First, it emphasizes that we are interested in the *differences* among syntactic forms of extraposed subject clauses concerning their information structure; hence, the different syntactic realizations are chosen as the parameter of variation on the *x*-axis. Second, the results are presented as percentages on the *y*-axis, because we must take note of the fact that the overall number of hits per syntactic category varies considerably in the corpus data.

Figure 5.3 illustrates the proportions of given and new information with different syntactic types of an extraposed subject clause. It thus

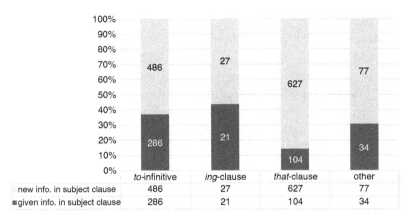

| | to-infinitive | ing-clause | that-clause | other |
|---|---|---|---|---|
| new info. in subject clause | 486 | 27 | 627 | 77 |
| ■given info. in subject clause | 286 | 21 | 104 | 34 |

**Figure 5.3** Frequency of given and new information in extraposed subject clauses
Data is from Kaltenböck 2005.

shows the different strengths of the association of the subject clause types with the dependent variable, given or new information. In particular, it highlights that finite *that*-clauses differ from the rest. Note, however, that presenting results only in the form of percentages can be misleading, since the chart would hide how much the absolute numbers within each category are different (for example, that there are considerably fewer *ing*-clauses than *that*-clauses in the data set). When presenting your own work, you should therefore add absolute numbers, in the form of a table (as we have done in Figure 5.3), for the sake of transparency.

In sum, the findings on the syntactic realization of extraposed subject clauses have confirmed the assumption that the syntactic type of an extraposed clause is a formal variable that interferes with the characteristic distribution of information in *it*-extraposition. An obvious reason for this interference is the length of the subject clause: Since non-finite clauses tend to be shorter, they are also more likely to be chosen as a syntactic realization when encoding given information. The pattern of variation that we have seen thus also confirms the validity of the Principle of End-Weight.

Based on the section, it is now possible for you to analyze a collection of attestations for *it*-extraposition. Go to Exercise 1 to retrieve instances of the construction from a text and to Exercise 2 for analyzing extraposed subject clauses as containing retrievable or irretrievable information. See Exercise 5 of the Level 2 exercises for an alternative visualization and interpretation of the data discussed in this section.

In order to find out more about the construction in discourse, we will now apply the text-linguistic perspective.

## 5.2.2 The Role of Discourse: Extraposition or Non-extraposition?

So far, we have looked at the internal properties of *it*-extraposition, that is, its syntactic realizations and information structure. In this analysis, the role of discourse resulted from the influence of the *co-text*, which determines what is given and what is new information. We now turn to the textual *context*, that is, to the types of discourse in which the construction is likely to occur.

The role of the discourse context, in the form of the surrounding register and genre (for more on this, see Chapter 9), raises at least two questions here. First, we are interested in the use of extraposition and non-extraposition in different types of discourse. This question can be answered by looking at the rates of occurrence of the construction in different registers. More specifically, however, we also want to find out if the discourse context affects the extent to which the information-packaging principle applies to the construction, as discussed in Section 5.2.1. In other words, one might plausibly assume that the discourse context in which extraposition is used is a relevant predictor for the distribution of information within the construction. As you will see, corpus results again enable us to investigate this assumption.

Let us first look at the occurrence of extraposition and non-extraposition in the two registers of speech and writing in Table 5.3. What the frequencies recorded in Table 5.3 (based on an equal amount of spoken and written words in a text corpus) tell us is that extraposition seems overall to be more common in writing. However, the numbers in Table 5.3 also indicate that sentences with a non-extraposed subject clause occur to a different extent in the two registers. The reason is that sentences with a subject clause that *could be* extraposed, that is, contain a matrix and a subordinate clause, are also more common in writing. The results given in Table 5.3, which are absolute rates of occurrence of the construction, do thus not prove a proper effect of the discourse type on the choice of the construction. Rather, they reflect the frequency of occurrence of that type of complex sentence as a whole.

Table 5.3 *Extraposition and non-extraposition in two registers*

|  | Non-extraposition | Extraposition |
|---|---|---|
| Speech | 79 | 730 |
| Writing | 138 | 971 |

Data is from Kaltenböck 2004.

Transforming the results from Table 5.3 into the graph in Figure 5.4, based now on percentages, illustrates that the choice of non-extraposition amounts to about ten percent of all complex sentences of that kind, regardless of register. Contrary to our initial assumption, we therefore have to note that speech and writing as different registers do not

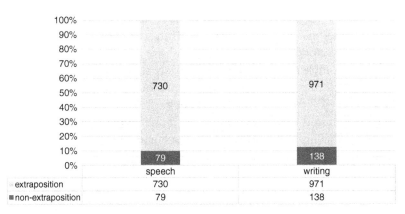

**Figure 5.4** Proportions of non-extraposition and extraposition in two registers Based on Table 5.3.

have a significant effect on whether speakers prefer a non-extraposed over an extraposed variant of these sentences.

Now let us return to the information-packaging function of *it*-extraposition in discourse. Is the information structure within *it*-extraposition dependent on the type of discourse in which the construction is used? Table 5.4, an expanded version of Table 5.2, which you saw in Section 5.2.1, contains the absolute frequencies of *it*-extraposition with given versus new subject clauses in speech as opposed to writing. Percentages are given in brackets. In this case, Table 5.4 enables us to detect a register difference: The information-packaging function of the construction, that is, its preference for the subject clause to contain new information, is only obvious in the context of writing, whereas the register of speech does not show a strong preference in that respect.

Table 5.4 *Information status of subject clause in* it-*extraposition*

| Information status | in speech | in writing | Total number (in %) |
|---|---|---|---|
| New information | 410 (56.1 %) | 807 (83.2 %) | 1,217 (71.5 %) |
| Given information | 321 (43.9 %) | 163 (16.8 %) | 484 (28.5 %) |
| Total | 731 (100 %) | 970 (100 %) | 1,701 (100 %) |

Data is from Kaltenböck 2005: 129.

Table 5.4 has told us an interesting difference, which we again want to visualize. Turning the numbers from Table 5.4 into the bar chart in Figure 5.5 illustrates the different proportions. Using percentages is unproblematic here since both corpora were of equal size and all frequencies, given again in the table together with the chart, are sufficiently high.

The graph in Figure 5.5 to some extent modifies the outcome of our discussion of Table 5.1 above. Although *it*-extraposition with new information in the subject clause is the more common pattern in both contexts, there is a clear effect of the discourse type on the function of the construction: in this case, this is an effect of the register resulting from the medium. The assumption that the main function of *it*-extraposition is information-packaging in fact only applies to the written medium. Note that the effect is not exclusively a matter of text-linguistic variation, since the overall frequencies of the construction in both contexts, as given by Table 5.3 (731 as opposed to 970),

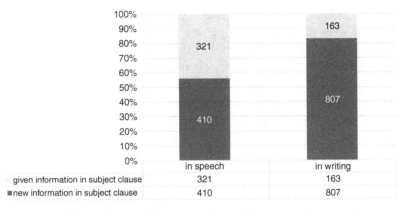

| | in speech | in writing |
|---|---|---|
| given information in subject clause | 321 | 163 |
| ■ new information in subject clause | 410 | 807 |

**Figure 5.5** Subject clauses with given and new information in two registers

are not strikingly different (the average rates of occurrence per text being 1.5 in speech and 1.9 in writing). Instead, the text type influences the discourse function of the construction, in that the assumed preference for an extraposed clause to contain new information only holds true for writing.

There is not much evidence on the occurrence of extraposition in more specific types of discourse, due to the fact that searching for the construction in a corpus is a challenge. We have seen before that lexical shortcuts can be a solution, so one possibility for retrieving instances of *it*-extraposition from a corpus is to search for specific lexical subtypes. For example, you could investigate the construction with specific semantic predicates, using lemmas in the matrix clause such as (*be*) *good, bad, true, apparent, likely*, or the like.

You could now turn to Exercise 6, where a corresponding project is proposed.

## 5.3 *It*-Clefting

The term clefting is used to describe a syntactic process that divides a single clause into two constituent parts. One of the two parts becomes foregrounded, while the other one is backgrounded (Huddleston &

Pullum 2002: 1414). There are two main constructions that are referred to as clefting: *it*-clefting (*it's the cake there that I like*) and *wh*-clefting (*what I like there is the cake*). In an *it*-cleft construction, *it* becomes the subject of the matrix clause, with a relative clause appearing as a modifier within an NP structure. At first sight, the construction therefore resembles extraposition, as you can see in (18) and (19). However, in contrast to the extraposed subject clause in (19), the embedded clause in an *it*-cleft, like (18), is a relative clause (*[whom] we met there*).

(18)    It was Lucky we met there. (*it*-clefting)

(19)    It was lucky that we saw four rhinos. (*it*-extraposition)

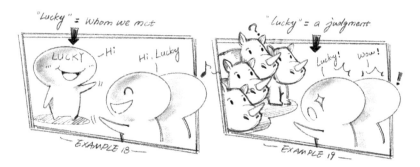

You may be familiar with the construction in (18) from constituency tests in syntax since the matrix clause in an *it*-cleft predicates, and thereby highlights, the existence of one clausal constituent. By contrast, in *it*-extraposition, the matrix clause is a comment or judgment. Turning sentences (18) and (19) back into more basic, canonical clauses makes this difference become apparent: for (18), the canonical clause would be *We met Lucky there*, and for (19), *That we saw four rhinos was lucky*.

Note that there are cases of *it*-clefting which turn out to be ambiguous. The ambiguity can be due to the fact that *it*-clefts can be used to highlight elements with different syntactic functions. While, in (18) above, the highlighted element is the grammatical object, there are also matrix clauses that introduce other clausal elements. In (20) and (21), for example, the highlighted element is an adjunct:

(20)    It's *about six weeks ago* I last took my bike to get to work.

(21)    It's *only on rare occasions* that I bike to work.

The examples in (20) and (21) not only have a non-clefted, but also a non-extraposed counterpart (*That I last took my bike to get to work is about six weeks ago; That I bike to work is only on rare occasions*). The ambiguity results from the ellipsis of the subordinator (*that* or *when*), which is what we have in (20) and (21). More complete versions of each sentence are given in (22) through (25), illustrating which of the two constructions is present:

(22)  It's about six weeks ago when I last took my bike to get to work. (*it*-clefting) corresponding non-cleft: *About six weeks ago I last took my bike to get to work.*

(23)  It is about six weeks ago that I last took my bike to get to work. (*it*-extraposition) corresponding non-extraposition: *That I took my bike ... is about six weeks ago.*

(24)  It's only on rare occasions when I bike to work. (*it*-clefting) corresponding non-cleft: *Only on rare occasions I bike to work.*

(25)  It's only on rare occasions that I bike or walk to work. (*it*-extraposition) corresponding non-extraposition: *That I bike to work is only on rare occasions.*

It is not always easy to tell what speakers have in mind at the moment of uttering a sentence like (20) or (21); most likely, the speaker will not be able to tell you either. But, as we have seen, the cases where we encounter problems distinguishing *it*-clefting from *it*-extraposition result from the possibility of dropping the relative pronoun or the complementizer in these constructions.

In the following, we turn to the discourse function of *it*-clefting as a syntactic variant in Section 5.3.1 and to its text-linguistic variation in 5.3.2. As you will see, there is not a lot of quantitative evidence to report in this area, since retrieving the construction based on a limited number of search strings is more than a challenge, and lexical shortcuts for the construction are not easily available. We will therefore explore the discourse function of *it*-clefting mainly by way of contextualized examples.

## *5.3.1 Functions of* It-*Clefting: Foregrounding, Focus, and Presupposition*

As we have seen so far, while the discourse function of *it*-extraposition has to do with presenting new information as the end-focus, *it*-clefting is a construction that syntactically highlights a particular sentence element. For example, in (18), the noun phrase *Lucky* is highlighted, while the rest of the predication becomes a syntactically subordinate relative clause.

This function of highlighting can also be described as **foregrounding** an element by way of the cleft construction. If you utter (18), rather than simply *We met Lucky there*, you turn the element *Lucky* into the complement in a new matrix clause. As a result, *Lucky* becomes a constituent of the new main clause and, with that, the new focus of the entire construction. The remainder of the original predication is placed within a subordinate clause ([*whom*] *we met there*), so that it appears to provide only background information. This division into foregrounded and backgrounded material is, in principle, independent of the information status of the two components. In the example in (26), a corpus attestation that is similar to Example (18), we see from the context that *Bill* is given information; nonetheless, *Bill* is foregrounded and syntactically marked as the focus.

(26)    Imitating the old man's adventure never entered my mind, but Bill Langland's taste for adventure required more actual participation than mine. *It was Bill who first suggested that we try to catch a big fish – any big fish –* on a handline. (COCA, Academic, 1997)

In contrast to extraposition, which attributes end-focus to a subject clause by placing the clause sentence-finally, *it*-clefting marks its focus syntactically and, as a result, makes the material in clause-final position appear less important. The syntax of the *it*-cleft also prevents an unintended, end-focus interpretation (Lambrecht 1994).

This focus-marking function of *it*-clefting is independent of the different conditions of given and new information in the foregrounded and backgrounded part of an *it*-cleft. We could see in (26) that the foregrounded element can easily be given information: *Bill* is highlighted but the information is not new. By foregrounding it, the sentence expresses the focus is on *Bill* and, with that, it creates a meaning of contrast: it was *Bill*, and not somebody else, who was able to do this. This effect of expressing a syntactically "stressed," contrastive focus is one of the two discourse functions of *it*-clefting (Prince 1978). The contrastive focus function is typically present when the focused element contains given information (see Figure 5.6).

**Figure 5.6** Focus marking and information structure in two types of *it*-clefting

As for the backgrounded part of the cleft-construction, this part may contain new information, as in (26), or old information, as in (27). However, in contrast to the foregrounded element, the backgrounded part in an *it*-cleft is always presented as if it were somehow already known. This effect is due to the background part being, syntactically, a subordinate clause. For example, in (27), due to the complex sentence structure of the *it*-cleft, the fact that *somebody killed the DREAM Act* (the name of a legislative proposal that grants conditional residency to certain undocumented immigrants in the US) is not presented as an issue in itself. What is highlighted is that the information (*that somebody killed the DREAM Act*) is already known from the previous discourse. The idea is strengthened, or sometimes properly created, that the backgrounded part of the cleft-construction contains information that was to be presupposed.

(27)    This wasn't Republicans who killed the DREAM Act. *It was Democrats who killed the DREAM Act.* (COCA, Spoken, 2011)

Not all instances of the *it*-cleft truly background given information, like in (27), and consequently receive a contrastive focus interpretation. In (28), for example, both the focused element and the backgrounded part of the sentence constitute new information.

(28)    It was on a snowy day just two years ago when I stood before you on
        this very spot in this beautiful and historic chamber to take the oath
        of office as Maryland's new governor. (COCA, News, 2017)

The element highlighted by the *it*-cleft in (28), originally an adjunct (*on
a snowy day*), would have been a plausible point of departure for the
clause, since adjuncts providing a temporal orientation tend to be
placed sentence-initially (as discussed in Chapter 3). Why is this element additionally foregrounded? The function of the *it*-cleft in (28) is not
so much about the element that is syntactically highlighted, but relates
to the backgrounded component. The *it*-cleft does not affect the order
in which the two parts appear in the discourse (~~it was~~ *on a snowy day
just two years ago when I stood before* ...). So, the difference that is
created only results from the syntactic subordination of the remainder
of the clause (*when I stood before you* ...). This subordinated part of
the *it*-cleft is again presented *as if* already known. The second type of *it*-
cleft, in which new information is expressed as the focus, thus presents
the subordinate clause as if it were "known to some people although
not yet known to the intended hearer" (Prince 1978: 899). Its function
is to evoke a **presupposition**, which comes about through foregrounding one part of the predication as the sentence focus and presenting the
rest *as if* it could already be presupposed (see Figure 5.6).

Summing up the discussion in this section, Figure 5.6 highlights that
the focus-marking and foregrounding function of *it*-clefts are independent of the distribution of information in the construction. The foregrounded element contains given or new information in comparison to
the rest of the clause; this element always ends up being marked as focus.
Depending on the information status of the foregrounded constituent,
the function of the *it*-cleft is either to express a stressed and contrastive
focus (*the Democrats*, nobody else), or to signal the presupposition that
the backgrounded part (what happened *just two years ago*) is not entirely
new, but something that is possibly already known. In Section 5.3.2, we
will turn to the question of how these two discourse functions of *it*-
clefting are associated with different types of discourse.

## 5.3.2 It-*Clefting in Different Types of Discourse*

Much like *it*-extraposition, *it*-clefting can be found in almost all
types of discourse. For example, the *GSWE* (Biber et al. 2021)

notes that *it*-clefts, although especially frequent in academic texts, also commonly occur in conversation or in fiction. The use of *it*-clefting in discourse is therefore not register-specific. However, as we will see, there is some variation regarding the element that the construction is meant to highlight. As illustrated in Figure 5.6, following the information status of that element, there are two types of *it*-clefting that we distinguish: the contrastive focus *it*-cleft and the presupposition *it*-cleft. Is either of these more characteristic in certain kinds of discourse?

Let us look at the foregrounded part of *it*-clefting again, this time at the information status as possibly varying by the type of text in which the *it*-cleft occurs. Figure 5.7 is based on 701 *it*-clefts from four spoken and written registers (Hedberg 1990): conversational speech, fiction, commentaries, and historical narratives.

We can see in Figure 5.7 that the *it*-cleft with given information, that is, the contrastive focus cleft, is the more common type in three out of the four types of discourse. However, we also see that new information in the foregrounded element is not uncommon in any of these registers. Figure 5.7 further highlights that this presupposition cleft, that is, the one that foregrounds new information, is the more common type of an *it*-cleft only in fiction (53.3 percent).

This outcome brings us to a final, interesting pattern of the use of *it*-clefting in actual discourse, a pattern that we also saw when dealing with (28). The example showed an *it*-cleft foregrounding new

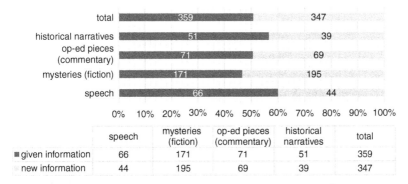

|  | speech | mysteries (fiction) | op-ed pieces (commentary) | historical narratives | total |
|---|---|---|---|---|---|
| ■ given information | 66 | 171 | 71 | 51 | 359 |
| new information | 44 | 195 | 69 | 39 | 347 |

**Figure 5.7** Information status of foregrounded element in *it*-clefts. Data is from Hedberg 1990, as cited in Gundel et al. 2001: 292.

information, but we also noted that the backgrounded part (*I stood before you on this very spot* ...), although syntactically subordinate, contains new information as well. It might strike us in Example (28) that the subordinate clause is comparatively long and drives the discourse forward, rather than adding just some background information. This use of the *it*-cleft is a pattern that occurs especially in narration. Although the construction highlights information by making it the sentence focus (*on a snowy day just two years ago*), this element is truly only an opener for the story or episode to follow. In the end, the backgrounded part turns out to be even more noteworthy. Similar occurrences are the examples in (29) and (30), which are, like (28), from story beginnings.

(29)    It was on a summer day in 2012 that I had to practically chase my 58-year-old spouse out of the house for a long-overdue physical exam I'd booked for him. (COCA, Magazine, 2014)

(30)    It was on a snowy night, after you'd bitten me again, that you rose up in a way, a levitating way, and your head was not yours but belonged to a pharaoh or a prince, and I caught a glimpse of what was behind the coral curtain in your village, and it was so exactly as you'd said, bowls and bowls and your mother's cup, your lips to your mother's cup, and then I saw the bus, and [...]. (COCA, Fiction, 2015)

This use of *it*-clefting, as illustrated by (28) through (30), is an interplay of syntactic foregrounding, the information in the foregrounded and the backgrounded components, both being new, and of the position in the text where the *it*-cleft occurs. As we saw, foregrounding one element by way of an *it*-cleft makes the rest of the sentence appear like known information, that is, presupposed. Using this mechanism for an upcoming narration helps to present a story *as if* some knowledge of it were shared by the reader, an effect that reduces the distance between writer and reader. The pattern tends to be used in fiction, which is what we saw in the higher proportion of the presupposition *it*-cleft in Figure 5.7 and in Example (30). However, as our discussion of examples (28) and (29) has shown, the pattern also occurs in non-fictional discourse, for example, in news texts or magazines.

You should now be able to detect and analyze the function of *it*-clefts in different kinds of texts and to distinguish *it*-clefting from *it*-extraposition. Go to Exercises 3 and 4 to test your analysis skills and to Exercises 7 and 8 (Level 2) for dealing with the discourse function of *it*-clefting. Also find out more about a possible common origin of the two constructions in our Good to Know box.

Good to Know: Extraposition as Possible Origin of Both Constructions

In this chapter, we have looked at the functions of *it*-extraposition and *it*-clefting in discourse, and we have seen that both share the function of marking an element as the focus of the sentence. We have also noted that the two constructions are formally similar, due to the pronoun *it* being used as a dummy subject. These similarities might raise the question of whether there is perhaps a common historical origin of the use of *it* in the two constructions.

You know *it* to be a personal pronoun, and there are sentences that look like an *it*-cleft, but in which *it* is in fact a personal pronoun, referring to something or someone. Note, for example, the sentence in (31):

(31)   A:   What a strange object you have over there!
       B:   It is the vase I received for Christmas

In contrast to *it* in an *it*-cleft, *it* in (31) is a referential pronoun, referring back to the strange object speaker A has been pointing to. The relative clause *I received for Christmas* modifies the NP headed by the noun *vase*, that is, together they form a single constituent (*the vase I received for Christmas*). By contrast, in the *it*-cleft in (27), the sequence *Democrats who killed the DREAM Act* is not a single constituent NP. By the analysis we presented when discussing this example, the *it*-cleft in (27) highlights the noun phrase *Democrats*, which is a predicative complement of the main clause. This clausal structure makes the relative clause not a modifier of *Democrats*, but of the subject pronoun *it* (*it/the ones who killed the DREAM Act was/were the Democrats*). Only, for reasons of end-focus and end-weight, this modifier is moved to the end of the sentence.

This analysis can explain the similarity of clefting and extraposition. If the subordinate clause in the *it*-cleft is a relative clause belonging to the subject NP, and not to the antecedent noun, both constructions can be said to result from the extraposition of a subordinate clause. We also saw in this chapter that there are cases in which it is difficult to keep clefting apart from extraposition: In particular, this is the case when the clefted element is an adjunct, as in the examples in (32) below (based on the *it*-cleft in (20) above):

(32)      It's about six weeks ago they did the job. (*it*-clefting)

(32)   a.  It's about six weeks ago when they did the job. (*it*-clefting)

(32)   b.  Six weeks ago they did the job. (non-clefted version)

(32)   c.  It's about six weeks ago that they did the job. (*it*-extraposition)

(32)   d.  That they did the job is about six weeks ago. (non-extraposition)

In view of these parallels, historical syntacticians have wondered if the two constructions are ultimately related. Do they have a common historical origin, or did one develop based on the other? There is some evidence discussed by historical linguists in favor of the position that *it*-clefting originates in extraposition, rather than the other way round (Patten 2014). For example, historical corpus data has shown that the earliest attested form of an *it*-cleft is the one with a focused NP. By contrast, those instances that foreground an adjunct, such as a PP or a clause, seem to be a later phenomenon. Also, from the point of view of the two types of *it*-clefting we discussed in Section 5.3.1, the *it*-cleft that highlights given information (the contrastive focus cleft) is attested earlier than the type of clefting where the backgrounded part is presented as if it could be presupposed. Taken together, these historical findings suggest a more likely origin of the cleft-construction in extraposition. Furthermore, in Old English, it was easily possible for a pronoun to be modified by a relative clause. And it was not uncommon for such relative clauses to occur sentence-finally, that is, to be extraposed (*it/the ones who killed the DREAM Act was the Democrats* becoming *it was the Democrats who killed the DREAM Act*). In that sense, the extraposition of a subordinate clause, which could be a proper subject clause or a relative clause modifying the subject NP, is possibly the common origin of both constructions.

## 5.4 Summary

In this chapter we have dealt with two constructions that serve the expression of the sentence focus, that is, of the most important part of the message in a sentence. We first explored sentences resulting from the extraposition of their subject clause and the characteristic distribution of given and new information within these sentences. We saw that discourse types and registers also play a role here and that only the written medium truly favors new information that is extraposed.

We then turned to the use of *it*-clefting in discourse: a construction which places the focus on one sentence element by turning the clause into a complex sentence. Depending on whether this element carries given or new information, the function of an *it*-cleft in discourse is either to create a meaning of contrast, or to present new information as if it were already known to the listener or reader. We looked at evidence for these functions in discourse and noted a characteristic pattern of use for narrative types of text.

On the way, we also discussed alternative formats for visualizing quantitative evidence from corpora and highlighted the importance, as well as the limits, of presenting proportional frequencies when dealing with data sets of a different size.

## 5.5 Exercises

### Level 1: *Classification and Application*

1. Find the occurrences of *it*-extraposition in the following text excerpt from Monica Macaulay's book *Surviving Linguistics: A Guide for Graduate Students* (Macaulay 2011). For each occurrence, give the corresponding, non-extraposed version.

---

A. Most graduate advisors do their best to train their students, but often they forget just how explicit they need to be. It's easy to forget, for example, that it's not obvious how submission of abstracts works or how examples should be laid out. It's also easy to overlook the fact that many linguistics graduate students don't come into the field with a background in science, [...]. (Macaulay 2011: xi.)

---

2. The instances of *it*-extraposition given below were collected from COCA, using the matrix predicate *be bad* or *be great*. Have a look at each attestation and its co-text provided and decide for each case whether the extraposed subject clause constitutes given or new information. What kind of evidence can you use to come to a decision?

| Preceding text | *it*-extraposition | Given or new? |
|---|---|---|
| A: I'll ask Betty to order some takeout. You still a vegetarian?<br>B: Yes, but not vegan anymore.<br>A: Just tell me what you eat.<br>B: Vegetables. Cheese. Beans. No meat.<br>A: What about one of those Greek salads from Dino's?<br>B: Fine. Dressing on the side. | 1. A: *It's great that you're still a vegetarian.* (COCA, Fiction, 2015) | |
| Regardless of the project, assessment, or unit we are working on with students, the important element is not only the assessment, but the Big Think that occurs for students afterward. It is too easy for teacher-librarians to be content when they finally get that elusive teacher to collaborate with them. | 2. *It is great to finally work with that teacher.* (COCA, Academic, 2010) | |
| With Boone in Los Angeles with me while I work on those safe houses for abused women and families, I've discovered just how amazing living together can be. I had no idea I'd adapt so quickly to having someone in my life 24/7. Add in B. J. and instant motherhood, and it's been the most incredible few months ever. | 3. *"It really is wonderful to see you so ecstatically happy,"* Gabi told her. (COCA, Fiction, 2013) | |

(*cont.*)

| Preceding text | *it*-extraposition | Given or new? |
|---|---|---|
| A: Now you have had a colored career, you're one of the more successful restaurateurs in the world. You could have gone anywhere. You stuck with New York.<br>B: First of all, it is my city, I grew up here, and second of all, the integrity of downtown especially | 4. B (continues): *It is great to see the way the people responded.* (COCA, Spoken, 2002) | |
| A: I think it does become competitive. It's almost like you want to prove that you're working harder than somebody else.<br>B: Right.<br>A: And is it part of what makes America great? I mean, we say it sometimes like oh, | 5. A (continues): *it's bad that we work so hard.* (COCA, Spoken, 2007) | |
| It is inconceivable to me that the city fathers want to emulate Beijing and Shanghai with their populations in the millions. | 6. *It is bad enough that L.A. is almost 4 million with continued high density, intolerable traffic and parking problems, unaffordable housing and all while undergoing a continued drought.* (COCA, News, 2016) | |

3. Is the sentence marked in this excerpt from P. D. James's *Devices and Desires* an instance of *it*-extraposition or of *it*-clefting? Find the answer by trying to produce the corresponding canonical version for each option.

B. There were after all a dozen appropriate texts he could have quoted. "Darkness and light are both alike to Thee." But they were not alike to a sensitive ten-year-old boy. *It was on those lonely walks that he had first had intimations of an essentially adult truth*, that it is those who most love us who cause us the most pain. (James, *Devices and Desires*, 2004)

4. For each of the following instances of *it*-clefting, produce the corresponding non-cleft version and name the syntactic function of the sentence element that is highlighted.

   a. It was you who introduced me to the track chair guys, right? (COCA, Spoken, 2015)
   b. It is because the State has recognized this fact that the law has insisted that, for a legal life and personality, these groups and societies must get the authority of the State, and submit to its conditions. (BNC, Academic, 1991)
   c. The anonymity of doctors who provide these details will be guaranteed. If these practices are not stamped out it is the public who will be the ultimate victims. (BNC, Academic, 1980)
   d. He looked up. On the pavement opposite a small boy watched him. The shouting grew fiercer, and the gates opposite were thrown open. It was the woman who had put the flowers on the place where Harry Lawrence had died, [...]. (BNC, Fiction, 1991)

## *Level 2: Interpretation and Research Design*

5. Figure 5.8 shows an alternative visualization of the results given as Table 5.2 and the graph shown as Figure 5.2. Figure 5.8 visualizes the absolute frequencies of different types of subject clause and their information status. Compare Figure 5.8 to 5.2 and discuss how the two diagrams highlight different research outcomes. Figure 5.2 already highlighted the relevance of syntactic form for the occurrence of extraposition. Which finding on different syntactic types of extraposed clauses does Figure 5.8 emphasize?

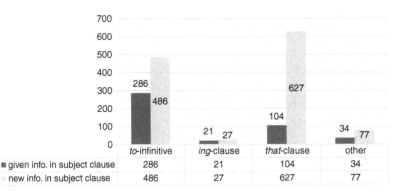

| | to-infinitive | ing-clause | that-clause | other |
|---|---|---|---|---|
| given info. in subject clause | 286 | 21 | 104 | 34 |
| new info. in subject clause | 486 | 27 | 627 | 77 |

**Figure 5.8** Information structure within different syntactic types of extraposed clauses (absolute frequencies)
Data is from Kaltenböck 2005: 131.

6. Replicate the analysis described in Exercise 2 with matrix predicates that express some kind of belief (e.g., being *true, apparent,* or *likely*). Find a search string for a related lemma search, combining the pronoun *it*, any form of the verb *be* and an adjective such as *true, apparent, likely,* or other. Based on an analysis of a randomized set of twenty attestations and their previous co-text, what is the proportion of given and new subject clauses? Do the findings confirm the hypothesis that extraposition occurs more often with new information in the subject clause?

7. Recall the function of an *it*-cleft, as discussed in Section 5.3.1, focusing either given or new information, and look at this example of *it*-clefting from the novel *Frankenstein*. Discuss the occurrence of an *it*-cleft in its relation to what you see (and possibly know) about the co-text and the context and a possible association with the genre of a suspense novel.

---

C. It was eight o'clock when we landed; we walked for a short time on the shore enjoying the transitory light, and then retired to the inn and contemplated the lovely scene of waters, woods, and mountains, obscured in darkness, yet still displaying their black outlines. (Shelley, *Frankenstein*, 1993 [1818]: ch. 23)

8. In Section 5.3.2 we pointed out that the type of cleft focusing given information, adding a meaning of contrast, is overall the more common type and that *it*-clefts with long and noteworthy information in the subordinate component, creating a presupposition, are a characteristic of narrative discourse. Find three *it*-clefts from a fictional and from an academic text of your choice. Classify them as belonging to the contrastive focus or the presupposition type. What do you observe? Which function seems to be more common in which type of discourse?

## Further Reading

- On the function of *it*-extraposition in discourse, notably academic discourse, see, for example, Zhang (2015). On information structure in *it*-clefts and their relation to *wh*-clefts, see Hedberg & Fadden (2007).
- On the use of *it*-clefting in child language development, see Aravind et al. (2018) or Thornton et al. (2018). For a more theoretical discussion of the relationship between extraposition and *it*-clefting, also contrasting their treatment within the conceptually very different frameworks of Generative Grammar and Construction Grammar, see Patten (2014).

# PART III

# Grammar of Discourse

# 6 | Connectives

## 6.1 Introduction

With this chapter, we will turn to the grammar *of* discourse. We will start with the most direct interface of the sentence and the discourse, which is the expression of connections between sentences. This means that grammatical aspects of the discourse itself will now become part of our discussion. Although we are still dealing with elements of grammar, we will explore how they connect to form units beyond the level of the sentence. The discussion will therefore center no longer just on sentence analysis, but will turn to concepts and ideas closer to the field of discourse analysis (see our note on this subfield of linguistics in Chapter 2).

While there are two ways of expanding a sentence, subordination and **coordination**, discourse proceeds through the sequence, that is, the coordination, of sentences (or non-clausal units). Within the sentence, the elements that can be coordinated are phrases or clauses: Example (1) illustrates the coordination of two noun phrases and (2) the coordination of two clauses. Coordinating conjunctions, such as *and*, *but*, and *or*, also commonly referred to as "coordinators," are the lexical category for elements that signal phrasal or clausal coordination.

(1)   Jimmy likes apples and pears.

(2)   Jimmy likes apples and Jimmy likes pears.

Coordinators connect elements of equal syntactic status. None of the constituents in (1) or (2) is a dependent element, which is why coordinate structures within the sentence are also described as "non-headed" constructions (Huddleston & Pullum 2002: 1275).

It is only a small step from a non-headed structure, that is, from coordination within the sentence, to the coordination of utterances in discourse. Coordinators also connect units of discourse, although, in writing, we often feel a little uncomfortable about using an item like *and* or *but* at the beginning of a new sentence. However, in speech, initiating a new turn using one of these coordinators is common, even when the next turn is uttered by a different speaker. This is shown in Example (3), where speaker B adds an utterance (*And Jimmy likes pears*) to the one made by speaker A (*Jimmy likes apples*).

(3)    A:   Jimmy likes apples.
       B:   And Jimmy likes pears.

The overt expression of the coordination of utterances is something very common in natural discourse, starting already in early childhood speech. In Example (4), which is from the CHILDES corpus, a large database of child interaction with their caretakers, the clause beginning with *and* easily connects two utterances across the turns of two different speakers (there will be more on connectives in language acquisition in Section 6.2).

(4)    CHILD:      Nina has dolly sleeping.
       ADULT:      The doll is sleeping too?
       CHILD:      And the man's sleeping on the big bed.
       [Nina; 2 years, 2 months] (example from Diessel 2004: 159)

The early and natural use of a coordinator for expressing connections in discourse, that is, without constructing a proper coordinate sentence, shows that the discourse-related function of coordinators, that is, their use as connectives, is part of their grammatical function.

Leaving the domain of grammar *in* discourse and turning to the grammar *of* discourse also means that the elements we will be looking at are more loosely connected to the core clause. For example, one could argue that, in a sequence like (3) or (4), *and* does not establish a syntactic connection at all, but works as a discourse marker (a category to be discussed in more detail in Chapter 8). Think of sentence connectives not so much as a way of expanding the core clause, but of adding a new one. This means you are adopting a discourse-oriented view: The function of a coordinator as a discourse connective is more to initiate than to truly connect (Biber et al. 2021: 87). Still, *and*, for example, does not carry all properties of a real extra-clausal element (these properties will be discussed in detail in Chapter 8). For instance, sentence-initial *and,* as in (3) and (4), is not mobile in position, unlike a connective adverb like *however,* and is not usually set off by intonation or punctuation from the rest of the clause (*Jimmy, *and/however, likes pears*).

Using a term from discourse analysis here, the relationship between sentences as units of discourse is called **conjunction**. Note that this term has no plural here because it refers to an area of the grammar of discourse and not to the part-of-speech class of conjunctions. Conjunction in this new sense covers all words and expressions that connect sentences or sections in a text. In discourse analysis, conjunction constitutes one crucial area of discourse cohesion, which is the cover term for all sorts of linguistic ties in a text, including lexical ties, substituting expressions, or the phenomenon of ellipsis. Conjunction is a grammatical type of cohesion, referring to the grammatical ties that express the semantic and pragmatic relationships in a text. To put it most simply, conjunction expresses how what is to follow in a text is connected to what has come before.

We will start this chapter with a discussion of what is at first sight the most basic semantic type of conjunction: additive conjunction. This choice might surprise you, since the idea of "addition" seems to mean rarely more than just continuity in a text or discourse. Which raises the question: Why express addition in discourse at all? There is no obvious answer to this question, which is exactly why we want to ask why, in the case of a simple additive relation, the next sentence in a discourse does not always open *without* a connective. This option is what we call a "zero" coordination. The contrast to the coordination with *and* is illustrated in Examples (5) and (6).

(5)  Jimmy likes apples. And Jimmy likes pears. (sentence coordination with *and*)

(6)  Jimmy likes apples. Jimmy likes pears. ("zero" coordination)

In this chapter, we will explore this opposition of sentence coordination by *and* or zero more closely, using both the variationist and the text-linguistic approach. We will then proceed by discussing other semantic types of conjunction and see how their usage varies within and across texts.

> Go to Exercise 1 to apply the distinction between the coordination of clauses and of sentences.

After reading this chapter, you will be able to:

- distinguish coordination within the sentence from the use of grammatical elements as discourse connectives;
- recognize and classify different elements that function as connectives;
- identify the four semantic types of conjunction and their different forms of expression;
- investigate characteristic patterns of the expression of conjunction in different types of discourse.


### Concepts, Constructions, and Keywords

*additive relation, adversative connectives, causative connectives, clausal coordination vs. sentence coordination, conjunction, connective adjuncts, coordinators, narrative mode, temporal connectives, "zero" expression of sentence coordination*


## 6.2 Additive Conjunction from a Variationist Perspective: Overt Marking vs. "Zero"

Additive conjunction expresses a relation of "addition" in the discourse. The connective element can be one of the additive coordinators, that is, *and* or *or*, or it can be an adjunct with additive meaning. Additive adjuncts include the adverbs *moreover* or *furthermore,* and prepositional phrases such as *in addition* or *in the same way*. Using a syntactic coordinator, most notably using sentence-initial *and*, is therefore only one out of several syntactic options to initiate a new sentence and to connect it to the preceding discourse.

An additive relation can also apply if there is no overt discourse connective (as in (6) above: *Jimmy likes apples. Jimmy likes pears.*). There is no real semantic difference between (5) and (6): Additive conjunction constitutes a proper case of variation in the area of discourse syntax. The choice of marking or zero must therefore be one governed by the discourse. Which contribution to the discourse does *and* as a connective make at all, in the light of this semantic equivalence? Does it make a difference whether a speaker or writer uses initial *and* or not? Discourse analysts have shown that, within a sequence of utterances, a change from zero connections to sentence- or turn-initial *and* signals some kind of "turn" within the discourse (Schiffrin 1987). By analogy, a change from *and* to zero can have a similar effect. This means, if there is a preference in a given context to use *and*, or no *and*, this is exactly what leaves the speaker with the possibility for a switch in order to express some kind of contrast.

Let us turn to an example. You are probably aware that many style manuals do not consider *and* at the beginning of a sentence in written text to be a good choice. In contrast to speech, where we often continue by using *and*, a written text, like a novel, will mostly contain zero connections between sentences. Still, we sometimes find individual occurrences of sentence-initial *and* in such texts, for example, when *and* signals the end of an episode, which is what you see in Example (7).

(7)    Deep down here by the dark water lived old Gollum, a small slimy creature. I don't know where he came from, nor who or what he was. He was a Gollum – as dark as darkness, except for two big round pale eyes in his thin face. He had a little boat, and he rowed about quite quietly on the lake.

Gollum got into his boat and shot off from the island, while Bilbo was sitting on the brink altogether flummoxed and at the end of his way and wits. Suddenly up came Gollum and whispered and hissed:

"Bless us and splash us, my precioussss! It guess it's a choice feast; at least a tasty morsel it'd make us, Gollum!"

*And* when he said Gollum he made a horrible swallowing noise in his throat. That is how he got his name, though he always called himself "my precious."

(Tolkien, *The Hobbit*, 1991 [1937]: 84)

In Example (7), the function of the connective *and* in the penultimate sentence of the passage results from the contrast to the regularity of zero connections, as explained above. With the use of *and* at the beginning of the last paragraph in (7), the episode ends and *Gollum* is now readily introduced into the discourse. This function is similar to the one of the formula *And they lived happily ever after*, which we know from many fairy tale endings.

In contrast to written texts, in which sentence-initial *and* is used scarcely overall, the overt expression of additive conjunction is common in spoken discourse. The reason is that, in natural speech, *and* easily supports the mere continuity of the discourse, for example, as a filler item or a marker of progression. We all know oral storytelling that proceeds by the typical *and then*-connections, associated, in particular, with early childhood speech (see Figure 6.1).

In early childhood speech, children do not yet connect their utterances by way of a coordinator. Conjunction comes to be expressed approximately around their second birthday (Bloom et al. 1980), the first coordinator, in fact, being *and*. Based on data from the CHILDES corpus, we know that *and* is used as a discourse connective before it is used as a syntactic coordinator, that is, it connects turns or discourse units before connecting clauses *within* the sentence (Diessel 2004). The evidence for this finding is intonation, in that the uses of *and* connecting

**Figure 6.1** *And then*-connections in early childhood storytelling

sentences in discourse, and not constituent clauses, are preceded by an intonation pattern and/or a pause indicating the end of that utterance. Children tend to use independent utterances beginning with *and* especially after a speaker change (Diessel 2004: 159), like in (8):

(8)  CHILD:        Piggy went to market.
     ADULT:        Yes.
     CHILD:        And piggy had none.
     [Naomi; 2 years, 7 months] (example from Diessel 2004)

In (8), which was produced by a child aged two years and seven months, *and* occurs as a marker of speech continuity. This function of *and* is similar to a pattern we also see in adult speech, from which the children obviously learn this.

Another reason why *and* is common in speech is that it can connect elements on all levels of discourse organization. These elements can be units of content or information, as in Example (8), or different verbal acts. This means that sentence-initial coordinators have a semantic or a pragmatic function. In that respect, they differ from many other discourse connectives. Take, for example, the dialog in (9), where a nutritionist is discussing Halloween snacks. Some of the uses of *and* relate to the content of the talk, for instance, the different Halloween giveaways (*gum*, *pretzels*, *tattoos*). Other links in the text connect different verbal acts, such as explaining (*And kids like gum*) and, later, recommending (*and actually, the kids will have these a lot longer*).

(9)  A:   So this could be a good idea, but brush your teeth.
     B:   Afterwards. Absolutely. *And* over here, gum is good for your
          teeth, too, right?
     A:   Sugarless gum. Yes. *And* kids like gum. So look for specials at the
          wholesale clubs. They've got the big boxes for less money. You
          could buy them in strips like this.
     B:   These are some other great . . .
     A:   Hundred-calorie packs.
     B:   Hundred-calorie packs.
     A:   Moms love these, portion control. *And* pretzels are benign, *and*
          they come in fun Halloween orange, fun shapes, goons, goblins.

B:    Mm-hmm. *And* if you don't want to do the candy or the food giveaways, I mean, these are just some great things that you can throw in there, as well. *And* actually, the kids will have these a lot longer, right?

A:    Yeah. *And* tattoos are a good idea, as well. My kids love when they get tattoos. (COCA, Spoken, 2007)

It is a characteristic of *and* as a discourse connective that it can establish both semantic and pragmatic links among the units of a discourse. By contrast, some connective adverbs and phrases, like *in addition*, provide semantic links only, that is, they connect ideas (as in *Sugarless gum. [. . .] In addition, there are pretzels*), but less easily different verbal acts (*?In addition, the kids will have these a lot longer.*)

To summarize, we have seen that the basic function of an additive connective in discourse is to signal continuation and that this is ultimately the most basic way of turning utterances into discourse. If *and* is used, the additive link can support a semantic and/or a pragmatic relation between utterances. In spoken discourse we find the expression of additive meaning to be much more common than in written discourse, where it is subject to a prescriptive attitude (see our Good to Know box on prescriptive grammar below). Another reason is that a written text, like an essay or a blog entry, already possesses a material continuity through the medium or genre, making the support of mere continuation less obvious.

We have also seen how the discourse function of *and* as a connective arises from the contrast to zero, that is, we have so far looked at the connective using the variationist approach (as introduced in Chapter 2). Turning to the text-linguistic approach in Section 6.3, we will explore how the use of sentence- and turn-initial *and* varies across different types of discourse.

Good to Know: Prescriptive Grammar and Sentence-Initial Coordinators

The interest in grammar in discourse is something that linguists share with language instructors. Perhaps you have experienced yourself a rather negative attitude against the use of coordinators at sentence beginnings. School teachers often express a critical attitude toward sentence-initial *and* when they supervise and grade young children's writing (Crystal 1995). Nowadays, grammar checkers also play a role: By putting a wavy line under any sentence-initial coordinator, they also impose a rule against them. Other sources adopt a more descriptive attitude. *The American Heritage Dictionary* notes the existence of a prescriptive grammar rule that judges sentence-initial *and* as "incorrect," but goes on to state that "this stricture has been ignored by writers from Shakespeare to Joyce Carol Oates" (www.ahdictionary.com). A usage-based reference grammar, such as the *GSWE* (Biber et al. 2021), comments on the existence of the proscription, but takes an interest in it only as far as the attitude helps to explain register variation. For example, the proscription of sentence-initial *and* is influential for the expression of conjunction in academic prose, but much less so in informal texts. Overall, while prescriptive sources have an impact on patterns of language use, they do not necessarily have an impact on grammar development. We return to this distinction in the account of textual variation that follows in Section 6.3.

## 6.3 Text-Linguistic Variation: Additive Conjunction in Different Types of Discourse

So far, we have seen that additive conjunction is the most obvious relation of continuity in discourse and, in that, competes with the zero expression of sentence coordination. Following this discussion based on the variationist approach, we now turn to the text-linguistic perspective. Note that this perspective means that we will look just at the occurrence of *and* at the beginning of sentences and no longer compare zero beginnings and uses of *and*. Following our explanation given in Chapter 2, a text-linguistic approach here means that the object of investigation is the pattern of occurrence of additive conjunction in different types of texts.

Let us first turn to written discourse, where we can expect a strong influence of the prescriptive attitude against sentence-initial *and*. For example, the *GSWE* describes the prescription as being "most influential in academic prose," whereas the use of *and* as a connective is higher in fiction and news texts, mostly because these also contain embedded dialog (Biber et al. 2021: 87). Interestingly, there is also corpus data from academic discourse in which the connective *and* does not turn out to be all that infrequent. One study found that sentence-initial *and*, compared to other additive connectives (e.g., *moreover*, *furthermore*, or *in addition*), was "the most frequently occurring additive marker in academic writing" (Bell 2007: 184). Figure 6.2 illustrates the occurrence of sentence-initial *and* in the corpus of that study (average rates per 100,000 words as the dependent variable on the *y*-axis), showing the results here for five different academic journals (the predictor variable on the *x*-axis).

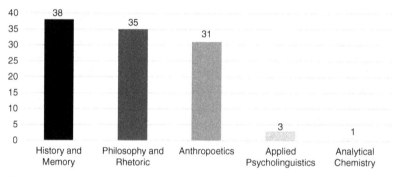

**Figure 6.2** Initial *and* in five academic journals
Per ~100,000 words. Data is from Bell 2007.

As we can see in Figure 6.2, sentence-initial *and* is used in academic texts, but particularly in journals from disciplines in the humanities (history, philosophy, anthropology). By contrast, the use of initial *and* seems to be much lower within disciplines from the natural sciences (psycholinguistics, chemistry). We can explain this finding if we come back to one aspect of the use of *and* that we discussed in Section 6.2. We saw there that it can help structuring the discourse by switching from zero to the use of *and* in order to signal a certain turn in the discourse. Similar to the shift from zero to *and* in Example (7), where the sentence with *and* concluded a chain of actions, *and* in humanities discourse was also found to conclude "argument chaining" (Bell 2007: 194). As an illustration, check out Example (10):

(10)    Gilligan's reporting also relied solely on a single Downing Street
        source, Minister of Defense employee and former UN weapons

inspector David Kelly. Kelly claimed that [. . .]. In the end, this series of events, one of many narratives surrounding the Iraq war and the intelligence that enabled the war, would lead to the August 2003 Hutton Inquiry in Britain, an attempt to explore Kelly's death that also engaged prewar intelligence and the reporting of the BBC. *And* it is with the Hutton inquiry that dramatic historiographies of the nascent Iraq War began to make their way to the British stage, [. . .]. (COCA, Academic, 2007)

The text excerpt in (10) contains *and* at the beginning of the last sentence, which is also the end of the author's chain of argument. By using *and*, the writer is able to mark a contrast: Since one form of connection, namely zero, has been the norm so far, deviating from that norm of connection is apt to signal that something different is coming. In (10), for example, when using *and*, the author turns from the listing of facts to a generalization and thereby concludes the line of argument.

Turning to spoken discourse, for the reasons we discussed in Section 6.2, we can expect that sentence- or turn-initial *and* is considerably more frequent. In contrast to the results for written discourse shown by Figure 6.2, in which all rates per 100,000 words are below 50, a simple search for initial *and* in different sections of COCA (described in the toolbox of this chapter) enables us to confirm this assumption. For example, when we did this search, there was a rate of occurrence of almost 1,000 per 100,000 words in spoken news (9,629 per 1 million words in Fox, details in the toolbox). The toolbox also demonstrates again (see also Chapter 2) how to calculate the rates of occurrence for different sections, and Exercise 5 (Level 2) asks you to discuss more data on the use of *and* in some written sections of COCA.

Studying Rates of Occurrence of Connectives in a Corpus

When we want to retrieve sentence-initial *and* in an electronic corpus, we can use the corresponding part-of-speech (POS) tag for the word class of conjunctions and add a full stop plus capitalize *and*. For example, having applied this search to four sections in the COCA corpus, we received the following number of hits (note that, if you are using a corpus such as COCA, to which text samples are constantly being added, the exact frequencies increase from year to year): 1,719 tokens in academic writing (field of education), 4,375 in academic writing (humanities), 60,662 in spoken news (Fox) and 131,478 in spoken news (NPR). These numbers confirm our understanding that sentence-initial *and* is much more typical of spoken discourse, but they also seem to offer a challenge in that the number in one type of speech is twice as large as in the other.

We therefore need to take into account that the four sub-corpora in COCA are different in size. When we did the search in 2019, the Fox news section had 6.3 million words, while the National Public Radio (NPR) corpus had 17.4 million words. In the academic sub-corpus, the sub-corpus for education had 9.4 million words and the humanities one had 11.9 million words. As a next step, we therefore need to calculate normalized rates of occurrence, as described in Chapter 2, which will provide us with averaged values for the occurrence of sentence-initial *and* for each corpus section.

Using the formula given in Chapter 2 (which is: (raw count ÷ total word count) × reference size in number of words), the rates of occurrence per million words look like this:

Fox: $(60{,}662 \div 6{,}300{,}000) \times 1{,}000{,}000 = 9{,}629$

NPR: $(131{,}478 \div 17{,}400{,}000) \times 1{,}000{,}000 = 7{,}556$

Acad./Edu.: $(1{,}719 \div 9{,}400{,}000) \times 1{,}000{,}000 = 183$

Acad./Hum.: $(4{,}375 \div 11{,}900{,}000) \times 1{,}000{,}000 = 368$

These numbers clearly confirm that written and spoken discourse differ considerably in the use of *and* at sentence beginnings. Both academic disciplines have much lower rates than the spoken news. By contrast, the difference within the discourse type of spoken news now appears to be less distinct. What looked like a noticeable difference when dealing with absolute frequencies (131,478 on NPR being more than twice of the 60,662 occurrences in Fox) has turned out to be one due mainly to corpus size. However, the finding that some academic texts contain considerably more occurrences of *and* at sentence beginnings than others has remained robust.

A final aspect of our discussion of the use of connective *and* in different types of discourse will concern the mode of discourse (see Figure 2.2 in

Chapter 2). Next to the opposition of speech and writing, which we have dealt with so far, we want to show that it is the presence of the rhetorical mode of narration that is also more closely associated with the expression of additive conjunction than other modes of discourse. To understand why the discourse we refer to here is more about mode, rather than genre, note that narration not only means telling personal stories and anecdotes, or writing fiction, but is a term that also captures the way information is presented in the discourse of news, politics, or science. Narration is described as a "basic" mode of structuring a text, one that applies to many genres (Virtanen 1992). Note that speakers also narrate extensively in conversations, which is why the analysis of oral storytelling is an important issue in conversation analysis.

Why is a **narrative mode** relevant to the phenomenon of additive conjunction? The defining property of narration is that the discourse verbalizes experience, which is why narrative discourse typically deals with past events that happened in a sequence. Discourse in which the sequence of two, or more, sentences corresponds to the sequence of events has been described as possessing a "narrative syntax" (Labov 2013). To cite a famous example by E. M. Forster (1927), the sequence *The king died. And then the queen died.* has narrative syntax, even though it does not necessarily have a plot, which would suggest some kind of causal relationship (as in *The king died. And then the queen died of grief.)* A narrative mode of discourse therefore means that the text has a structure that is based on experience and chronology.

The connective *and*, the basic form of expression for continuity, is highly suitable for this mode of discourse and for the narrative syntax (also compare Figure 6.1), which is supported by observations based on spoken discourse. For example, in a study based on the Fisher corpus, a corpus of American telephone conversations, by far the most typical pairwise combination of connective elements in sentence-initial position was *and* in combination with *then* (Lohmann & Koops 2016). The score for *and then* was about three times as high as the next combination with *and* in the hierarchy (which was *and so*). Without going into the exact measure of how the difference was calculated (if you are interested, you could consult the reference), this finding reflects a close association of the occurrence of connective *and* with narrative syntax and temporal continuity in a text. Interestingly, the reversed sequences also occurred at distinctly different frequencies: *so and*, but not *then and*, was also observed (see

Lohmann & Koops 2016: 442 and Section 8.4 on discourse marker sequences).

Let us also turn to written discourse, which will highlight that, despite the close association with oral storytelling, the use of sentence-initial *and* in narration is not necessarily a matter of an oral or colloquial style. The excerpt in (11) is from a historical academic text, taken from Robert Hooke's *Micrographia*, which is a famous scientific text of the seventeenth century. We know that, in those early days of science, scientists often reported, that is, narrated, their scientific activities, rather than presenting a proper argument (Dorgeloh 2005).

(11)    About eight years since, upon casually reading the Explication of this
        odd PHÆNOMENON, by the most Ingenious DES CARTES, I had a
        great desire to be satisfied, what that Substance was that gave such a
        shining and bright Light: *And* to that end I spread a sheet of white
        Paper, *and* on it, observing the place where several of these Sparks
        seemed to vanish, I found certain very small, black, but glittering
        Spots of a movable Substance. [...]

                                            (Robert Hooke, *Micrographia* [1665] in
                                            Helsinki Corpus TEI XML Edition 2011)

The passage illustrates what we have just described as a "narrative" syntax: The sequence of the clauses and sentences corresponds to the sequence of the steps in the experiment. Using *and* to initiate a new sentence (*And to that end I spread ...*) or clause (*and on it ... I found*) reflects the narrative mode of this discourse, which was common in those early scientific texts.

In sum, we have seen that, from the text-linguistic perspective, *and* is a discourse connective that turns out to be associated with spoken and with narrative discourse. In addition to this text-linguistic pattern, we have seen that *and* in written discourse is not altogether uncommon and enables the writer to mark an argumentative shift.

> Go to Exercise 2, which is about the association of the con-
> nective *and* with the narrative mode of discourse, and to
> Exercises 6 and 7 (Level 2) for interpreting data on sentence-
> initial *and* in written discourse. Find out more about the use of
> *and* in spoken discourse in Exercise 3.

## 6.4 Connective Adjuncts

So far, we have dealt with one semantic type of conjunction, the expression of additive conjunction. We concentrated our discussion on the discourse connective *and,* which belongs to the lexical class of coordinators but also functions as a discourse connective. We now turn to other connective elements, which differ from *and* syntactically (they are adjuncts rather than syntactic coordinators) as well as semantically (by expressing a relation beyond mere addition).

As we discussed in Section 6.2, a connective adjunct can be an adverb or a phrase. There are simple adverbs, such as *so* or *then,* which just express the relation in discourse, while more complex adverbs and connective phrases combine the meaning of a discourse relation with an element referring back to something in the previous discourse. These different items could be ordered in a cline of increasing complexity, in which the meaning of the discourse connection, expressed either by the adverb or by the preposition, is enriched by more and more material. An example of such a cline (for temporal connectives) is shown in Figure 6.3.

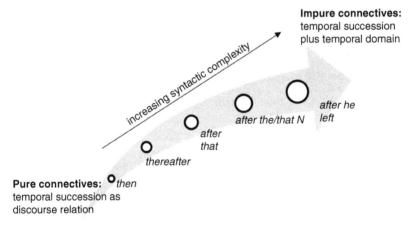

**Figure 6.3** Cline of temporal connectives

The categorical distinction corresponding to the beginning and end of the cline in Figure 6.3 is the one between "pure" and "impure" connective adjuncts (Huddleston & Pullum 2002: 777). For example, *then* is a pure connective, as it just expresses a temporal succession in discourse. By contrast, phrases with a temporal preposition (*after that/the N*) do not just connect, but also specify the temporal domain within which the clause applies, which is why they are impure connectives. Whereas impure connectives also add content, pure connective adjuncts are just functional elements within the grammar of discourse.

We can equally apply this distinction to the other types of conjunction: For example, a connective adjunct for expressing a result or reason can come from the lexical class of adverbs, like *so* or *consequently*, but it can also be a phrase, such as *as a result* or *for this reason*. These phrases do not just connect, but combine the connective element with a way of pointing backward: *As a result (of this)* or *for this reason*, for example, establish a causal relation and refer backward to *this* or *this reason*. Similarly, *under these circumstances* is an additive connective, but at the same time functions as a clausal modifier, carrying abstract locative meaning.

Impure connective adjuncts belong more closely to the core clause and are *not only* a phenomenon of the grammar of discourse. The borderline status between sentence adjunct and discourse connective can be made obvious by checking whether the adjunct can be the focused element in an *it*-cleft construction (see Chapter 5 for more on cleft constructions). See, for example, the contrast between (12a) and (13a), where only the impure connective adjunct in (13a) can be foregrounded by a cleft construction, as in (13b):

(12)  a.  Jimmy likes fruit. Consequently, he likes apples.

(12)  b.  Jimmy likes fruit. *It is consequently that he likes apples.

(13)  a.  Jimmy likes fruit. For this reason, he likes apples.

(13)  b.  Jimmy likes fruit. It is for this reason that he likes apples.

Still, the distinction between pure connective elements and clausal modifiers as impure connectives remains a little fuzzy. For this reason, when turning to the semantic types of connective adjuncts in Section 6.5, we use pure connectives as examples wherever possible. Just bear in mind that there are many more items that can be used within each category.

Consult Exercise 3 for an opportunity to retrieve the different syntactic categories that function as connectives in a text.

Turning now to the semantic types of links that different connectives provide within discourse, we use an established semantic classification. According to this classification, there are four main types of discourse relations, which are listed in Table 6.1.

**Table 6.1** *Semantic types of conjunction and their syntactic realizations*

| Examples of . . . | . . . additive adverbs | . . . additive prepositional phrases |
|---|---|---|
| Additive | *also, alternatively, besides, moreover, similarly* | *in addition, for instance* |
| Adversative | *however, yet, conversely, instead* | *despite this, by contrast* |
| Causative | *so, hence, consequently* | *as a result, for this reason, because of this* |
| Temporal | *first(ly), then, finally, previously* | *after that, at the same time, in the end, next time* |

Next to additive conjunction, discussed at length in Section 6.3, you see in Table 6.1 that there are three other core semantic types. Let us look at each of these below by variation on a single example. You will see two instances for each semantic type, because we also want to distinguish between semantic and pragmatic uses of these relations in discourse. As discussed above when looking at the discourse function of *and*, this distinction relates to the question of whether the link is one based on the content of the discourse or on what the speaker/writer is doing (the verbal act).

- Adversative: The adversative relation is similar to the additive relation but adds something to the discourse in a contrastive sense.

(14)  In this class, you do not have to submit a paper. *Instead*, you are required to write at least a paragraph for every session. (adversative, semantic)

(15)  In this class, you do not have to submit a paper. *Instead*, let me tell you how I would like you to work here. (adversative, pragmatic)

- Causative: The semantic type of causative (also sometimes referred to as "causal") connectives expresses relations such as result, purpose, and reason.

(16)    In this class, you do not have to submit a paper. *Consequently*, there
        will be more time for reading. (causative, semantic)

(17)    In this class, you do not have to submit a paper. *So* what do you have
        to do instead? (causative, pragmatic)

- Temporal/sequential: Temporal relations express a proper temporal
  progression, or they relate to the internal relations of ordering or
  structuring the discourse.

(18)    In this class, you do not have to submit a paper. *Next time*, this will be
        different. (temporal, semantic)

(19)    In this class, you do not have to submit a paper. *Now*, what are the
        reading assignments? (temporal, pragmatic)

When looking at examples (14) through (19), you may have noticed
that some connective adjuncts, like *instead*, express a semantic or a
pragmatic connection in discourse. Others, notably *so*, *now* and *then*,
characteristically express a pragmatic relation. As you will learn
in Chapter 8, this latter type of adverbs is likely to become a real
extra-clausal element, that is, a discourse marker. Classifying them as
discourse markers means that one emphasizes their function as a
**bracketing** device within the discourse, while dealing with them as
connectives here means we focus on the connections that they express.

Turning to the role of discourse in the use of connectives, we will take
a closer look at academic texts in Section 6.5. Choosing these texts is
not random, since connectives are often used to support scientific
argumentation. Before turning to this discourse type, you should go
to Exercise 4 to identify the four semantic types that we have discussed
in this section.

## 6.5 Connectives in Academic Discourse

To conclude our discussion of connectives, we will look at the usage of
connectives in academic English. The findings that we discuss here are
mainly about research articles and textbooks, but we will also turn to
some differences between professional academic and student writing.
For a first look at some findings, the obvious question to ask is whether
all semantic types discussed in Section 6.4 are used in academic writing
to roughly the same extent. For example, since doing science usually

means presenting evidence in order to develop or contradict a position, it is plausible to assume that expressions of causative and adversative relations are more likely in academic texts than temporal or additive connectives. This means that we expect causative and adversative connectives to be more pervasive in academic texts than expressions of the other two relations.

Table 6.2 gives us a first idea whether this assumption is borne out by corpus-based results. The data was collected for a study of connective adjuncts in English (and Chinese) academic writing (Gao 2016). The table shows the results for English academic articles, based on a corpus of research articles from four different disciplines.

Table 6.2 *Normalized frequency of connective adjuncts in academic articles*

| Semantic type of connective adjunct | Rate of occurrence (per 10,000 words) |
| --- | --- |
| Additive | 1.14 |
| Adversative | 0.73 |
| Causative | 0.58 |
| Temporal/sequential | 0.43 |
| Total | 2.88 |

Data is from Gao 2016.

The results in Table 6.2 are normalized rates of occurrence, which show that, counter to our initial expectation, additive conjunction is the most pervasive semantic type expressed by connectives in academic texts: Its frequency is about twice as high as the frequency of causative or temporal connectives. More in line with what we predicted, the adversative type is also quite common in academic texts. With regard to our initial assumption, causative conjunction occurs to a lower extent than expected.

Remember that, since we are using the text-linguistic approach here, this data documents a pattern as characteristic of a discourse type. Academic discourse is dense in both information and argumentation, which is what the presence of additive and adversative connectives plausibly reflects. Other work dealing with academic registers has found similar proportions in related discourse types. For instance, in academic textbooks the most frequent connective adjuncts are *however*, *thus, for example*, and *therefore* (Biber 2006).

It is interesting to compare this pattern of professional academic discourse to the academic texts produced by students. A data set that allows for this comparison is shown in Table 6.3, based on writings from the field of literary studies (Shaw 2009). The table gives the results (rates of occurrence) for five connective adjuncts, and not for all adjuncts used in the text, which is why the numbers do not reflect the overall use of connective items. However, the total of connectives is given in the final row.

**Table 6.3** *Frequency of five connective adjuncts in academic writing*

|               | student corpus literary writing | professional corpus literary writing | professional corpus adjusted for density |
| ------------- | ------------------------------- | ------------------------------------ | ---------------------------------------- |
| *however*     | 122.6                           | 61.9                                 | 93.3                                     |
| *yet*         | 104.0                           | 57.5                                 | 86.7                                     |
| *thus*        | 80.5                            | 55.2                                 | 83.2                                     |
| *therefore*   | 86.7                            | 16.7                                 | 25.2                                     |
| *for example* | 50.8                            | 22.0                                 | 33.2                                     |
| all connectives | 844                           | 560                                  | –                                        |

The table shows the frequency per 100,000 words of five specific connectives and the overall number of connectives in different types of academic writing. Data is adapted from Shaw 2009.

By looking at the first three columns of Table 6.3, we may be surprised to see that the frequency of the five connectives is higher in the texts written by students than in professional academic writing. We could speculate on whether or not this difference is due to a lack of experience, resulting in an overuse, but one could also argue that it can be due to a difference in genre. After all, student essays are not (yet) exactly the same type of writing as published research articles.

Apart from this difficulty of comparison, the results in Table 6.3 pose another challenge, which is dealt with by the numbers in the fourth column. Since it turned out in the data that there is an overall higher frequency of connectives in the student corpus, the results for the professional corpus had to be adjusted for their density. This adjustment was necessary because, ultimately, the author of that study wanted to know how frequent each of the five connective elements was in comparison. For example, how frequent would *however* have been if both groups of writers had used connectives to the same extent? To this end, the frequency of each adjunct had to be adjusted for density. An adjusted frequency results from multiplying each individual rate of occurrence by the ratio of the total frequencies, that is, here by 844/560. For example, *however* has an adjusted frequency of 93.3 (844 ÷ 560 × 61.9). This value would be its rate of occurrence in professional literary writing if this discourse had overall the same rate of occurrence for connectives. In this way, the adjusted numbers in the fourth column of Table 6.3 inform us about the frequency that each item would have if the overall density of connectives were the same in both corpora.

Resulting from this adjustment, Figure 6.4, based on Table 6.3 (columns two and four), with normalized rates of occurrence as the dependent variable on the *y*-axis, enables us to compare the two types of discourse for their pattern of use of the five connective elements.

Figure 6.4 highlights two outcomes. On the one hand, it shows that the texts produced by students by and large have a similar pattern of occurrence for these five connectives as the professional discourse. For example, both groups of writers use *however* and *yet* most frequently. On the other hand, there are also differences, for example, in that four out of the five connectives show higher rates of occurrence in the writing by students. One might conclude that students overuse these connective expressions, but we also have to bear in mind the limitations of the data

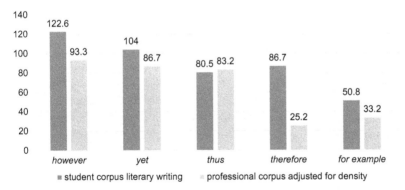

**Figure 6.4** Five adjuncts in student and professional literary criticism
Data is from Shaw 2009; frequency for professional writing has been adjusted for density.

set (with just five lexical items). It would equally make sense to assume that the professional writers used a wider range of connectives, including *and* or *but*. Exercise 8 (Level 2) will return to this question.

In sum, the occurrence of connectives in academic texts has indicated that the different semantic types and expressions of conjunction do not vary randomly, but with the discourse type. It has also become obvious that the overt expression of conjunction is to some extent dependent on the experience of the writers and on the genre. In the literature, many other patterns of genre variation are discussed (for some, see our notes for Further Reading at the end of this chapter). For example, there is a well-known preference for temporal connectives in narrative and instructive texts and for the expression of additive conjunction in descriptive and informative texts. It can also be quite interesting to look at your own academic writing, which is what we suggest in Exercise 9.

## 6.6 Summary

In this chapter, we have introduced you to one area of the grammar of discourse, looking at the various syntactic elements that function as discourse connectives. We started with one semantic type of conjunction, the additive relation, and explored the use of *and* as one possible connective for expressing this relation. We discussed the close association of the use of sentence- or turn-initial *and* with spoken and narrative discourse, as reflected in corpora by higher rates of occurrence in the corresponding discourse types. We also saw that, in discourse where additive relations are less commonly expressed, switching to *and* at the beginning of a sentence enables the writer to signal the end of a chain or some kind of turn.

We then turned to the different semantic classes of conjunction and looked at their syntactic realizations as well as at their occurrence in academic texts. We learned that there is a characteristic usage of the four types of conjunction within the academic register, but that their use also depends on the writer. For example, we saw that students tend to use more connectives, but show less variation, compared to the texts written by more experienced academics.

We also touched on the procedures for dealing with the frequencies of connectives as gathered from large-size corpora. For corpus sections of a different size, we saw how to deal with normalized rates rather than absolute frequencies. For interpreting rates of occurrence against the background of a different density of the overall category, you learned how to adjust frequencies of individual items for their density.

## 6.7 Exercises

### *Level 1: Classification and Application*

1. Identify all cases of clausal coordination within the sentence and of the use of a coordinator as sentence connective in excerpt A. What are the criteria that you go by? Looking at the occurrences that you find, and considering that this is a children's book, is there a pattern you expected to see?

---

A. Once upon a time there was a deep and wide river, and in this river lived a crocodile. I do not know whether you have ever seen a crocodile; but if you did see one, I am sure you would be frightened. They are very long, twice as long as your bed; and they are covered with hard green or yellow scales; and they have a wide flat snout, and a huge jaw with hundreds of sharp teeth, so big that it could hold you all at once inside it. This crocodile used to lie all day in the mud, half under water, basking in the sun, and never moving; but if any little animal came near, he would jump up, and open his big jaws, and snap it up as a dog snaps up a fly. And if you had gone near him, he would have snapped you up too, just as easily. (Rouse, *The Crocodile and the Monkey*, 2019)

---

2. Discuss whether the occurrence of *and* as a discourse connective in excerpt B is from the context of a narrative or a non-narrative mode in the discourse. What are the linguistic signals that indicate the presence of narration? Why do you think *and* is used, in contrast to the sentences beginning with zero-connections?

---

B. Wim Wenders' "Alice in the Cities" is about a disinterested togetherness between a German journalist (with a heart of a poet) in the middle of a creative block and a pre-adolescent girl who unexpectedly found herself in his care. It is also about a unique psychological atmosphere which is created by these two protagonists and which becomes the very style of the film – relaxed, tender, warm, more than just life. Thirdly, the film is about creative process when the object of creative effort is life itself. *And*, finally, it is about the geography of two cultures, American pre-globalist (and impulsively entrepreneurial) and European post-fascist (knowingly existential). (CORE, mixed register, 2009)

3. Underline all connective adjuncts in passages C and D. Indicate whether they are formally adverbs or prepositional phrases. Which ones are pure connectives (in that they do not add content, but only structure the discourse, as explained in Section 6.4)?

C. In a nutshell, can you explain the process? First we break down the shot to determine the number of layers that will be needed based on the subject matter, shot length and camera movement. Then the individual elements are rotoscoped out so that they can be manipulated independently. Next we apply depth and roundness to the individual elements using proprietary software and then we need to paint in the occlusions that were created by offsetting those objects as part of the depth process. Basically we round the objects and then shift them left and right to create the offset that would appear if you were in the position of the camera. Then we clean it up so that the viewer doesn't know it's been manipulated. (CORE, Interview, undated)

D. Incredibly, you can design three identical websites using exactly the same design and wording but with only the colours changed between them and elicit entirely different responses from visitors to each of the sites. For this reason alone, colour should be your main consideration when looking at the design of your website or even your company's corporate colours. (CORE, Advice, 2012)

4. Classify all sentence connectives (in italics) in the following examples by the four semantic types of conjunction (additive, temporal, adversative, causative).

(20) [...] when I returned from the bedroom, Thomas Jefferson and his toolbox were gone. I went outside to look for him and saw that his bright yellow van was still parked out front. I waited a few moments, not knowing what to do. *Finally* I approached the van and saw that Thomas Jefferson was sitting inside, holding his face in his hands. (COCA, Fiction, 2012)

(21) The volume highlights three particular assumptions that are inherent to and embedded within current trauma discourse. *First*, this discourse operates on the basis of a strongly individualist approach to human life, with a marked emphasis on the disengaged self and on intrapsychic conflicts. *However*, this notion of the self may not be valid in many non-western cultures, which are predicated on alternative notions of the self and its relationship to others. *Secondly*, it is assumed that the forms of mental disorder that are described by western psychiatry map unproblematically onto those found elsewhere. *However*, in non-western contexts, it is likely that the idioms of distress vary considerably; the emergence of a particular symptom does not necessarily mean that it has the same meaning or significance across different cultures. *Finally*, the emergence of a professionalized trauma discourse has tended towards the handing over of memory to experts to pronounce on its meaning and significance. (COCA, Academic, 2008)

(22) Adolescent relationships often take unexpected twists and turns. *Therefore*, it is important to regularly reflect on the process and outcomes associated with peer network interventions. (COCA, Academic, 2013)

(23) An experimental randomized design would allow for an evaluation of whether implementation of the SCS model itself, rather than other potential variables (e.g., school policies, other programs), cause observed outcomes. *Therefore*, the current study was implemented to utilize a randomized design within a large urban school district with more than 80,000 students. (COCA, Academic, 2013)

## Level 2: Interpretation and Research Design

5. Table 6.4 contains the results from a search in COCA for occurrences of *and* at sentence beginnings. Why are the results difficult to compare, and what could you do about this? Which news sections are similar in their use of *and*, and can you try to explain why?

**Table 6.4** *Frequency of connective* and *for three written sections of* COCA

|  | NEWS (Local) | NEWS (National) | NEWS (Sports) |
|---|---|---|---|
| sentence-initial *and* | 3,013 | 4,709 | 9,523 |
| size of section (words in million) | 6.0 | 6.6 | 14.0 |

The table shows the absolute frequency of connective *and* and the corpus size for three written sections of COCA.

6. Collect your own set of data about the usage of sentence-initial *and* in two different genres from a corpus (use, for instance, subsections of magazine and newspaper texts in COCA). Set up a table with absolute as well as normalized rates of occurrence. Choose a diagram that is suitable to illustrate your results.

7. In Section 6.2. we argued that *and* at the beginning of a sentence is much more likely to occur in speech than in writing. In a study of differences across types of professional spoken discourse, Iyeiri et al. (2010) found the following rates of occurrence for the use of turn-initial *and*:

|  | Range of rates of occurrence in three speech files (per 10,000 words) |
|---|---|
| Speech at press conferences | 0.6 – 1.3 |
| Speech at meetings on reading tests | 11.9 – 23.2 |

In the light of what you have learned in this chapter about the discourse functions of initial *and*, discuss possible reasons for the difference.

8. It has been suggested that a possible reason for the higher frequency of connective adjuncts in student writing is that professional writers hesitate less to use *and* and *but*, instead of connective
adjuncts like *furthermore* or *however*. Look at the frequencies
(taken from Shaw 2009) as given in Table 6.5. Do they confirm
this assumption? Write a short text to discuss your observations.
As background of your discussion, take into account what we
noted in Section 6.2 about the negative attitude that many adult
speakers have toward the use of sentence-initial coordinators in
written discourse.

Table 6.5  *Occurrence per 100,000 words of four types of connectives*

|  | student corpus literary writing | professional corpus adjusted for density |
|---|---|---|
| *however* | 122.6 | 98.3 |
| *furthermore* | 6.2 | 13.8 |
| *and* | 6.2 | 48.0 |
| *but* | 27.2 | 57.0 |

Data is from Shaw 2009.

9. Analyze a sample of your own academic writing for the expression of conjunction. Which connectives do you commonly use?
Imagine an editor criticizing your language use for containing
sentence-initial coordinators (*and* or *but*) or connective adverbs
(like *so*, *now*, and *then*). If you had a conversation with this
editor, what would you say from a linguistic perspective?

## Further Reading

• One classic reference work for the grammar of discourse, or cohesion, in English, on which this chapter also builds, is Halliday &
Hasan (1976). Its basic classification scheme for cohesion, as also
used in this chapter, is covered by most textbooks on discourse
analysis or discourse studies; see, for example, Renkema &
Schubert (2018: ch. 6).
• Sanders (1997) introduces the distinction of semantic and pragmatic
relations in discourse. See Spooren & Sanders (2008) on the

acquisition of discourse relations and van Silfhout et al. (2015) on experimental work that documents how readers benefit from connectives as processing signals in texts.

- For connectives in academic writing, see, for example, Bell (2007) and Gao (2016). The acquisition of sentence coordination in early childhood is described in Diessel (2004: ch. 7). Rezvani et al. (2017) document the frequency of connectives in different sections of the BNC and COCA. Dupont (2021) describes the occurrence of adversative connectives (contrasted with French) based on large corpora of editorials and research writing.

# 7 | Pronouns and Ellipsis

## 7.1 Introduction

In Chapter 6, we started dealing with the grammar *of* discourse, that is, with elements of grammar that have a function across the boundary of the single sentence. We saw that each sentence, as an upcoming unit of discourse, is related to the previous discourse by different types of relations and that these relations can be expressed by different connectives. In this chapter, we turn to another type of sentence connections: those created by pronouns and ellipsis. For example, when talking about a friend, perhaps in one sentence you call this friend by name and, in the next, using a pronoun (*he, she, they*). Given that you and your interlocutor already know what or who you are talking about, you could also omit the reference to that person altogether (*Sue? Is not here.*). In this way, pronouns and ellipsis also establish ties across sentence boundaries, which originate in so-called "chains of reference."

Reference is the technical term for the relation between a linguistic expression and its referent. The relation is illustrated in a famous model, the **semiotic triangle**, which you see in Figure 7.1. The model highlights that the meaning of a linguistic expression cannot be said to be directly the object (or any other aspect of the world) that the speaker is dealing with. Instead, any real-life entity that language can be about has an indirect relation to its linguistic expression, the two being linked via a learned mental representation (called the concept) in the speakers' minds. For example, when talking about your friend as *my neighbor* or *the guy next door*, you refer to that person by uttering these noun phrases since you have learned that the lexemes *neighbor* and *guy* can both express the concept of a male adult person.

It is very common that speakers and writers refer to the objects, persons, or ideas they talk about more than once. The relation between several linguistic expressions which have the same referent is called

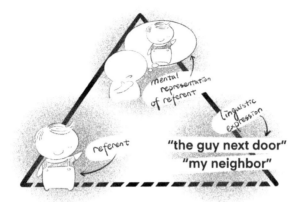

**Figure 7.1** The semiotic triangle
Based on Ogden & Richards 1972.

*co-reference*. It results in a sequence, or "chain," of co-referential elements, which point backward or, more rarely so, forward in the text. Co-referential elements in discourse can be lexical expressions, that is, when the same lexeme is used more than once, or pronouns, the category of grammar for expressing co-reference.

As an example, take a look at the excerpt in (1), which is a text about two professional basketball players. In the magazine article, one player, *Nurkic*, is quoted talking about a colleague, *Lillard*. In the beginning, Lillard is referred to by his name and as *the guy*, that is, by two noun phrases with a lexical head, which set up Nurkic's use of pronouns for referring to his colleague. In the last sentence of (1), reference to that player is omitted altogether (*Ain't no fake*).

(1)     I talked to Nurkic earlier this season, before his injury, and in the middle of a career year, he credited Lillard, the guy who's never going to let his big man walk away to the end of the bench. "It's hard to explain day-by-day what *he* means to us," Nurkic said. "But I think the most important thing for me, and for anybody on the team. *He* never changes. No matter what happens to the team or to us as individuals, *he*'s the same person. Ain't no fake." (COCA, Magazine, 2019)

So, the entire chain of co-reference in (1) looks like the one in Figure 7.2.

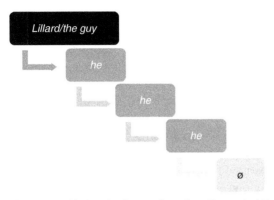

**Figure 7.2** Chain of reference based on Example (1)

While the last sentence in (1) contains an elliptical reference (henceforth **ellipsis**), in the three previous clauses Nurkic refers to Lillard using a pronoun. A pronoun is thus the grammatical expression of a co-referential noun phrase. Note that, at the discourse level, the grammar of pronouns works somewhat differently from the grammar inside the clause. In formal linguistics, inside the clause, co-reference is shown by what is called coindexing, which means two elements within a structural unit refer to the same referent. For example, the sentence *John said he would be late* can be interpreted with coindexing (*John$_i$ said he$_i$ would be late*), shown by adding the same index $_i$ twice, but would also be grammatically correct with no coindexing, that is, with *John* and *he* being different persons (*John$_i$ said he$_j$ would be late*). By contrast, co-reference in discourse never relies on coindexing, but is always established pragmatically. Co-reference in discourse relies on retrieving the most likely referent for a pronoun from the previous discourse.

Like connectives, which we discussed in Chapter 6, pronouns and ellipsis contribute to the grammatical cohesion within discourse. By contrast, using different words for the same referent establishes lexical cohesion. For example, if *Nurkic* in (1) had wanted to use lexical instead of grammatical cohesion, he could have referred to *Lillard* by his name or as *my colleague, somebody's brother* or *friend*, or the like. In this chapter we will only deal with co-reference in as far as it is expressed by grammatical cohesion.

In the following, we will first look at the different types of pronouns and ellipsis. We will then explore some characteristic patterns of occurrence of pronouns and ellipsis as observed in different kinds of discourse. We will see that these patterns are closely related to the thematic structure of a text. Stories, for instance, deal with a limited number of characters and therefore often possess more referential continuity than, say, non-fictional texts, such as dictionary entries. But there are also systematic differences among different kinds of stories. For example, research on reading comprehension found that stories for children tend to contain more continuous chains of reference, since this is less demanding for the working memory (Oakhill & Garnham 1988). Researchers have also observed that, for persons with reading difficulties, a text with fewer pronouns and more lexical repetition is easier to process (Yuill & Oakhill 2010). We will return to some psycholinguistic aspects of pronouns and their interpretation in sections 7.2 and 7.3. We will also discuss that some types of discourse contain fewer pronouns than others because they require a high degree of precision, for instance, professional texts in science or law. We will touch upon such differences when turning to the text-linguistic approach in Section 7.4.

After reading the chapter, you will be able to:

- detect the different forms of pronominal reference and types of ellipsis in texts;
- describe and explain the patterns of the occurrence of pronouns and ellipsis in different types of discourse;
- interpret and develop a research design for studies of referential expression in discourse.

## Concepts, Constructions, and Keywords

*accessibility, anaphoric/cataphoric reference, demonstrative pronouns, ellipsis, endophoric/exophoric reference, extended reference, givenness, personal pronouns, reference, semantic/pragmatic principles (of pronoun interpretation), subject ellipsis, textual/situational recoverability, world knowledge*

## 7.2  Types of Pronominal Reference

Pronominal reference is one of the cohesive ties within the system of cohesion as proposed by the classic text-linguistic work of Halliday & Hasan (1976). Within that system, reference is described as the semantic relation between two elements in discourse that refer to the same entity, as illustrated by Example (2):

(2)    *Sue* left. Maybe *she*'s sick.

*Sue* and *she* in (2) are co-referential. Pronouns express co-reference by virtue of being grammatical pro-forms, that is, they instruct the reader to search in the surrounding discourse for an interpretation. In (2), the pronoun is pointing backward, which is called *anaphoric* reference. When a pronoun is pointing forward, this is called *cataphoric* reference. In contrast to anaphoric reference, which easily connects noun phrases across sentence boundaries, cataphoric pronouns are more challenging to interpret and are therefore more likely to be used within the sentence. For example, in (3), *she* is likely to refer to *Sue* while, in (4), it could also be the case that somebody else left for the reason of *Sue* being sick.

(3)    Since she left, I suppose that *Sue* is sick.

(4)    She left. I suppose that *Sue* is sick.

More complexity is added by the fact that the pronoun *they* can be used as a singular or plural pronoun. So, in a sentence like *Since they left, I suppose that Sue is sick, they* could or could not be used cataphorically. If you're interested in pronouns and language change, read our Good to Know box on singular *they*.

Good to Know

Word of the Decade: Singular *they*

The American Dialect Society voted *they* as "Word of the Decade" in 2020, recognizing the growing use of the pronoun to refer to an individual person without making any assumption about their gender identity (American Dialect Society, 2020). (Note what we just did? We used *their* to refer back to the singular noun *person*, which is exactly what this usage note is about.) The use of *they* to refer to an individual person is also known as "singular *they*." Singular *they/them/theirs* is not exactly new. It dates back to the fourteenth century and can be found frequently in the works of much-admired writers, like Jane Austen ("they say every body is in love once in *their* lives") and William Shakespeare ("There's not a man I meet but doth salute me, as if I were *their* well-acquainted friend" Shakespeare, *The Comedy of Errors*, 1981 [1623]: IV.iii). *They* is also not the only pronoun that can be used to refer back to singular and plural antecedents. Most people who think that singular *they* creates unhelpful ambiguity don't seem to be too bothered by the fact that the pronoun *you* can also refer to singular or plural antecedents and that sentences like *You are right* are, if seen in isolation, just as ambiguous as sentences with *they*. It should be noted that in many of the examples of singular *they*, *they* refers back to an antecedent that is

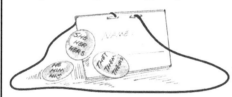

notionally plural. The pronoun *everybody*, to go back to the example from Jane Austen, for example, is grammatically singular (we would say *Everybody is happy*, not *Everybody are happy*), but notionally *everybody* refers to more than just one person. This is not really what the rise of "singular *they*" is all about. No, singular *they* was crowned Word of the Decade because it is increasingly used as a pronoun referring to an individual, in response to the need of a pronoun that doesn't classify individuals as either male or female. People may prefer to be addressed as *they* because they think of gender as a non-binary category, in which case neither *he* nor *she* nor a more complex expression like *he or she* would be appropriate to refer to them. Therefore, we should really be talking about the rise of *they* as a *non-binary* pronoun instead of just "singular *they*." At American universities and schools, for example, it is now quite common for students and instructors to state their pronouns when they introduce themselves, with *they* being a common choice, and everyone is expected to respectfully use the pronouns a person selects for themselves.

In 2017, the *Associated Press Stylebook*, the most influential style guide for journalists in the US, updated its section on gender to reflect that "[n]ot all people fall under one of two categories for sex or gender, according to leading medical organizations, so avoid references to both, either or opposite sexes or genders as a way to encompass all people" (Easton 2017). Specifically, in stories "about people who identify as neither male nor female or ask not to be referred to as *he/she/him/her*: Use the person's name in place of a pronoun or otherwise reword the sentence, whenever possible. If *they/them/theirs* use is essential, explain in the text that the person prefers a gender-neutral pronoun." For example, in a picture essay about people who returned to New York City beaches as soon as they re-opened in summer 2020 after the first wave of the COVID-19 epidemic, *The New York Times* wrote about a person called Kelsey Rondeau, "who uses they/them pronouns," that "Rondeau was laid off from their work as a live entertainment performer when the pandemic began" (Rosa 2020). Note that in this example the use of singular *they* is established as a personal choice before the pronoun is actually used, so that readers will not be startled. They likely would not be. In 2019 the non-partisan Pew Research Center found that 42 percent of adult Americans say that forms should list a gender option other than "man" or "woman" for people who don't identify as either (Geiger & Graf 2019). In the same year, Merriam-Webster announced that its dictionary would now include the non-binary use of *they* ("used to refer to a single person whose gender identity is nonbinary") as one of the four standard meanings of anaphoric *they*. That same year several states in the US started offering "non-binary" as a third gender option on driver's licenses. Social media platforms like Twitter, Instagram, or LinkedIn now allow users to include their pronoun choice in their profiles. Non-binary *they* has spread so quickly because it fills a need (better than newly created pronouns like *zir* or *zem*). It clearly deserves the Word of the Decade crown.

The process of pronoun interpretation, or, more technically speaking, anaphora resolution, is a fascinating topic. In principle, the meaning of a pronoun is very vague, as illustrated by the following Haiku, written by the American poet Clement Hoyt (van den Heuvel 2000):

*In the lightning flash –*

*through the night rain – I saw it!*

*... whatever it was.*

(van den Heuvel 2000: 89)

In real life, however, interpreting pronouns works pretty smoothly. Many discourse linguists have claimed that there is a principle of "natural sequential aboutness," which means that we tend to interpret pronouns as referring to something or somebody that has just been mentioned (Bosch 1983). This principle holds as long as our semantic and pragmatic expectations do not tell us otherwise. For example, following this principle, in (5), *She* and *Sue* are likely to be interpreted as co-referential while, in (6), they are not.

(5)    She was sick. That's why Sue took the day off.

(6)    She screamed. That's why Sue ran away.

In (5), both the discourse expectations triggered by the connective expression *that's why* and our general knowledge conform to an interpretation whereby Sue left because she was sick. In (6), however, this natural interpretation of the second sentence being about the same referent as the first is blocked by our **world knowledge**, which suggests that screaming is probably not a reason why a person is leaving. We can therefore generalize that pronoun interpretation follows syntactic principles, as in (3), and an expected continuity of aboutness in discourse, as in (5), but that beyond the sentence there must also be a semantic and pragmatic plausibility.

   The role of general, pragmatic knowledge in pronoun interpretation is an issue that has interested, in particular, psycholinguists. Ehrlich (1980) carried out several famous experiments in which the interpretation of pronouns required either just grammatical knowledge or also a check for pragmatic plausibility. For example, in the sentence *Jane blamed Bill because he spilled the coffee*, the difference in gender determines that there is only one person that can be co-referential with the pronoun (assuming that both Jane and Bill choose traditional binary pronouns). By contrast, in *Steve blamed Frank because he spilled the coffee* the pronoun can refer to either of the two males. The interpretation that it was Frank, the one being blamed, who spilled the coffee thus requires a pragmatic **inference**, and not just grammatical knowledge. In Ehrlich's experiments, it turned out that the subjects who were shown sentences of that type and then had to pick a referent for the pronoun, completed this task faster with those sentences that required just grammatical knowledge. It took them longer to interpret the pronoun if the two noun phrases were of the same gender and the subjects also needed to apply their world knowledge for pronoun interpretation. The insights gained from these experiments established a position most linguists nowadays agree with: Readers first apply grammatical knowledge when interpreting a pronoun and only turn to their wider, general knowledge when they need to.

Since the 1980s, more psycholinguists have sought to understand the details of the process of pronoun understanding. Two classic approaches stand out, which were originally in conflict with one another (for references, see the Further Reading section). According to one approach, speakers are found to apply grammar-based strategies when interpreting pronouns, such as a "subject assignment" or "grammatical role parallelism" strategy. For example, in an experiment subjects interpreted the referent of *her* in sentences like (7) and (8) differently, preferring the subject as the pronoun's antecedent. By contrast, in a sentence like (9), listeners or readers are likely to interpret *her* as referring to Sally, presumably because they watch out for a "structural parallelism," that is, for the same syntactic role of both the pronoun and its referent (Chambers & Smyth 1998).

(7)  Sue defeated Sally, and all their friends criticized her. [*her* = Sue]

(8)  Sally was defeated by Sue, and all their friends criticized her. [*her* = Sally]

(9)  Sue defeated Sally, and the trainer insulted her. [*her* = Sally]

(10)  Sue defeated Sally, and their trainer congratulated her. [*her* = Sue]

In contrast to such grammar-based strategies, in a sentence like (10), *her* is again more likely to refer to Sue, but this time due to the semantics of the verb *congratulate*. This interpretation relates to the world knowledge that readers and listeners have about the act of congratulating. Similarly, when subjects in an experiment were asked to complete a sequence like in (11) or (12), the difference in the last word of the first sentence caused different interpretations of the pronoun *they*. Here, it is again world knowledge about what kind of entities can be delighted and what kind of entities can be delicious which contributes to picking the right referent (Mitkov 2014).

(11)    The children had sweets. They were delighted.

(12)    The children had sweets. They were delicious.

The findings about sentences like examples (10)–(12) support what is called in the literature a "coherence-based" approach to pronoun interpretation, in contrast to the grammar-based strategies we illus-trated above. Many linguists nowadays agree that there is truth in both theories and that neither a coherence-based approach nor grammar-based principles "can do it alone" (Ariel 2013: 39; Kehler & Rohde 2013). This position is in line with the treatment of pronouns as an area of discourse syntax, that is, with the view that pronouns are subject both to grammatical rules and usage-based principles.

Another property of pronouns is that they support the thematic continuity of a text. This function in discourse is not limited to third-person pronouns, which are most of the time interpreted as expressing an *endophoric* kind of reference. **Endophoric reference** means that the referential relation is located within the discourse (like the relation between *the guy* and *he* in Ex. (1)). By contrast, first- and second-person pronouns express a situational (technically termed *exophoric*) kind of reference, which means that the listener or reader is instructed to retrieve the referent within the discourse situation (for instance, the speaker being the referent of the pronoun *I* in the sentence *I talked to Nurkic* in (1)). Exophoric pronouns do not establish ties among them-selves, but they can also be co-referential and contribute to the thematic continuity within a text. For example, in a textbook like this one, we sometimes address you, our readers, by the second-person pronoun *you* and thereby also create a continuity of reference. Note, however, that the distinction between first- and second-person pronouns as exophoric and third-person pronouns as endophoric pronouns is not absolute: Like *it* in the Haiku shown above, a third-person pronoun can also refer to an object or person outside the discourse, which means it can also be used exophorically.

To complete the set of pronouns within the system of grammatical reference, the last group to consider are demonstrative pronouns. Demonstrative pronouns are the elements *this, that, these,* and *those,* which in principle can be pronouns or demonstrative determiners (like in *this book* or *those problems*). Demonstrative pronouns contribute to grammatical cohesion since they are used, not only exophorically, referring to the local or temporal discourse situation, but also endophorically, referring back (or forward) in the text. When referring within the discourse, demonstrative pronouns often have what is known as a "propositional referent," which means they refer to an entire proposition (Webber 1991). A case of propositional reference is illustrated in (14), contrasting with (13), where *it* co-refers only with the NP (*a book*).

(13)    Charlotte wrote a book. *It* was a difficult read but the sales were spectacular.

(14)    Charlotte wrote a book. *This* was a difficult job but the sales were spectacular. (Çokal et al. 2018: 276)

Psycholinguists have observed that readers have a clear preference for interpreting the pronoun *it* as referring to entities in discourse, and for *this* as referring to a proposition, like in the second sentence in (14). Measuring the reading times of subjects under different conditions in an experiment (*it/this* referring to either a proposition or an NP), researchers observed that it takes a subject longer to read sentence pairs different from the ones in (13) and (14), that is, sentences in which either a proposition is referred to by *it* or an NP referent is referred to by *this* (Çokal et al. 2018). Similar outcomes were achieved with children for whom it had turned out to be more difficult to process the pronoun *it* when its antecedent was a proposition rather than a noun phrase (Megherbi et al. 2019). These insights from psycholinguistics and language acquisition show that the processing of demonstrative pronouns in discourse is different, to some extent, from the one of personal pronouns: Demonstratives tend to instruct the reader to combine the subject and the predicate when resolving the pronoun's reference. For this reason, demonstrative pronouns often have the function of expressing **extended reference** in discourse.

To sum up the types of pronominal reference we have discussed so far, take a look at Figure 7.3, which contains the different types of pronouns within the overall system of grammatical cohesion.

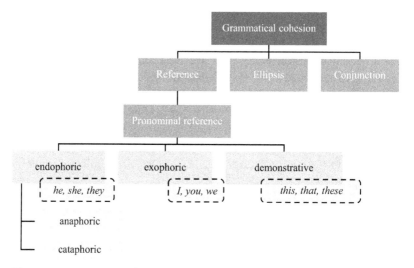

**Figure 7.3** Pronouns within the system of grammatical cohesion

Using the typology in Figure 7.3 to detect and classify pronouns in discourse, you should now be able to take on Exercises 1 and 2.

## 7.3 Pronouns within Discourse

We now turn to the question of how pronouns are used in discourse, starting with a well-known pattern that most of you will know from reading or analyzing literature. Fictional narration makes frequent use of pronouns since, as noted in the introduction, telling a story typically entails some continuity of the characters. As examples, let's have a look at the excerpts in (15) and (16), the initial paragraphs of two famous nineteenth-century English novels:

(15) There was no possibility of taking a walk that day. *We* had been wandering, indeed, in the leafless shrubbery an hour in the morning; but since dinner (Mrs. Reed, when there was no company, dined early) the cold winter wind had brought with it clouds so sombre, and a rain so penetrating, that further out-door exercise was now out of the question.

   *I* was glad of it: *I* never liked long walks, especially on chilly afternoons: dreadful to *me* was the coming home in the raw twilight, with nipped fingers and toes, and a heart saddened by the chidings of Bessie, the nurse, and humbled by the consciousness of my physical inferiority to Eliza, John, and Georgiana Reed. (Brontë, *Jane Eyre*, 1981 [1847]: 1)

(16) Emma Woodhouse, handsome, clever, and rich, with a comfortable home and happy disposition, seemed to unite some of the best blessings of existence; and had lived nearly twenty-one years in the world with very little to distress or vex *her*.

   *She* was the youngest of the two daughters of a most affectionate, indulgent father; and had, in consequence of her sister's marriage, been mistress of his house from a very early period. Her mother had died too long ago for *her* to have more than an indistinct remembrance of her caresses [...]. (Austen, *Emma*, 1985 [1815]: 37)

In a literary studies class, you may have learned that it is the perspective of narration that determines most the choice of pronouns in a novel. If the story is told by a first-person narrator, first-person, exophoric pronouns are typically used (as in (15)). By contrast, as in (16), if the story is told by a narrator who is not a character, a novel is likely to contain more third-person pronouns. More specific aspects of pronoun use in literary discourse are discussed at length within stylistics. For example, in so-called "unreliable" narration, the referents of pronouns are often left opaque. A well-known example is the first sentence of the novel *One Flew over the Cuckoo's Nest*, "They're out there," in which the anaphoric pronoun *they* cannot be familiar to the reader and is therefore used to signal the presence of an unreliable narrator (Short 1996: 268).

   It is a general requirement, and one not limited to fictional narration, that interpreting a pronoun requires an NP that is retrievable. From the discourse perspective, this means that the referent of a pronoun must be given information, a status whose relevance we already pointed out in Chapters 3 to 5. We discussed there that the givenness of information is not always determined just by the discourse, but that givenness ultimately refers to a state of knowledge on the part of the addressee. Applied to pronouns, this means that whether or not a pronoun is felicitous ultimately depends on the status of the referent in the reader's or listener's mind, resulting from conditions of both memory and attention. We know that speakers also use and comprehend so-called "unheralded" pronouns, which have no explicit co-referring noun phrase, but make reference to knowledge and beliefs shared by the interlocutors (known as the "common ground"). For example, in a corpus study dealing with telephone speech, it was found that such unheralded, long-distance pronouns made up to between 5 percent (for *he* and *she*) and 13.9 percent (for *they*) of third-person pronouns, that is, in these cases a pronoun was used although another referent, to which the pronoun might also have referred, had intervened (Gerrig et al. 2011). For example, speakers on the phone variably referred both to their friends and parents as *they* and just assumed that their conversation partner would be able to interpret the pronoun from the context (e.g., *They're coming back tomorrow night*).

From a psycholinguistic viewpoint, the givenness expressed by a pronoun reflects the mental accessibility of an element in discourse (Ariel 1988). For example, referring to somebody by name usually marks a lower degree of accessibility than referring to that person by using a pronoun. Similarly, a definite noun phrase (*the guy*) marks a referent as being more accessible than an indefinite one (*a guy*). However, researchers have noted that what precisely determines different degrees of mental accessibility is a complex matter, influenced by many conditions in the discourse. Factors discussed in the pertinent literature range from the inherent prominence of referents in some situations (such as babies being almost always prominent in their parents' mind) to being the topic of the discourse, to having been more or less recently cued or mentioned (for a summary, see Ariel 2001). In addition, the discourse itself creates expectations about the continuity of reference. For example, eye-tracking experiments have shown that subjects expect referential information to be less accessible if the discourse they listen to contains markers of disfluency (e.g., hesitation markers of fillers like *uh* or *um*). By contrast, fluency of the discourse and, in particular, deaccented noun phrases created an expectation of givenness, which led the subjects to choose the most directly accessible entity as the most likely referent (Arnold & Tanenhaus 2011).

In view of these many factors that influence what is more and less accessible to the reader or listener, it is helpful to look at pronouns in relation to other forms of reference. In a classic model, the different syntactic realizations of a referring expression are ranked in a so-called "givenness hierarchy" (Gundel et al. 1993), in which the respective degree of givenness reflects a state within the addressee's mind. As you see in Figure 7.4, pronouns rank high in these conditions: (stressed) third-person pronouns have the attribute "activated." The ranking further highlights the unidirectional entailment of all options, showing that pronouns (*he, she, it, they, this,* and *that*) represent a kind of givenness that includes a familiar, identifiable, and referential status.

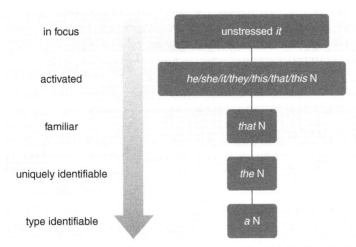

**Figure 7.4** Pronouns in the givenness hierarchy of Gundel, Hedberg & Zacharski (Gundel et al. 1993: 275).

The position of pronouns within the hierarchy in Figure 7.4 shows that they are close to the "in focus" end of the scale. This means that the referent of a pronoun must be in the short-term memory, either due to the immediate co-text or to the context of the discourse (Gundel et al. 1993: 278). However, how an entity enters the short-term memory, and how long it stays there, is again a complex question, to which psycholinguists have also dedicated a lot of research. For example, there are experiments designed to find out if reference is retrieved faster if the co-referential expression in the preceding sentence is focused. This would mean that a constituent highlighted within a cleft construction would be retrieved faster than a constituent that is not focused (e.g., it is easier to retrieve a giraffe as a target referent with a preceding sentence like *What the kids like best about the zoo is the giraffes* rather than *It is only the kids that like the giraffes best about the zoo*) (Cowles & Garnham 2011). The results confirm the role of the previous discourse, even if they are not always conclusive because there are many other effects, for instance, grammatical subjects being always "preferred antecedents" (Kaiser 2011: 1659). Other experiments found effects of the structure of the discourse: In a text completion task, where students were shown text fragments with a protagonist that was either expressed by a noun phrase or proper name or by a pronoun and were then asked to continue the story, pronouns in the fragments caused participants to continue the same episode, whereas full noun phrases or proper names often prompted them to carry out a more substantial topic shift, for instance, they introduced a new character (Vonk et al. 1992).

Good to Know
*The Secret Life of Pronouns* – What Using Pronouns Can Tell about Speakers

James W. Pennebaker, the author of a famous book titled *The Secret Life of Pronouns*, is a psychologist who has done numerous studies based on automated word counts from large and diverse corpora. Much of his work has dealt with the question of the extent to which the frequency of certain word classes, especially pronouns, allows us to make predictions about the speaker. In Pennebaker's work we find an in-depth look at some gender stereotypes, such as the one that women talk more emotionally and therefore use more personal pronouns (with less specific information) than men. Other findings from his work correlate a low use of pronouns, notably first-person singular *I*, with lying and self-deception. For example, in dating ads, the use of first-person pronouns was found to be the "best general predictor of honesty" (Pennebaker 2011: 156). In other work, Pennebaker and various co-workers have been able to show that higher frequencies of pronouns in discourse go together with a lower social status and fewer chances of power, leadership, and academic success.

Such research outcomes are fascinating but, at the same time, they point to the limits of the area of discourse syntax as we have defined it. Yes, we are interested here in how grammar works in language use, that is, in discourse, but discourse syntax does not cover the question of how speakers of different character and background deal with different topics at different occasions. As we pointed out in Chapter 2, variation based on the background of the speaker is a core area of sociolinguistics. Out of the many aspects that define a discourse situation, aspects of social role and personality of speakers are highly complex variables for the study of language variation and fall outside the scope of this book.

---

Overall, both the position of pronouns within the givenness hierarchy and the insights from psycholinguistic work we discussed lend support to the position that pronouns are used "to maintain reference" (Cowles & Garnham 2011: 317). This means they are generally associated with a high degree of continuity in discourse. We will now explore how this generalization accounts for different referential strategies within different types of discourse.

## 7.4 Pronouns across Types of Discourse

Before turning to pronouns, let us briefly consider the question of how spoken and written texts are likely to differ with regard to their patterns of reference in general. These patterns concern both the number of referents and the form of referring expressions preferred in a discourse. It is helpful to recall the semiotic triangle (Figure 7.1) here, because it highlights that referents are the different persons or objects dealt with in a text, while referring expressions are the linguistic forms chosen to write or talk about them. As we could see in the givenness hierarchy in Section 7.3, pronouns are only one linguistic option for expressing reference and thus only one aspect of the pattern of reference in a text.

Recall our initial example. When discussing the text excerpt on NBA basketball players in (1), we saw that different expressions (*the guy* and *he*) are used for dealing with the same referent. Similarly, the text excerpt in (17), which is about dog training, contains several references to dog owners: The writer uses the expressions *dog owners*, *owners*, *puppy owners*, and *them*. The text therefore has a similar referential continuity as Example (1), discussed at the beginning of this chapter, but, in comparison, we see it has fewer pronouns.

(17)    Dog training can be a pretty overwhelming task, but proper training and socialization are very important for every dog. So many *dog owners* choose not to skip this step. Armed with snacks and patience *owners* usually get pretty good results at getting their puppies to listen to *them*. Although some *puppy owners* are not afraid to take this task to a whole new level. Take for instance Anna Brisbin, a voice actress, and a YouTuber from Los Angeles, who decided to train her dog, not in English but in Harry Potter spells. (Andželika 2019)

It requires an automated text analysis to investigate different types of discourse with respect to both the number of referents and of referring expressions, which is why we only report some general tendencies here. Overall, research comparing spoken and written discourse has found that conversation has the highest density of referring expressions, including many pronouns, and at the same time the lowest frequency of different referents. By contrast, academic and technical discourses possess a high frequency of different referents, but a lower total of referring expressions. News texts are characteristically high both in the total number of referring expressions and in the number of different referents. Fiction is found to possess the lowest total number of referring forms and a comparatively low number of different referents (all findings from Biber 1992). Note that these findings are about the overall number of referring expressions in the discourses investigated, not just about pronouns.

While determining the extent of all references requires a complex procedure of text analysis, varieties of discourse are more easily compared just for the occurrence of pronouns. Any corpus tagged for word classes enables you to do so, that is, retrieve and compare the frequency of pronouns across different discourse types in a corpus. For example, in COCA (where the part-of-speech tag for personal pronouns is _pp*), our search across different corpus sections at the time of writing this book yielded the frequencies shown in Table 7.1 (for dealing with individual frequencies per section, see the toolbox in Chapter 6). Bear in mind that the exact numbers will have changed by the time of your reading this chapter, since COCA, like many other corpora, is constantly being modified and enlarged. Note that, as explained in Chapters 2 and 6, the numbers from COCA that we use here are normalized frequencies, not the absolute frequencies of occurrence.

**Table 7.1** *Rates of occurrence of personal pronouns\* in five sections of COCA*

| Spoken | Fiction | Magazine | News | Academic |
|---|---|---|---|---|
| 87,508 | 91,321 | 42,026 | 38,693 | 19,009 |

\* Per million words.

The bar chart in Figure 7.5 shows the frequency of pronouns in the five registers from Table 7.1 (the rate of occurrence per one million words is now the dependent variable on the y-axis). Figure 7.5 conforms to what we have already noted about the general pattern of reference in spoken as opposed to written discourse: Spoken discourse is distinctly higher in the frequency of pronouns than most written discourse. However, what we also detect is that the frequency of pronouns in fiction is even higher than in speech, reflecting that most fiction is narration, which usually has a high continuity in reference (the story characters). Another reason why spoken discourse has comparatively fewer pronouns than fiction may be the occurrence of non-clausal units in spoken language: Many utterances in spoken discourse are not complete sentences and contain few or no noun phrases at all (e.g., utterances like *Fine* or *Great*). As for written non-fiction, Figure 7.5 shows that magazine and news writing are considerably lower in pronoun use than speech, with academic texts being very low.

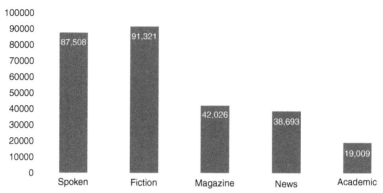

**Figure 7.5** Distribution of personal pronouns in five registers
The rate of occurrence is per 1 million words.

The results in Figure 7.5 can also be understood in the light of the
distinction of **endophoric** and **exophoric reference** we introduced
above. Returning to the psychological conditions of pronoun interpretation (illustrated in Figure 7.4), an activated information status, the
prerequisite for pronoun use, requires a shared discourse situation. In
written discourse, this referential activation can rely on the physical
continuity of the text, which ensures the interpretation of both endophoric and exophoric pronouns (like in examples (15) and (16)). By
contrast, spoken discourse relies mostly on shared situational knowledge and is therefore typically higher in exophoric than in endophoric
reference. Dissolving this distinction of speech versus writing a bit, we
touch upon pronouns in electronic discourse in our next Good to Know
box.

For practicing the retrieval and analysis of pronouns in discourse, turn to Exercises 3 and 4. We suggest in both exercises,
not only to identify the number of pronouns, but to contrast these
findings with the overall number of noun phrases. If applied to a
single text or a small corpus, this analysis can easily be done
manually, enabling you also to look at the proportion of grammatical, as opposed to lexical, forms of reference. Exercises 7 and 8
(Level 2) deal with the interpretation of data on pronoun use in
other types of discourse.

Good to Know
Pronouns in Digital Discourse – Written Speech or Spoken
Writing?

Over the last twenty years, web-based language use, such as the
discourse of emails, text messages, postings or blog entries, has
received a considerable amount of attention in discourse-related
work (e.g., Squires 2016). A core point of interest in this research is
the question of whether electronic discourse is more like spoken or
written discourse (e.g., Renkema & Schubert 2018, see also Chapter
9 for a more in-depth discussion). Since we saw in this section that
spoken and written language differ distinctly with regard to the
expression of reference, pronouns as a core area of grammatical
cohesion are a good candidate for dealing with this issue.

   Early work on electronic discourse emphasized that its use of pronouns is similar to speech. One study, for example, found a proportion
of about 64 percent of all pronouns were first-person in computer
conferencing (a genre comparable to forum postings; Yates 1996).
Other studies have found the language of weblogs to be more diverse.
For example, early corporate blogging turns out to contain a considerable amount of exophoric, first- and second-person pronouns
(Puschmann 2010), while other blog texts appear to be more exclusively based on endophoric reference (Hoffmann 2012). In addition,
blogs usually show a characteristic use of exophoric, demonstrative
pronouns, with which their writers refer to other web-based material,
such as pictures or videos. Web-based discourse is therefore not only
constituted by grammatical cohesion within the text itself, but also
relies on references to the many other components presented throughout the web. In addition to reflecting connections within the text or to a
shared context, **digital discourse** thus certainly inheres a specific kind of
givenness, which is due to its web-based environment.

## 7.5 Types of Ellipsis

Ellipsis is another type of grammatical cohesion in discourse. It results
from the omission of an element that the listener or reader is able to

recover, either from the previous discourse or from the discourse situation. Before we consider the discourse conditions of ellipsis, let's explore which syntactic elements can be affected.

In the most common cases of ellipsis, the omitted element is a word, typically a noun, as in (18), but other types of lexical material are also possible, as illustrated in (19)–(21):

(18)   These dogs are trained in English, those (*dogs*) in Harry Potter spells.

(19)   I don't train my dogs in English. Do you (*train your dog in English*)?

(20)   That's how you keep your dog from running away. (*Do you have*) Any questions?

(21)   (*I*) Didn't manage to keep the dog from running away today. (*I*) Had a horrible time.

Apart from these cases of ellipsis, there are also so-called "compressed" clauses (*if necessary, when in trouble*) (Wiechmann & Kerz 2013), which often have a formulaic character. These formulaic clauses are less directly triggered by the discourse context, which is why they will not be included in our discussion.

When ellipsis occurs, the reader or listener must recover the missing information from the discourse or the discourse situation. For this reason, discourse in which ellipsis occurs is usually highly interactive, such as conversation or texting. In conversation, the resulting utterances are often only clause fragments. For example, in its chapter dedicated to the grammar of conversation, the *GSWE* shows a proportion of 38.6 percent of the units of conversation in the corpus to be non-clausal (Biber et al. 2021: 1065). A dialog with non-clausal utterances is shown below in (22a): a sequence in which only three out of seven utterances are full clauses. The remaining four utterances are non-clausal (*really, training dogs, yes, do you?*), as illustrated by (22b) and (22c).

(22a)   A:   So, you train your dog in Harry Potter spells?
        B:   Really?
        C:   What are you talking about?
        A:   Training dogs.
        D:   Yes. I don't train my dogs in English. Do you?

(22b)   (We are talking about) training dogs.

(22c)   Do you (train your dogs in English)?

Ellipsis is common in spoken discourse for a variety of reasons, including speed and economy. The instances in (22a) are all follow-up questions or remarks within an ongoing dialog, in which knowledge of the previous utterance is easily presupposed. Verb phrase, or verb plus noun phrase ellipsis, is therefore a particularly common feature of highly interactive discourse.

Subject ellipsis, as in (21), is the most common subtype of noun phrase ellipsis, since, as also discussed in Chapter 4, the subject role is normally associated with givenness and being the topic. The phenomenon of subject ellipsis is also known as "zero anaphora" for languages other than English in which the subject position can be left empty (like Chinese or Japanese). However, sentences with no overt subject are not uncommon in informal spoken English (e.g., Oh 2005, 2006). For example, subject ellipsis is again found to occur in utterances that are close follow-ups of a preceding utterance (a sequence like *You know what I did last night? Ø Did a terrible thing ...* ; Oh 2005: 278).

We will focus on subject ellipsis in the remainder of this chapter, because it is an interesting characteristic of some informal types of written discourse, such as casual notes or informal letters, diary entries (Haegeman & Ihsane 1999; Nariyama 2004; Weir 2012), or texts and emails. See examples (23) and (24) from online blogs of the CORE corpus:

(23)  Yesterday had a fairly slow day. Went for a walk up Mt Rogers. Then had Nat and Andrew over to play [...] (CORE, Personal Blog, 2009)

(24)  Can't eat, can't rest. Went to see my doctor today who wrote me a letter to show them. (CORE, Personal Blog, 2007)

Focusing on subject ellipsis, we now turn to some patterns of its use in both spoken and written discourse.

Turn to Exercise 5 for identifying cases of subject ellipsis in a text.

## 7.6 Subject Ellipsis: The Discourse Perspective

In this section, we will directly combine the variationist *and* the text-linguistic perspective, exploring both the most common syntactic variants of subject ellipsis and the discourse types in which it occurs. Let's start with the question of which syntactic types of subjects are preferred. One highly common type is ellipsis with the first-person singular (*I*) as subject NP, as in Example (25).

(25)   When we moved into this house, *inherited* a then-5 yr old Thermador glass cooktop. We've now been here 10 years, so it's celebrating its' 15th year. We remodeled the kitchen 3 years ago, with new appliances, but I chose to keep the Thermador. *Took awhile* to learn how to regulate the heat properly, [...] (COCA, Web, 2012)

In a study of informal discourse (covering natural conversation, TV dialogs, and letters), the proportion of first-person subject ellipsis, like in (25), ranged from 20.4 percent (conversation) to 47.2 percent (TV dialog) to 82.4 percent (letters) of all omitted subjects (Nariyama 2004). This shows that first-person subjects are truly common, but not necessarily the most common type of subject ellipsis in all registers. For example, the same study found that ellipsis with the impersonal pronoun *it* made up 61.2 percent in conversation. It could be a matter of discussion whether conventionalized formulas such as *doesn't matter* or *sounds good*, which also fell into this category, should be seen as proper, that is, syntactically productive, instances of subject ellipsis. However, it was rightly observed that many of these formulas also reflected a view of the speaker (*doesn't matter* [to me], *sounds good* [to me]). For this reason, one could conclude that most subjects in subject ellipsis are "centred on the first person" (Nariyama 2004: 258).

   These outcomes show subject ellipsis as being closely associated with interactive, speaker-centered discourse, but the subjectless clauses found in letters also indicate that the personal, informal character is easily transferred to other registers. Especially in written discourse, where we expect sentences to be complete and explicit, violating this expectation can cause an inference of "casualness both in register and content" (Nariyama 2004: 248). So, *(I've) gotta go* sounds more evasive and less binding than the complete sentence *I've got to go*, which implies a more concrete commitment on the part of the speaker. This effect of subject ellipsis is typically achieved in those kinds of written discourse that are *meant to be* informal or occur under limitations of space. An interesting register to look at in this regard is blog writing, the discourse we also used for illustration in (23) through (25). In a corpus of 204,997 words taken from blogs, there were 235 occurrences of subject ellipsis (Teddiman & Newman 2007). Note that it would be even better to be able to relate the occurrence of subject ellipsis to the number of sentences in the corpus; however, as for this study, no syntactic parsing was carried out so that no number of clauses is indicated. Figure 7.6 gives the results for this data set, illustrating the proportions of the different types of subjects that were omitted. (This time we are presenting proportions as a pie chart; see our discussion of proportional frequency charts and Figure 2.6 in Chapter 2.)

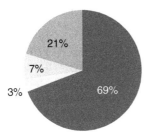

■ 1st pers.sg.    1st pers.pl.    2nd pers.    ■ 3rd pers.

**Figure 7.6** Proportions of omitted subjects in online blogs
Data is from Teddiman & Newman 2007.

Figure 7.6 illustrates that, again, by far the majority (69 percent) of all cases of ellipsis in the corpus result from the omission of the pronoun *I* (sentences like *hope this is alright, decided yesterday to do the trip*). The study thus confirms that the main syntactic pattern of ellipsis, reflecting the speaker's prominence, is not only a characteristic of informal speech, but also applies to informal writing.

Let us conclude our discussion of ellipsis in discourse by pointing out some parallels with the use of pronouns. When exactly do speakers make use of subject ellipsis *within* a given text or discourse? The core condition is similar to pronouns, namely that the referent needs to be accessible; for subject ellipsis, this means that it must be fully recoverable. In an elliptical reference, the referent is either anaphorically recoverable from the preceding text, or situationally recoverable, if the referent is retrievable within the surrounding situation.

Textual **recoverability** is illustrated by the contrast between (26) and (27). While the sequence of sentences in (26) is fine, in (27) subject ellipsis sounds odd and is unlikely to occur.

(26)    Sue is very tired today. She came home late last night. (She) missed the
        bus.

(27)    Sue is very tired today. She came home late last night. Bill couldn't
        drive her. ?(She) missed the bus.

The reason for the difference between (26) and (27) is that, in (27), it is
almost impossible to interpret *Sue* as the referent of the missing subject.
To achieve this interpretation, the speaker would at least have to use a
right-dislocation (*Missed the bus, Sue*).

   The referent of a third-person pronoun (like *he, she,* or *they*), if
omitted, can normally be retrieved from the preceding sentence. By
contrast, *it* can also be a pronoun with an extended reference. As noted
in Section 7.2, both *it* and *this* potentially signal reference to a proposition or a longer stretch of discourse as a whole. In (28), for example, *it*
in the third sentence subsumes the entire previous sentence, that is, it
refers to both events expressed by the constituent verb phrases.

(28)    My mom is sick. I visited her yesterday and brought her a cake and
        flowers. (It) seems to have done her a lot of good.

Situational recoverability applies to the omission of subjects whose
referent is identifiable, not within the text itself, but within the discourse situation. These subjects are most often first-person pronouns,
like in the examples (23) and (24) already discussed above. However,
other pronouns, such as *you, he* or *she,* and *they,* are sometimes also
recovered situationally. In these cases, the situation clarifies the reference, which is what you see in Example (29):

(29)    (I/you/we/he/she/they) should've known better.

Many conventionalized expressions rely on situational recoverability, such
as *wouldn't mind/mind (a drink, coffee, …), will do,* or *see you later.* These
sentences are hardly perceived as cases of subject ellipsis, but they nonetheless require discourse conditions where the subject must be recoverable.

Turn to Exercise 6 for analyzing utterances taken from dialogs,
applying the distinction between the textual and situational
recoverability of subjects in ellipsis.

When doing Exercise 6, you will notice that the examples you are asked to analyze are from dialogs of TV series. The nature of this task highlights that the construction is often used in scripted dialog to indicate casual talk.

## 7.7 Summary

In this chapter, we have dealt with the grammatical ties in discourse that result from pronouns and ellipsis. We introduced the concept of co-reference and looked at different types of pronouns. We saw that, when expressing endophoric reference, pronouns establish co-referential ties, and, with that, chains of reference within discourse. By contrast, when used for exophoric reference, pronouns in the first place point to a shared situation. We also discussed principles of pronoun interpretation and the concept of givenness in discourse from a psycholinguistic viewpoint. We explored givenness in discourse in the sense of an entity being recoverable for the interlocutor, which means that the referent is mentally accessible. We then saw that this status of a referent is equally a condition of elliptical references and, more specifically, of subject ellipsis in discourse.

We discussed data concerning the use of both pronouns and ellipsis in discourse and saw that there are some characteristic patterns of text-linguistic variation. While exophoric pronouns and ellipsis are primarily indicators of an interactive and oral language use, we also looked at patterns of variation within the written medium, for example, pronouns in literary or electronic discourse and subject ellipsis in informal types of writing.

## 7.8 Exercises

### Level 1: Classification and Application

1. Highlight all pronouns in the passage below, which is the beginning of the prologue of the story *The Moon Maid* by Edgar Rice Burroughs (2002). Classify each pronoun according to the boxes in Figure 7.3 (double-dipping is possible). Considering what you have learned about anaphoric and cataphoric reference and that this is the beginning of the book, would you expect the discourse to begin like this?

A. I met him in the Blue Room of the Transoceanic Liner Harding
the night of Mars Day – June 10, 1967. I had been wandering
about the city for several hours prior to the sailing of the flier
watching the celebration, dropping in at various places that I
might see as much as possible of scenes that doubtless will never
again be paralleled – a world gone mad with joy. There was only
one vacant chair in the Blue Room and that at a small table at
which he was already seated alone. I asked his permission and he
graciously invited me to join him, rising as he did so, his face
lighting with a smile that compelled my liking from the first.

(Burroughs, *The Moon Maid*, 1972 [1923]: 1)

2. The referent of *he*, a boy named Julian, in the passage above is
introduced in more detail a bit later in the novel. An excerpt of this
section is given below. Identify all pronouns and classify them
according to the classification scheme presented in Section 7.2.
Are there cases of extended reference?

B. My name is Julian. I am called Julian 5th. I come of an illustrious
family – my great-great-grandfather, Julian 1st, a major at
twenty-two, was killed in France early in The Great War. My
great-grandfather, Julian 2nd, was killed in battle in Turkey in
1938. My grandfather, Julian 3rd, fought continuously from his
sixteenth year until peace was declared in his thirtieth year. He
died in 1992 and during the last twenty-five years of his life was
an Admiral of the Air, being transferred at the close of the war to
command of the International Peace Fleet, which patrolled and
policed the world. He also was killed in line of duty, as was my
father who succeeded him in the service.

At sixteen I graduated from the Air School and was detailed to
the International Peace Fleet, being the fifth generation of my
line to wear the uniform of my country. That was in 2016, and I
recall that it was a matter of pride to me that it rounded out the
full century since Julian 1st graduated from West Point, and that

during that one hundred years no adult male of my line had ever owned or worn civilian clothes. (200 words)

(Burroughs, *The Moon Maid*, 1972 [1923]: 9)

3. Analyze the text given in Exercise 2 for its rates of occurrence (per 100 words) of both nouns and pronouns (count strings of two nouns, like in *Peace Fleet*, even if not hyphenated, as one noun). How many different referents does the proper name *Julian* refer to in the text? How many referring expressions in the passage refer to the narrator's grandfather, *Julian 3rd*?
4. The passage below is a history text about the peace treaty ending World War I. Look at the pattern of reference that the text shows and compare your observation to the results of your analysis from Exercises 1–3 above. Using the givenness hierarchy of Figure 7.4, find out which noun phrases in the text refer to a referent that is fully activated. Which ones have a referent that is only familiar or uniquely identifiable?

C. On 11 November 1918, an armistice came into effect ending the war in Western Europe – but this did not mean the return of peace.

The armistice was effectively a German surrender, as its conditions ended any possibility of Germany continuing the war. Similar agreements had already been signed by Bulgaria, Turkey and Austria. However, the peace treaties which officially ended the First World War were not signed until 1919.

In the interim, fighting continued in many regions, as armed groups pursued nationalist, revolutionary or counter-revolutionary aims. Russia was torn apart by a civil war, which claimed more Russian lives than had the world war.

The peace settlements were imposed by the victors, rather than negotiated, and have since been criticised as laying the foundations of future conflicts. In fact, the conditions imposed

> upon the defeated powers were not unduly harsh, but the treaties contained many compromise solutions to difficult issues. As a consequence, their long-term success was limited, but they did not in themselves make the Second World War inevitable. (Imperial War Museum, 2021)

5. Identify the cases of subject ellipsis in the following discourse. Which ones rely on anaphoric recoverability, and which ones on situational recoverability? Is there a case of an extended reference for the omitted pronoun *it*? Which kind of discourse do you think this is from?

> D. If the conservatory connection can be isolated from main house, it's allowed (or was when I installed a rad in mine). Who's going to know anyway!! Quite. Ours already had two radiators connected to the main supply, and also a building regs certificate. I'm guessing they fitted the radiators after the certificate was issued? Anyway, keeps the room usable all year round. We've got an air conditioning unit in ours, was fitted by the previous owners. Seems to work really well on the few occassions we've used it to warm it up. They're supposed to be pretty efficient too, no idea on how much they cost to buy/install though. I've just gone through the rubbish job of lifting the old conservatory floor tiles and the screed to instal Heatmat on Thermal Insulation Boards ... messy job, but oh my the difference is incredible, now have a room that can be used all year round. Got electric u/f heating in ours and it's OK but uses a LOT of watts so given up with it for the winter. For the odd weekend that we do want to use the conservatory, esp over Xmas, I fire up a gas space heater, ten mins and it's too hot. (CORE, Interactive Discussion, 2012)

6. How is the referent of each of the grammatical subjects omitted in the following utterances (taken from dialogs from the Corpus of American Soap Operas) recoverable in the discourse? Distinguish between anaphoric and situational elliptical reference (disregarding

distance as a factor of recoverability). Discuss how your findings can be seen as being typical of scripted dialog.

ANGELO: Oh, the hotshot lawyer. Yeah, I thought you looked familiar. Can't believe your brother turned out to be a baby-napper. Seemed like such a stand-up kid. (SOAP, *Young and Restless*, 2011)

CLAYTON: I found a relatively new investment group. Seemed like a good opportunity, but the past day or so I haven't been able to access my account. (SOAP, *Guiding Light*, 2009)

KENDALL: It's your journal. I carry it with me everywhere I go. I read it all the time. Makes me feel closer to you, like you're still with me. (SOAP, *All my children*, 2011)

CARLY: The Galaxy Club. South of Market. I was very good at my job. Made great tips. (SOAP, *As the World Turns*, 2010)

BROOKE: And that's something that Ridge could never get past. Took me a long time to realize that. (SOAP, *Bold and Beautiful*, 2009)

## Level 2: Interpretation and Research Design

7. In Section 7.4, we discussed the differences between spoken and written discourse and the properties of electronic discourse regarding pronoun use. Table 7.2 gives you the average rates of occurrence for the pronoun *you* across different types of blogs from the CORE corpus (CORE being an acronym for the Corpus of Online

Table 7.2 *Frequency\* of* you *in five sections of the CORE corpus*

| Opinion blog | Religion blog/ sermon | Personal blog | Travel blog | News report/ blog | Informational blog |
|---|---|---|---|---|---|
| 9,312.26 | 7,964.45 | 11,677.85 | 9,216.78 | 6,069.48 | 11,999.82 |

* Per million words.

Registers of English). Discuss these findings in the light of the psycholinguistic background on pronoun interpretation, as discussed in Section 7.3. What kind of results would you predict for the occurrence of third-person, i.e., endophoric, pronouns against the general assumption which we discussed that pronouns are used to maintain reference?

8. Choose samples of two text varieties (approximately 500 words each) about the same topic and from the same medium (for example, a short news report and a commentary on the same topic). How do they differ either in their proportion of endophoric and exophoric pronouns or in the occurrence of personal and demonstrative pronouns? Formulate your research question (paying special attention to being specific about the object of investigation, which is in this case the textual varieties) as well as a hypothesis and a prediction about the difference that you expect to find. Present your findings both in the form of a table and as a suitable graph.

9. In Section 7.6, we discussed certain formulas containing subject ellipsis, such as *doesn't matter*, *sounds good*, or *would be nice*. Can you think of other conventionalized expressions containing subject ellipsis? You may use your own speech, or look at some dialogs in series, films, or fiction.

10. Both newspaper headlines and advertising are well known for the frequent use of ellipsis. Collect five instances of elliptical sentences from each kind of discourse and compare them. How are they different in the form and function of ellipsis?

## Further Reading

- There is a lot of interesting evidence on the interpretation of pronouns in the psycholinguistic literature. Classic references on grammar-based factors and the so-called centering theory are Grosz et al. (1995) or Chambers & Smyth (1998). For the pragmatic, coherence-based approaches, see Ariel (2013) and Gardelle & Sorlin (2015). For more recent, empirical studies on pronoun resolution, see, for example, Holler & Suckow (2016).

- The notion of accessibility is also discussed in the literature as "salience." For psycholinguistic studies and the expression of accessibility/salience in discourse, including zero anaphora, see a special issue of *Discourse Processes* (Sanders & Gernsbacher 2004) or Branco et al. (2005). Classic work on anaphora in English discourse is Fox (1986, 1987), on English in comparison to other languages, see Fox (ed., 1996). Most work in stylistics also touches on pronouns in literary discourse, for instance, Toolan (2013) or Gibbons & Macrae (2018).

- On features of grammatical cohesion in web-based discourse, see Biber & Conrad (2019: ch. 7) and Squires (2016). Hoffmann (2012) discusses grammatical cohesion, including the expression of reference, in personal weblogs. On ellipsis in different registers (for instance, conversation as opposed to storytelling), see Travis & Lindstrom (2016).

# 8 *Discourse Markers*

## 8.1 Introduction

We now turn to some elements of discourse syntax which do not belong to the core clause but are placed outside, or inserted within, it. To start with an example, take a look at the sequence in Example (1) and its illustration in Figure 8.1, which is a sequence of utterances made by a literary critic on NBC.

You will notice that the elements marked in italics in (1) come from different syntactic categories: *well* is just a word, an adverb, whereas *you know* is, from a syntactic viewpoint, a minimal, somewhat incomplete, clause. However, we feel that these elements occur as rather separate from the rest of the construction, both in terms of their position and their function. For example, no content modification is added to the proposition of the sentence *I think fans of Stephen King will see a lot in it* by adding *well* and *you know*. The separation from the clause is also shown by the punctuation, which indicates that, in the original spoken discourse, the elements were set off by intonation.

The terminology used in the linguistic literature to refer to these elements is varied. *Discourse markers*, the term we are using here, is the most common term. Elsewhere, such elements outside or inserted within the clause are also referred to in the literature as discourse or pragmatic particles, parentheticals, or extra-clausal constituents.

This variety in terminology is symptomatic, in that it is a bit of a challenge to define both precisely and consistently what a discourse marker is. Syntactically, discourse markers are not only adverbs and considered "small" clauses, like the elements highlighted in (1), but also coordinating or subordinating conjunctions, such as *and*, *but* or *because* (or *'cause/coz*, since we are dealing with speech here). From the point of view of their function, many discourse markers in fact express

(1) A: *Well, you know*, I think fans of Stephen King will see, *you know*, a lot in it, *you know*, they will certainly appreciate it, but it also has an incredible visual look to it, *you know*, very kind of "Matrix"-like effects.
B: It does.
(COCA, Spoken, 2004)

**Figure 8.1** Discourse markers as separate from the clause

a connection, while others mark a boundary and thereby help organize speech. The borderline between connectives, as discussed in Chapter 6, and discourse markers is therefore a bit fluid. For example, the adverbs *now* and *then* can be temporal adjuncts, and also, when placed sentence-initially, temporal connectives, which is why we have already come across them both in Chapters 3 and 6. Now we will see that these adverbs also occur in discourse when no temporal connection is at play. While in the example in (2), *now* expresses a temporal connection, in (3), it does not provide a temporal frame for the clause that follows. In (3), the presence of another temporal adjunct (*on Tuesday*) further indicates that *now* is no longer part of the proposition, but that it only marks a boundary between two utterances.

(2) [...] when I met my husband I was this strong, independent woman. *Now*, with three kids, I want to be taken care of. (COCA, Magazine, 2011)

(3) Thanks for helping to elevate and maintain the standards in our society. *Now*, folks, on Tuesday, I told you about [...]. (COCA, Spoken, 1996)

When exploring additive connectives in Chapter 6, we noted a similar pattern for the varying uses of *and*. We saw that the conjunction variably expresses a semantic, additive relation between two propositions or a pragmatic turn, marking a boundary between utterances. As evidence for this distinction, we checked whether *and* can be replaced by *in addition*: if this is not possible, the relation is not semantic, but pragmatic, and *and* resembles more of a discourse marker than a connective (see Section 6.2).

Despite some overlap, discourse markers are therefore an area of discourse grammar that we will look at separately. In contrast to connective elements, one primary function of a discourse marker is to bracket speech or talk (Schiffrin 1987), in the sense of marking a link or signaling a boundary between discourse units, like in Example (3).

The other function of discourse markers is that they typically provide some clue about the speaker's or the listener's role in the discourse (their attitude, current action, or the like). If you look again at the discourse markers in (1), you will notice that, in the given context, *well* marks the beginning of the utterance as a response and *you know*, in addition to bracketing the sequence, invites the listener's participation or consent. Most discourse markers also have such an interactive function – they support the ongoing interaction.

In the following, we explore the role of several discourse markers and will take a closer look at these two functions. The discussion will focus on a selection of items, since the category of discourse marker comprises a large group of lexemes and lexicalized phrases, rather than a closed set of grammatical elements. We will start with a discussion of the category as a whole, focusing on its formal and functional characteristics in Section 8.2. We then turn to the functions of *then* as a discourse marker in Section 8.3 and to the question of discourse marker sequencing in Section 8.4. Section 8.5 deals with the discourse marker *you know* as used in different types of discourse and Section 8.6 with the question of how discourse markers emerge and develop. We are aware that a lot of interesting work in this area is about speaker-based variation, going beyond the role of discourse. See the boxes on *like* as a discourse marker as well as on discourse marker use and language proficiency later in this chapter and our recommendations for further reading at the end of this chapter.

After reading this chapter you will be able to:

- recognize and describe the two primary functions that define a discourse marker;
- find out where words like *and, because, but, now, or, so, then*, and *well*, or sequences like *you know* and *I mean*, are used as discourse markers, i.e., as units outside the clause, and where they are elements inside the clause;

- retrieve discourse markers from a corpus and analyze their function using information from the surrounding discourse;
- investigate patterns of variation concerning the position and sequencing of discourse markers.

## Concepts, Constructions, and Keywords

*discourse markers vs. freestanding markers (e.g., yes, ok), interjections (oh, ah), bracketing (speech or talk), inference, discourse marker sequence, comment/parenthetical clause, matrix clause hypothesis, grammaticalization*

## 8.2 Discourse Marker: A Category of Grammar?

Let's start by defining the category of discourse markers by those attributes that are most widely agreed upon in the literature (for example, Dik 1997; Schourup 1999; Kaltenböck et al. 2016). One attribute, which we have already discussed, is syntactic: an element is a discourse marker if it occurs outside or in addition to the core clause, that is, if it is optional. We saw in the examples in the introduction that this property often means that the discourse marker is set off from the clause by intonation. In scripted speech or online writing, punctuation has a corresponding function, although we must be aware that, especially in online writing, punctuation is often used quite creatively. Overall, a first characteristic of a discourse marker is that it tends to occur at syntactic boundaries, very commonly at sentence beginnings, but also parenthetically within the clause or in the right clause periphery, that is, at the end of the clause (for more on this, see Section 8.3 below). In (1), for example, we have seen the use of *you know* in all three positions: in the beginning, in the middle, and at the end of the clause (*you know, I think fans of Stephen King will see, you know, a lot in it, you know*).

This more peripheral syntactic status of the category of discourse markers has a semantic counterpart in that the presence of a discourse marker does not affect the propositional meaning of the sentence. For example, if we delete *now* from the sentence in (3), as in (4), the sentence does not gain a different interpretation in the sense of its proposition. Remember that, as outlined in Chapter 1, the proposition is the truth-conditional meaning of a sentence, which, in (4), remains unaffected.

(4)    Thanks for helping to elevate and maintain the standards in our society. Ø, folks, on Tuesday, I told you about [...].

The third defining feature of the category of discourse markers is their function in discourse. As we have already seen in the introduction, there are two main functions of a discourse marker: they are used to connect or mark a boundary within speech (bracketing function), and they provide cues for the understanding between speaker and listener (interactive function). Behind these tasks, there is perhaps a more general, superordinate function, relating to the discourse as a whole. Discourse markers contribute to the fact that a discourse, our talk, needs to make sense as a whole, that is, they support its coherence. Since discourse develops linearly (in contrast to sentence grammar, which largely builds upon hierarchical relations; as explained in Chapter 2), marking connections and boundaries simplifies the process of understanding for the hearer and thereby helps to "negotiate" what should be a meaningful whole (Jucker & Ziv 1998). For example, in (3) above, repeated here as (5), the occurrence of *now* enables the listener to recognize a turn in the discourse, which is the beginning of a new section of the talk.

(5)    Thanks for helping to elevate and maintain the standards in our society. *Now*, folks, on Tuesday, I told you about [...]. (COCA, Spoken, 1996)

Having discussed the core properties of discourse markers, let us turn to their syntactic realization. Since our focus is on grammar here, we will mainly deal with those items that could in principle also be used syntactically, that is, as elements *inside* the sentence. For a start, we will take a look at a set of discourse markers that is widely discussed in the literature. This set is based on Schiffrin (1987) and comprises the discourse markers *and, because, but, I mean, now, or, so, then, well*, and *you know*. Comparing this list to other possible elements that are also often seen as discourse markers (e.g., Brinton 1996), we can recognize which types of items could in principle be added. The difference is illustrated by Figure 8.2:

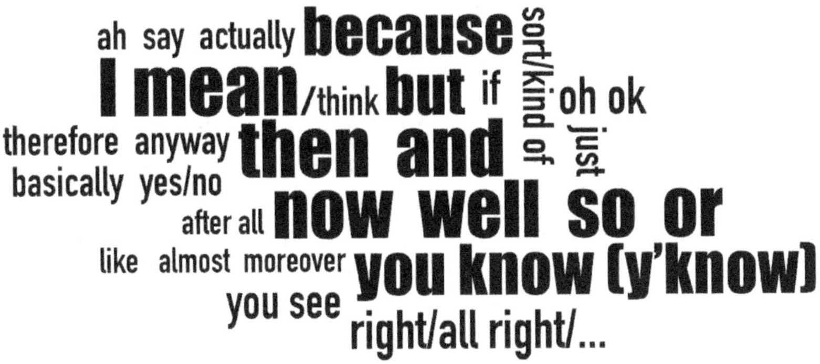

**Figure 8.2** Two inventories of discourse markers
Based on Schiffrin 1987 and Brinton 1996.

The discourse markers in the largest font size in Figure 8.2 are the ones we are going to focus on in the following. There are two reasons for this choice. First, several of the elements that are not highlighted do not necessarily precede, follow, or interrupt a clause. The items *oh*, *ok*, (*all*) *right*, and *yes/no* commonly occur just on their own, which means they are often freestanding markers. The other group of discourse markers we will largely neglect are those that occur almost anywhere in the clause and not necessarily at syntactic boundaries. Based just on the set of items contained in Figure 8.2, this property applies to *almost, basically*, and *like*, which are all commonly used as *phrasal* modifiers. Although they can also be filler items, in which case they meet the criterion of marking a boundary, these words do not share all properties of a discourse marker as described above, that is, they are not typically used for bracketing the discourse. While discourse markers characteristically mark the boundary of a clause or a sentence, phrasal modifiers commonly occur inside a clause. Look at the example in (6) for illustration:

(6)    *And, I mean*, amazingly, *you know*, this *like* chance meeting on a bench in Regent's Park resulted in this incredible company. (COCA, Spoken, 2017)

In (6), *and, I mean* and *you know* occur turn-initially and thus at the beginning of the clause. By contrast, *like* has a function that relates closely to the level of the phrase: It seems to have enabled the speaker to search for, or possibly emphasize, the word *chance meeting*. And although *like* can mark just a pause and is also found clause-initially (*Like, that's not happening*), leading some of the literature to distinguish *like* as a discourse marker from *like* within the clause being a mere particle (D'Arcy 2007), from our point of view *like* is a less typical instance, which is why we do not include it in our discussion (but see our box on *like* as a marker of the speech of an entire generation).

In contrast to modifiers within the phrase and to freestanding discourse markers, the elements highlighted in Figure 8.2 constitute very typical instances of the category of discourse markers. In addition, they all share the property that they can initiate a new grammatical unit: a new clause, sentence, or turn. Clause- or turn-initial occurrence could therefore be a fourth defining attribute for the category of discourse markers (Schourup 1999).

In addition to the challenge of delimiting discourse markers as a category, another issue one needs to decide is when exactly an item is used as a discourse marker and when it is still an element within the core clause. For example, the sequence *you know* also occurs within sentences when it is a true matrix clause. Often, like in Example (7), when *you know* is a main clause, the construction will keep the complementizer *that* but, as you see in Example (8), this is not necessarily the case. In (8), *you know* is still likely to be the main clause, since an alternative for the tag *right?* would be the tag question *don't you?*, rather than *isn't it?*.

(7)    You're just angry because you know that this is the right thing to do.
        (COCA, TV, 2017)

(8)    You know this isn't a competition, right? (COCA, TV, 2019)

In contrast to (7) and (8), where *you know* is not used as a discourse marker, in (1) and (6) above, the sequence *you know* was syntactically more "marginal" (Brinton 1996: 34). However, the boundary between uses as a main clause as opposed to a more marginal, parenthetical one is not always easy to draw, even if intonation, notably the presence of a pause, often indicates use as a discourse marker. We will come back to this distinction in our discussion of the development of discourse markers and their **grammaticalization** in the history of English in Section 8.6.

Exercises 1 and 2 provide an opportunity to identify elements as discourse markers and to distinguish syntactic from discourse marker uses.

Good to Know
*Like* – One of the Most Hated Words in English

In its usage note on *like,* dictionary publisher Merriam-Webster points out that the various uses of *like* are "a particularly bountiful source of irritation for people who get annoyed by the language habits of other people." Which uses are we talking about? The word *like* has many meanings and many different syntactic uses in English. It can be a verb (*Do you like broccoli?*), a noun (*We talked about our likes and dislikes*), an adjective (*The portrait is very like*), a preposition (*This cake tastes like a slice of heaven*), and a conjunction (*Looks like you don't remember his name*). There's also quotative *(be) like,* as in (9), whose function is to recreate speech or inner monolog in the narration of stories, as in (10). Quotative *(be) like* is often associated with the speech of young middle-class females from the San Fernando Valley in California, immortalized in the song "Valley Girl" by American song-writer Frank Zappa in the early 1980s.

(9)  [H]e asked me, "Can we switch seats?" And I was like, "Oh, yeah, sure. Okay." (GloWbE-US, 2011)

Quotative *(be) like* was first documented in the speech of speakers born in the 1960s and it was accelerated by speakers born ten years later. Those speakers are middle-aged today and still use quotative *like,* as do many others. We can't really say anymore that quotative *like* is a marker of the speech of adolescents.

Additionally, there is the use of *like* as a discourse marker, typically as an introductory element, as in (10), which is receiving just as much negative attention as quotative *like* by language prescriptivists.

(10)  They never went out in a small canoe. *Like,* we went from here to Cape Beale. They had great large war canoes. (D'Arcy 2017: 14)

In this context, *like* signals "exemplification, illustration, elaboration, or qualification" (D'Arcy 2017: 14) of a previous utterance. In (10), the first sentence makes a general claim about the use (or non-use) of small canoes. The second sentence, introduced by *like*, provides an illustration of that claim, which continues in the third sentence. Unlike quotative *like*, *like* as a discourse marker does not co-occur with *be* and is not grammatically required. Some people therefore think that it is just a filler word, a step up from *um* or *er*, but *like* clearly adds to the meaning of the sentence (if not in a propositional way). For a full account of *like* and its history see D'Arcy (2017).

Let's return to the functional properties of the category of discourse markers. We discussed above that discourse markers have two main functions: a bracketing function, which means to establish a connection and/or mark a boundary between units of talk, and an interactive function, providing an orientation for the listener. In this context, it is necessary to point out that the function of most discourse markers is variable since it depends on and is influenced by the context. Putting this more systematically, any function identified for a given marker is potentially multi-fold in two senses (Kaltenböck et al. 2016: 10). On the one hand, the function of a discourse marker can vary from discourse to discourse. A case that we already discussed in Chapter 6 is the use of *and* as a connective, which listeners or readers interpret, in accordance with the context, as additive, temporal, or causal. In (11), for example, *and* is additive, whereas in (12) it expresses a temporal succession.

(11)   Horses forever changed life on the Great Plains. They allowed tribes to hunt more buffalo than ever before. They tipped the balance of power in favor of mounted warriors. *And* they became prized as wealth. For Native Americans today, horses endure as an emblem of tradition and a source of pride, pageantry, and healing. (COCA, Magazine, 2014)

(12)   But go back to the example of the Bush tax cuts, which were supposedly temporary when they got passed. They worked. People liked them. *And* they became permanent law, which is where [...] we are today. (COCA, Spoken, 2017)

Similarly to these examples from written discourse, *and* in spoken language also either connects discourse segments or expresses a succession. In many contexts a given discourse marker will have more than one function, which is something we also see in (12). *And* not only expresses a sequence of facts here and is bracketing the sequence of information, it can also be said to introduce the speaker's next argument, that is, to have an interactive function.

With this co-presence of the functions of discourse markers in mind, let us now turn to more specific, individual functions within the set of items we want to look at here. The typical functions of these discourse markers are shown in Table 8.1, each now paired with an example for illustration. Examples (13) through (20) were retrieved from COCA, using the surface form of each discourse marker. As you see, we extracted the attestation plus more of the preceding discourse, which we did using the context + function (see our toolbox below on the need for contextual information and how to retrieve such information from a corpus such as COCA).

The reason why, with Table 8.1, we present illustrative examples rather than quantitative data on the occurrence in discourse, is that a category that is described by its function in discourse, like the one of discourse markers, can only be retrieved in a corpus that is parsed for syntactic structure (such as the *International Corpus of English*, which some of the studies we report from below have used). In an unparsed corpus, like COCA, the discourse markers are formally identical to their occurrence as elements *within* the sentence, which is why, with this area of discourse syntax, we reach the limits of basic corpus-linguistic, quantitative methodology. Instead, what we can do is to look at the concrete functions in actual discourse, taking into account that these functions are variable and influenced by the surrounding text, as discussed above. In order to do so, we need to be able to extract discourse markers from a corpus together with their surrounding text, which is described in the toolbox below.

Based on the functions illustrated in Table 8.1, we turn to work on discourse markers in Section 8.3. We will first discuss some properties of discourse markers using the variationist approach, namely their position in the clause and their sequences. From the text-linguistic perspective, we will then look at findings on the use of discourse markers in actual spoken discourse as well as in represented speech.

Table 8.1 *Typical functions of discourse markers**

| Element and its Discourse Function | Discourse Function in Context |
|---|---|
| *well*<br>marking response | (13) A: In a new direction – what do you mean?<br>B: *Well*, you know, I think of Stephen King will see, you know, a lot in it, you know […]. (COCA, Spoken, 2004) |
| *because, so*<br>marking cause and results | (14) Granted, $150 a year is a low recurring cost for a platform with such promising health benefits. *Because* have you seen a vet bill lately? (COCA, Magazine, 2015) |
| | (15) Google doesn't have an iPhone app. *So* it's limited to being used like other social media. (COCA, Spoken, 2011) |
| *now, then*<br>marking progression and succession | (16) Thanks for helping to elevate and maintain the standards in our society. *Now*, folks, on Tuesday, I told you about […]. (COCA, Spoken, 1996) |
| | (17) Who else drives you to one-up them the way that I do? Bane. No, he doesn't. Superman. Superman's not a bad guy. *Then* I'd say that I don't currently have a bad guy. (COCA, Spoken, 2017) |
| *you know, I mean*<br>marking information and participation | (18) […] it's clear that this company could not have become what it became without without the both of you. *I mean*, you both brought different skill sets to this. And, *I mean*, amazingly, *you know*, this like chance meeting on a bench in Regent's Park resulted in this incredible company. (COCA, Spoken, 2017) |
| *and, but, or*<br>marking discourse connectivity | (19) How insane not to have taken something more substantive than a thin silk wrap, as he'd suggested before they'd left. *But* despite the forecast, Vicki'd refused to believe the temperature would really drop so fast. (COCA, Fiction, 2012) |
| | (20) My aunt and cousin Vivian used to shop there the day after Thanksgiving. *Or* was it the day after Christmas? (COCA, Fiction, 2010) |

* Terminology is based on Schiffrin 1987.

Go to Exercise 3 for investigating the functions of discourse markers as attested in language usage.

How to Get Contextual Information from the Surrounding Discourse

The function of an element of discourse grammar, and of a discourse marker, in particular, does not depend just on the overall type of discourse in which it occurs. Corpus sections (like spoken, academic, news, and the like), which classify the source of an attestation according to its external situation, provide only insufficient contextual information. Rather than this source information, which comes automatically with the attestation, we need more information about the surrounding discourse, that is, about the *co*-text of an attestation (on the distinction of context and co-text, see the discussion in Section 2.2).

In COCA and the other corpora at the English Corpora interface, one gets access to a so-called "Expanded Context" after clicking on any of the fields with source information (corpus section, year of publication, or publication title). When the Context+ screen opens, you will be shown both more detailed source information and a longer stretch of the text the search item is from. Such an expanded co-text is useful particularly when you want to look closely at what was going on in the interaction before a marker occurs. Are different speakers taking regular turns here? What is the communicative function of previous utterances? Information like this enables you to identify functions such as presented in Table 8.1, that is, they help to determine whether an utterance is a response, serves the structuring or connection of arguments and information, and/or addresses specific roles of the discourse participants.

## 8.3 Variation in Position: Bracketing vs. Interactive Function of *then*

We have already pointed out that discourse markers have a strong tendency to occur sentence- or turn-initially. As discussed in Chapter 3, the relevance of the initial position is often explained by cognitive factors: we discussed them as signposts that guide the reader or listener through the discourse. We noted that this function applies to the sentence-initial placement of adjuncts and also saw in Chapter 6 that something similar is true for connectives.

Against this importance of sentence beginnings, the existence of "final connectors" may surprise us, although this is how adverbs like *then*, *though* or *anyway* in sentence-final position are sometimes referred to in the literature (e.g., Biber et al. 2021: 879; Lenker 2010). The late occurrence of a connective marker seems to be counter-intuitive, since expressing the type of connection for the sentence *after* its proposition might require that the sentence needs to be re-processed. Therefore, we need to ask why one might want to place a succession marker like *then*, not initially, as in example (17) in Table 8.1 above, but turn-finally, like in (21).

(21)    Superman's not a bad guy. I'd say that I don't currently have a bad guy, then.

*Then* in (21), used at the end of the second sentence, does not just mark a relation of sequence between the two utterances but seems to signal something else. What could this be? We have a true case of syntactic variation here, which means we should look at the placement of *then* using the variationist approach. Let's explore this case of variation in more detail.

As illustrated by Example (17) in Table 8.1, *then* typically marks a temporal succession within discourse. However, when used utterance-finally, we find that the meaning of *then* is no longer just temporal. In contrast to (17) and Example (22) below, where *then* does mark a progression; in Examples (21) and (23), *then* expresses a causal relation, that is, it signals more of a conclusion.

(22)    Then, where did you go?

(23)    Where did you go, then?

This causal meaning of utterance-final *then* can be explained by an inference: Since the marking of succession occurs only in retrospect, the utterance is interpreted "as the inferred result" of a preceding utterance or discourse segment (e.g., Haselow 2011: 3606; Biber et al. 2021: 870). The difference in function is also signaled phonologically: *then* in (23) would be uttered with rising intonation and preceded by a pause (*Where did you go, thén?*), in contrast to a temporal adjunct in sentence-final position (*Where did you go thèn?*; Quirk et al. 1985: 643). By placing *then* utterance-finally, the speaker signals that they are drawing a conclusion from, and not just continuing, the previous discourse. This means that sentence-final *then* is not so much a device of bracketing the talk by linking neighboring utterances, but that it situates the entire utterance into a wider context of assumptions and is therefore more interactive.

If the meaning of *then* is in fact different in these two positions, an interesting empirical question is which of these two meanings the main function for the discourse marker *then* is. Let us take a look at corpus-based data. According to one study (Haselow 2011), from a set of 1,000 attestations containing *then* (taken from the British component of the *International Corpus of English*), only 118 (12 percent) were in fact truly clause- or turn-initial. As illustrated by Figure 8.3, 24 percent of the instances of *then* occurred in final position, while the largest proportion of the occurrences of *then* (48 percent) were in fact those following a conjunction (*and* or *but*). However, in these combinations (*and then, but then*), *then* is no longer really autonomous, initiating the next utterance, but is linked more closely to the connective element and expresses a temporal relation between the preceding and the next utterance. In the presence of a coordinator, *then* functions more like a temporal adjunct again, no longer as a proper discourse marker. According to Figure 8.3, the discourse marker *then* is thus more common as an inferential marker than as a discourse marker of succession. We therefore have to conclude that the bracketing function of *then* is less frequent than the interactive one, that is, *then* as a discourse marker primarily signals something like a conclusion.

There are some other interesting properties going together with the utterance-final function of *then*. These aspects are exemplified in (24), which is an attestation of the sentence in (23) taken from the COCA corpus. In (24), speaker A reacts to speaker B's turn (*I didn't go home*), asking B for further information.

(24)   A:   Did something happen at home?
       B:   I didn't go home.
       A:   So, where did you go, then? (COCA, Movie, 1994)

In example (24), the speaker wants to get some information, and the inference expressed by *then* is that the previous discourse has made them

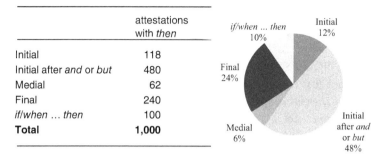

|                          | attestations with *then* |
| ------------------------ | :---: |
| Initial                  | 118   |
| Initial after *and* or *but* | 480 |
| Medial                   | 62    |
| Final                    | 240   |
| *if/when … then*         | 100   |
| **Total**                | **1,000** |

**Figure 8.3** Positions of adverb *then* in 1,000 attestations from the ICE_GB corpus/spoken component
Data is from Haselow 2011.

wonder. Like in this example, it has been found that *then* is typically used for performing such so-called "directive" speech acts. As you may know, with a directive, the speaker is seeking to get the listener to carry out a certain action (such as providing information, like in (24)). For example, out of about 200 utterances containing utterance-final *then* from two spoken language corpora, by far the majority (147 out of 181, or 81 percent) were utterances in which the speaker was seeking information (Haselow 2012). By contrast, according to the same study, and as shown in Figure 8.4, other utterance-final adverbs, like *though*, *actually* or *anyway*, occurred predominantly in so-called "assertives" or "other" speech acts, that is, in non-directive speech acts.

The fact that utterance-final *then* is associated with the presence of a directive speech act strengthens the analysis that its function is primarily interactive. This view is also supported by the data in Figure 8.5, which shows that by far the majority (94 percent) of all cases of final *then* occur in a contribution to the discourse that is made by a *new* interlocutor, and only rarely to one uttered by the same speaker.

In sum, findings on the positions of *then*, based on the variationist approach, have revealed interesting functional differences. Using final *then*, speakers do not just signal their progression to the next turn, but they typically express a request for information and ask their interlocutors to react. When in final position, *then* is more clearly interactive and dialogic than when placed utterance-initially. We can therefore generalize that different positions for a discourse marker are associated with different functions within discourse.

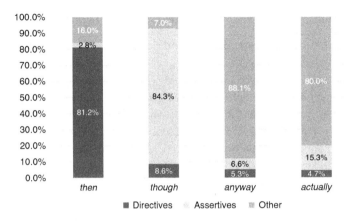

|           | then | though | anyway | actually |
|-----------|------|--------|--------|----------|
| Directives | 147  | 16     | 8      | 8        |
| Assertives | 5    | 156    | 10     | 26       |
| Other      | 29   | 13     | 133    | 136      |

**Figure 8.4** Final adverbs as discourse markers with different speech acts
Data is from Haselow 2012.

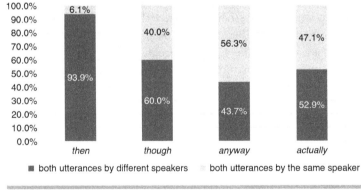

|                                   | then | though | anyway | actually |
|-----------------------------------|------|--------|--------|----------|
| both utterances by different speakers | 170  | 111    | 66     | 90       |
| both utterances by the same speaker   | 11   | 74     | 85     | 80       |

**Figure 8.5** Final adverbs in dialogic vs. monologic sequences
Data is adapted from Haselow 2012.

## 8.4 More Syntactic Variation: Discourse Marker Sequences

Another interesting aspect of discourse markers that we can explore using the variationist approach is their sequencing. As we have seen in several examples above, discourse markers typically occur in clusters, which raises two questions: which discourse markers are likely to co-occur? And how are they characteristically ordered? While these questions are mainly empirical, with many combinations being possible, they also lend support to the more theoretical position that discourse markers are a category of their own. The fact that sequences such as *you know and* or *and but* occur at all indicates that the elements involved are discourse markers, which obviously means being rather unrestricted by the syntax of the underlying grammatical category (Schiffrin 1987: 32).

As we saw when looking at the function of *and then* in narrative discourse in Chapter 6, initial connectives followed by a discourse marker are very common. The sequence *and then* appears to be the most frequent combination of two discourse markers, but the sequences *but then* and *and so* are also quite prevalent. According to one study, all three were among the ten most frequent sequences of two discourse markers, based on a statistical value that used both individual frequencies and the frequencies of the combinations and, on that basis, measured the so-called "association strength" (Lohmann & Koops 2016; the method is described in detail on p. 428). According to this measure, the ranking of the ten most frequently occurring combinations was as given in Figure 8.6.

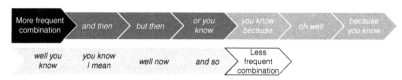

**Figure 8.6** Ranking of ten strongly associated combinations of discourse markers
Frequencies are based on Lohmann & Koops 2016.

For retrieving data on discourse marker sequences, one again faces the problem that a corpus does not distinguish discourse marker uses from other occurrences of the lexemes involved. For instance, for the sequence *and so*, we easily get more than 40,000 hits in COCA, but not all of these hits contain *so* as a discourse marker. Apart from the proper uses of *so* as a discourse marker, like the one shown in (25), there will also be many false positives (like in *and so it is,* or *and so on*), which one will first have to discard.

(25)    INTERVIEWER:    Really? *So* you were recruited by – what was it? – Boeing right out of school, right? You worked for them before you even graduated?

  INTERVIEWEE:    Correct, yes.

  INTERVIEWER:    *And so* tell us what your job is.

  INTERVIEWEE:    *So* I'm a rocket structural engineer.

  (COCA, Spoken, 2019)

The excerpt in (25) is from a job interview and illustrates the sequence *and so*, but also contains two single uses of the discourse marker *so*. These uses of *so* are clearly interactive: *so* introduces both a question (*So you were recruited … ?*) and an answer to a question (*So I'm a rocket structural engineer*), which corresponds to the function of *so* as marking a result (see Table 8.1) at the level of the exchange. For example, it is not the fact that the applicant is *a rocket structural engineer* that results from the previous question, but the answer by itself. In combination with *and*, this interactive function is augmented by a connective: *and so* now marks a new turn and establishes a connection, combining a bracketing function and an interactive function of this discourse marker sequence (see Section 8.2).

Let us also look at the reversed sequence *so and*, which is equally documented by corpus data. For example, in COCA, for *so and* preceded by a comma (which limits the search to the beginning of a syntactic unit or turn), we received a set of 76 occurrences, one of these being the utterance in (26). Studies in the area of discourse marker sequencing equally report a more than marginal number for this sequence (206, for example, according to Koops & Lohmann 2015), which indicates that, even if less common, the combination *so and* is attested and constitutes a true case of sequential variation.

(26)    The question is whether it's different if – if you're getting a normal
        night of sleep and then potentially trying to nap or not getting much
        sleep at all and then trying to nap, and by the way, *so and* then there's
        talk about potentially introducing this in some high schools? (COCA,
        Spoken, 2015)

In (26), which is about taking naps during school lessons, *so* does not
mark just a new turn in the discourse but occurs with a certain discon-
tinuity. Since talking about napping in general does not necessarily
result in talking about napping in some schools, the two topics are
connected at a more general level of thematic continuity. This function
of *so* in (26), resulting from a more abstract relation, is described in the
literature as *so* being a "main idea marker" (Müller 2005: 68).
Interestingly, this function almost never applies when *so* occurs in
second position (Koops & Lohmann 2015: 255), that is, following a
connective, like in (25). By contrast, in (26), the more abstract function
of *so* is further reflected by the insertion of *and*, strengthening the
connection.

Figure 8.6 also allows for some interesting observations concerning
the discourse marker *you know*, which, as we can see, is involved in five
out of the ten most common combinations. This finding is not a
surprise in the light of what we pointed out to be its typical function
(Table 8.1). Like in Examples (1) and (18), *you know* signals or invites
participation, which is a basic interactive function. A closer look at the
most common sequences containing *you know* reveals some more
unexpected patterns of use. In *you know because* and *you know I
mean*, based on clausal syntax, we would expect the reversed sequence.
Interestingly, based on a larger set of data, it turns out that sequences
with initial *you know* "constitute the bulk of the unpredicted cases"
(Koops & Lohmann 2015: 253). This observation is partly due to the
overall high frequency of *you know* in the data, which suggests that
another factor in discourse marker sequencing is the mere frequency of
the elements involved. However, this aspect does not seem to apply to
all elements to the same extent: *I mean*, for example, although generally
rather frequent in speech, only occurs once in the sequences given in
Figure 8.6.

There are two general insights about discourse markers that we gain
from this closer look at the issue of sequential variation. On the one
hand, discourse markers continue to have certain syntactic preferences,

and with that, to a certain extent, they remain related to their syntactic counterparts. On the other hand, the lexemes and clauses involved, when being discourse markers, possess more flexibility, a property which opens the possibility for a functional differentiation. Different sequences of discourse markers thus perform different functions in discourse, they have different "functional correlates" (Koops & Lohmann 2015: 256). This insight also highlights the nature of discourse syntax in general, being less driven by the syntactic principles of clause grammar, but rather by the surrounding discourse.

## 8.5 The Role of Discourse Type: Functions of *You Know* in Speech and Writing

Having dealt with the variationist perspective on discourse markers, let's now turn to their use in different types of discourse. From the discussion so far, we know that we should start with spoken discourse, since, as described above, discourse markers are elements with a primary bracketing or interactive function relating to speech or talk (e.g., Dik 1997: 381; Kaltenböck et al. 2016: 2). Of course, discourse markers equally occur in scripted speech or dialogs in fiction, such as in novels or films. For example, in the excerpt in (27) from *Alice in Wonderland*, Alice, talking to a mouse, uses *you know* like in natural spoken discourse. She uses it twice, and she certainly doesn't mean that the mouse is supposed to know what she is talking about.

(27)   "Are you – are you fond – of – of dogs?" The Mouse did not answer, so Alice went on eagerly: "There is such a nice little dog near our house I should like to show you! A little bright-eyed terrier, *you know*, with oh, such long curly brown hair! And it'll fetch things when you throw them, and it'll sit up and beg for its dinner, and all sorts of things – I can't remember half of them – and it belongs to a farmer, *you know*, and he says it's so useful, it's worth a hundred pounds! He says it kills all the rats and – oh dear!" cried Alice in a sorrowful tone, "I'm afraid I've offended it again!" For the Mouse was swimming away from her as hard as it could go, and making quite a commotion in the pool as it went.
       (Carroll, *Alice's Adventures in Wonderland*, 1991 [1865]: ch. II)

Contrary to the meaning of *you know* as a matrix clause, what Alice expresses by *you know* in (27) is that the information she is giving is

**Figure 8.7** *You know* in fictional dialog

new and newsworthy, probably even quite shocking, to her interlocutor, the Mouse. *You know* in this sense supports her presentation of content, which corresponds to the function of *you know* marking information and inviting participation (Table 8.1). Using *you know* as a discourse marker reflects a rather precise idea that Alice has about the Mouse as an interlocutor, particularly about its attitude regarding dogs (Figure 8.7). Research using the text-linguistic approach has highlighted this function of *you know* as marking shared information. For example, research on different registers found that there are higher rates of usage in conversations among friends than among strangers, and lower ones in the speech of high-status speakers or in discourse addressed to a larger audience (Jucker & Ziv 1998; Fox Tree & Schrock 2002).

For working with frequencies of *you know* based on a corpus, one faces the problem again that it needs to be retrieved with some reliability as a discourse marker, as separate from a syntactic matrix clause. One way out is to make use of punctuation here, that is, add a comma after *you know,* which works reasonably well (note that, in COCA, you have to separate the comma by a blank space). Based on this search strategy, Figure 8.8 shows the rates of occurrence of *you know* (normalized to one million words, as described in Section 2.4) in seven sections of COCA. It is not surprising that it is mainly spoken discourse and, to some extent, TV and movie scripts that show a high frequency of *you know*: this outcome is clearly in line with the general function of bracketing talk and/or serving interaction. By contrast, in written discourse, the rates of occurrence are extremely low and most likely result mainly from speech or dialog embedded within written text (like in example (27)).

In online discourse, which in Figure 8.8 is represented by blog and other web-based discourse, the occurrence of discourse markers also results from a more interactive nature of these discourse types. For example, in (28), taken from a blog titled "100 Reasons NOT to Go to Graduate School," *you know* is not used in the context of direct speech, but can certainly be said to have an interactive function.

(28)    Personally, I feel having a comfortable salary is better than doing something you love. So a high paid job you hate/are numb to is worth it? *You know*, that is an argument they make for law school, and I don't think it really holds water [...]. (COCA, Blog, 2012)

In (28), *you know* introduces information that provides background information to the main line of thought. Presenting "off-record" information is one of the interactive functions of *you know* (Fox Tree & Schrock 2002; Jucker & Ziv 1998), which has been found to apply in online writing similarly to speech (Fox Tree 2015: 68).

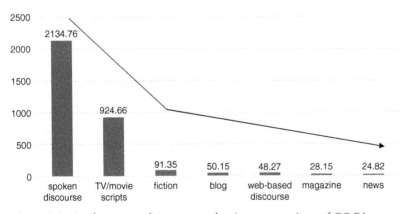

**Figure 8.8** *You know* as a discourse marker in seven sections of COCA
The graph shows occurrences per 1 million words.

Overall, using the text-linguistic approach has shown that the function of *you know* as a discourse marker applies to interactive discourse, rather than being limited to the written medium. As we will see in the final section, on the history of discourse markers, they often originate in functions that were just as common in writing as in speech.

> You should now be able to take on Exercise 4, which asks you to interpret frequency data on the positioning and the distribution of two other discourse markers.

## 8.6 Variation in Discourse over Time: The Development of Discourse Markers

As almost all grammatical elements, discourse markers are and have been subject to change. Several elements we dealt with in this chapter have been in use since Old English, but their function shifted with the documents in which they typically occurred. For example, the function of *then* (*Þa*) in Old English narratives was one of "peak-marking," signaling that the maximum point of tension in the story was reached, but became one of a mere "sequencer" in Middle English (Wårvik 1995). Some discourse markers became obsolete in the history of English, such as *methinks*, whereas several clausal discourse markers, like *I mean* and *you know*, emerged during the Middle English period (Brinton 2010).

There is an ongoing debate about the origin and development of these clausal discourse markers, which include a few other clauses (such as *I think*, *I guess*, or *you see*) and are also called "comment clauses" (Brinton 2011). There is historical evidence that, for example, the development of *you see* (or *see*) as a discourse marker has gone along with a rise of *you see* in matrix clauses with the complementizer *that* omitted. This observation has led to the assumption that the omission of *that* caused a syntactic reanalysis of *you see*, which thereby developed from a main clause to a parenthetical comment clause. This assumption is called the "matrix clause hypothesis" (e.g., Kaltenböck et al. 2011). Other historical linguists have argued that comment clauses must have evolved out of a broader variety of constructions. For example, *you know* and *I see* could easily have developed, not only from first-person matrix clauses, but also from other clauses, for instance, *as you know* and *as you see* (Brinton 2017). According to this view, it is not possible to say with certainty that the development of a discourse marker has been caused by a single pattern of syntactic variation.

There is more consensus in the literature that the most common process through which discourse markers come about is one of grammaticalization (some authors call it "pragmaticalization," since what changes is the expression of pragmatic functions). Grammaticalization typically begins with the loss of specific semantics, known as "bleaching," and with a loss of the categorial restrictions that applied to the original category. For example, as we discussed in Section 8.5, *you know* as a discourse marker has lost its original meaning as well as the syntactic properties of a matrix clause, in that it is no longer limited to occur in a fixed position (see Ex. (27)).

Grammaticalization is also the origin of discourse markers that have, syntactically, been adverbs. A well-known and more recent case is the use of *actually* as a discourse marker (Oh 2000; Clift 2001; Aijmer 2013), which is very common, especially in the speech of the younger generation (Waters 2009). Originally, *actually* was a VP adjunct, meaning "in fact" or "in reality," but the adverb has undergone a semantic change and turned into a discourse marker (e.g., Traugott & Dasher 2009). In contemporary discourse, *actually* is found not only within the VP, but in all sentence positions, that is, clause-initially as well as clause-finally. As examples, look at (29) and (30):

(29)  A:  You say in your piece that the wall was certified in 1995 by Jamie Gorelick. It *actually* started with Bush 41 and with Reagan. And all she did was recertify it. Not only that, but John Ashcroft recertified the very same things Jamie Gorelick did.

     B:  No.

     A:  And the 9/11 Commission was very specific about this, and they *actually* mentioned that in their report.

     B:  *Actually*, the law you're talking about, FISA, was enacted in 1978.

       (COCA, Spoken, 2006)

(30)  A:  Because President Trump promised to drain the swamp and he flooded his national security team with that exact swamp.

       B:  Well, I agree with that, *actually*.

         (COCA, Spoken, 2019)

Examples (29) and (30) illustrate that *actually* can be used as a VP adjunct (*actually started*, *actually mentioned*), but also occurs at the beginning or at the end of an utterance. Nowadays, in all three positions *actually* expresses an attitude of the speaker, indicating some kind of opposition or discrepancy between the interlocutors (Smith & Jucker 2000). For example, in (29), *actually* emphasizes that the clausal proposition is counter to expectation (*It actually started …* , *they actually mentioned that …*). At the beginning of a new turn, like at the end of (29), *actually* marks this turn as being a correction (*Actually, the law you are talking about was enacted in 1978*). In (30), in utterance-final position, *actually* softens the speaker's opposing view (*I agree with that, actually*).

These interactive functions, together with the variable position in the clause, justifies considering *actually* as a discourse marker rather than as a clausal adjunct. In addition, there is evidence from corpora that *actually* is today much more frequent in speech than in writing (e.g., Oh 2000; Aijmer 2013). Based on one corpus study that looked at a variety of registers (Aijmer 2013), Figure 8.9 shows the pattern of occurrence of *actually* in spoken and written discourse in comparison to its semantic correlate *in fact*.

As we can see in Figure 8.9, *actually* and *in fact* are both clearly more common in speech than in writing. However, we also see that, in dialog, *actually* is considerably more frequent than *in fact*. This finding suggests that *actually* is now commonly used as a discourse marker. By contrast, as you may know, its use in writing is often heavily criticized, for example, as being "the most futile, overused word on the Internet" (Carusillo 2014). The description as "futile" results from its semantic bleaching, which shows that *actually* has grammaticalized and is perceived now primarily as a discourse marker.

This is now a good time to check out Exercise 5, which looks at different positions of *actually*, contrasting spoken and written discourse.

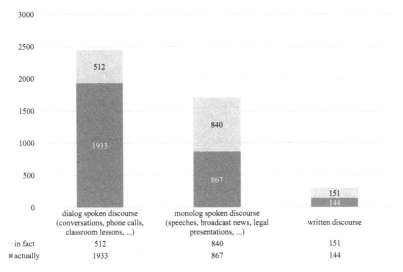

Figure 8.9  Frequency of *actually* and *in fact* in dialog, monolog, and written discourse
Occurrences per 1 million words; based on Aijmer 2013.

**Good to Know: Language Proficiency and Discourse Marker Use**

As we have seen throughout this chapter, discourse markers are common in speech and important for an efficient communication. Competence in using them is therefore also of importance for second-language learners. Research in this area indicates that discourse markers often fall short of a native-like usage. Learners rarely acquire this competence in the classroom, which is why characteristic differences often remain for a long time (Hellermann & Vergun 2007; Polat 2011).

For example, in a study of spoken discourse by American and German advanced speakers of English (elicited through the mutual retelling and discussion of a movie), many systematic differences were in fact observed (Müller 2005). While only *so* was most commonly used in the speech of both groups, the preferences for the other discourse markers differed quite substantially. The native group used *like* and *you know* more often, whereas the German speakers used *well* much more than those two. Overall, with the exception of *well*, all other discourse markers were used far more by the native speakers: *so* was twice as frequent, and *you know* and *like* even five times as frequent. And although *well* is particularly common in learner speech, it also became obvious that the functions of *well* are quite different. While, in the speech of non-natives, it is used mostly for managing the flow of the talk, most notably, as a marker of hesitation and pausing, *well* has more specific functions as a marker of response in native usage, for example, the expression of disagreement (Aijmer 2011; Buysse 2015).

## 8.7 Summary

In this chapter we have explored elements which are rather loosely connected to the grammar of the clause and primarily serve the needs of spoken, interactive discourse. We looked at several typical discourse markers, pointing out their defining properties and characteristic functions in discourse. We saw that discourse markers are placed in variable positions within the sentence, that these are associated with different functions in the discourse, and that discourse markers also occur in characteristic sequences.

We then turned to the use of discourse markers in different text types, showing that they are closely associated with the online production of spoken discourse. We also saw that they occur in embedded or scripted speech and online writing and that, ultimately, the function of a discourse marker is variable and has to be analyzed based on the surrounding text. Finally, we touched on the development of discourse markers and what to learn from their grammaticalization.

## 8.8 Exercises

### *Level 1: Classification and Application*

1. The discourse below is from a news interview, in which a film director (Kevin MacDonald = speaker A) tells a CBS moderator (Chris Wragge = speaker B) about the making of the YouTube documentary "Life in a Day." Circle all elements in this discourse that you consider to be

discourse markers and describe the bracketing and/or interactive function they perform. Are your findings in line with the properties of a discourse marker described in Section 8.2?

---

B: It was July 24, 20 – 2010, and I am sure a lot of thought must had gone into why you chose this day, right?

A: No. No. There was – there was very little thought. Well, the thought was it's after the World Football Cup, Soccer Cup –

B: Okay. All right.

A: – as you call it here. And I thought, well, during that nobody, except in America is going to take part because nobody in America is interested in soccer.

B: Yeah.

A: So we laughed all round in here.

B: That was like soccer what?

A: So – so and then we – we wanted to do it before the big – the big holidays in August.

B: Sure.

A: But the big thing was, you know, should we do it on a – should we do on a weekday or on a – on a weekend.

B: Weekend.

A: We went for a weekend because we thought more people would take part, and we were – we were right.

B: And finally where can people see this?

A: They can see it in theaters.

B: Yeah.

A: – starting this Friday. It's a limited release to begin with and then expanding out. So go and see it.

B: Life in a Day, folks. Really good stuff. Kevin, great – great to see you this morning. Thanks so much. We appreciate it.

A: Thank you, Chris. Thanks for having me on.

B: And just as another reminder for you Life in a Day opens in theaters this Friday, so go out there [...].

(COCA, Spoken, 2011)

---

2. In sentences a. to e., you will find uses of some of the elements discussed in Section 8.2. Decide if the element is used as a discourse marker or whether it has a grammatical function inside the clause. Are there borderline cases?

a. When designing flying vehicles, there are many aspects of which we can be certain but there are also many uncertainties. Most are random, and others are just not well understood. (COCA, Magazine, 2018)

b. [...] he has a radical plan to win community support: he wants to open up the long-isolated island to guided tours. The proposal has met with, well, mixed reactions. (COCA, News, 2000)

c. You traditionally have started with the "10 blue links" result, which has taken you to a place where you could often refine your search in a context specific fashion. What do I mean by context specific? I mean that this specific search allows you to specify attributes unique to the type of thing you are searching for. (COCA, Web, 2012)

d. A: So, do you think it's the right picture or not? B: I think you've got it down cold. So, I have a question for you, then. (COCA, Blog, 2012)

e. He didn't think she'd remember; he'd mentioned his birthday last week, but she hadn't taken it up then. (COCA, Web, 2012)

3. Apply the more specific functions of individual discourse markers, which are listed in Table 8.1, to the elements you found in Exercises 1 and 2. Are there uses where the element functioning as a discourse marker could be said to have more than one function?

4. In Section 8.3, we looked at the position of *then* as a discourse marker and saw by looking at the data in Figure 8.3 that, for *then* by itself, the initial position is less common than the final one. In Figure 8.10 on the next page, there is a similar set of results for the two other discourse markers we discuss in more detail in this chapter, *you know* and *actually*. Do these elements behave similarly to *then*, or is there a difference in the corresponding pattern of syntactic variation? In the light of what is said in Section 8.5 about the text-linguistic pattern of variation of *you know* as a discourse marker, would you expect to see differences in its positioning of these two in spoken vs. written text varieties?

5. Section 8.6 dealt with the process that led to the use of *actually* as a discourse marker rather than a VP-adjunct. Figure 8.11 shows the distribution of *actually* across different positions within the

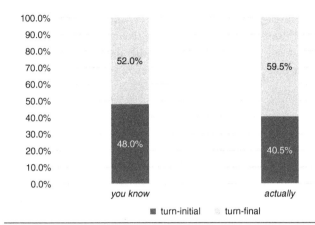

| | you know | actually |
|---|---|---|
| turn-initial | 49 | 98 |
| turn-final | 53 | 144 |

**Figure 8.10** Distribution of turn-initial and turn-final position of *you know* and *actually*
Data is from Haselow 2019.

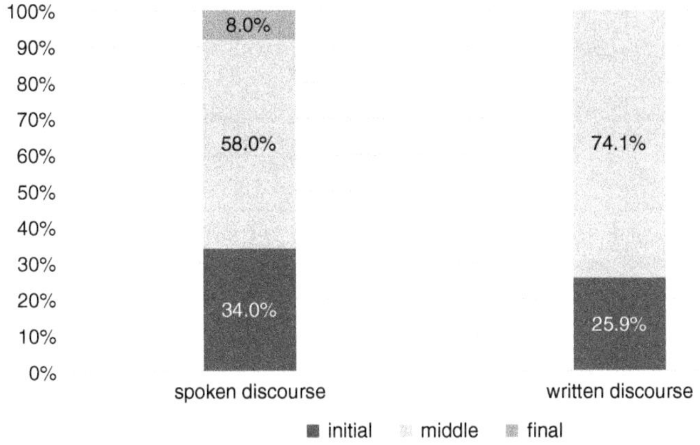

| | spoken discourse | written discourse |
|---|---|---|
| initial | 34 | 43 |
| middle | 58 | 123 |
| final | 8 | 0 |

**Figure 8.11** Positioning of *actually* in spoken and written discourse
Data is from Oh 2000.

sentence, contrasting the pattern of occurrence in spoken and written discourse. How does the use in these two text varieties differ? Why do you think the chart presents the data as proportional frequencies (in percentages), rather than as rates of occurrence?

## Level 2: Interpretation and Research Design

6. In Section 8.4, we pointed out that sequences of discourse markers going against the grammar of the underlying elements (such as *and but* or *so and*) are nonetheless possible. Which other sequences of the discourse markers dealt with in Section 8.2 do you consider unexpected from a grammatical point of view? Which ones do you nonetheless find attested in a corpus?
7. We saw in Section 8.5 that the main pattern of text-linguistic variation in the use of discourse markers reflects the opposition of spoken and written, as well as of more and less interactive, discourse. Below you see data on the occurrence of the discourse marker *well* in different types of spoken discourse. How do you account for the differences? What kind of chart would you choose as an illustration?

Table 8.2 *Occurrences\* of the discourse marker* well *in five types of spoken discourse*

|  | Private conversations | Telephone calls | Business transactions | Unscripted speeches | Broadcast talks |
| --- | --- | --- | --- | --- | --- |
| *well* | 6,965 | 9,943 | 5,646 | 4,843 | 735 |

\* Per 1 million words. Data is from Aijmer 2013: 26.

8. Think about a project in which you could look at the occurrence of discourse markers in scripted dialogs (such as from novels or film scripts). Which discourse markers would you choose to investigate? How would you go about retrieving these in a text corpus? Think about discussing your outcomes in relation to the question of how authentic (i.e., close to natural speech) scripted dialog is.
9. Do you observe any emergence of new discourse markers in online writing? How would you go about studying these when using a text-linguistic approach? Which aspect of the use of discourse markers in online discourse could one look at using a variationist research design?

## Further Reading

- An overview of the research concerning the history of discourse markers is provided in Brinton (2010). Individual work on discourse markers has been published in countless journal articles over the last thirty years (only some of which are included in our reference list) as well as in many edited volumes, for example, Fischer (2006) or Kaltenböck et al. (2016). Sequences of discourse markers are dealt with in Cuenca & Crible (2019) and Haselow (2019).
- On discourse markers in teenage speech, see, for example, Andersen (2001) and Tagliamonte (2005). On the use of markers as varying by age and gender, see Beeching (2016); for variation across varieties of English, see Aijmer (2013) as well, for example, as Burridge (2014) on *'cos* and *because* in Australian English. A considerable amount of work on discourse markers is also dedicated to their use by non-native speakers; see, for instance, Aijmer (2011) on *well*, or Buysse (2012, 2020) on *so* and *actually*.
- For a more theoretical discussion of discourse markers and attempts for a coherent definition, see Schourup (1999), Fraser (2006, 2009) or the introduction to Kaltenböck et al. (2016). On the topic of grammatical-ization and the rise of discourse markers, you could consult *The Oxford Handbook of Grammaticalization* (Heine & Narrog, 2011), especially the entry on the relationship between grammaticalization and pragma-ticalization (Diewald 2011), or Heine et al. (2021).

# 9 *Grammar and Genre*

## 9.1 Introduction: The Role of Register and Genre

We have explored throughout this book how syntax is influenced by the surrounding discourse, and we have noted that many types of discourse have characteristic features at various levels of sentence structure. For example, we discussed how syntactic variation happening at the beginning, in the middle, or at the end of a sentence can be triggered by the surrounding text (Chapters 3 to 5), but at the same time we saw that the use of these variants is also influenced by the discourse situation, by external, non-linguistic factors such as the medium, topic, and the purpose of a text. In Chapters 6 and 7, we turned to the expression of discourse cohesion and looked at connectives, pronouns, and ellipsis and their occurrence in different types of text, for instance, the use of connectives in the academic register, of pronouns in fiction, or of ellipsis in informal speech or writing. Finally, in Chapter 8, we explored elements used as discourse markers, which is a characteristic of spoken discourse.

In this final chapter, we now turn to a discussion of discourse varieties as such, which means we will look at some of their features in the area of grammar. We will explore a few selected registers and genres more closely. Before we start you should note that, as discussed in Chapter 2, we are using the terms register and genre here in accordance with the approach of Biber & Conrad (2019), where both concepts are described as referring to situational varieties of language use. This means we follow their approach of considering register and genre as being different perspectives for analyzing discourse, and "*not* as different kinds of texts or varieties" (Biber & Conrad 2019: 2). This approach entails that one can in principle look at every kind of discourse both from a register and from a genre perspective. While, with the register perspective, the analysis focuses on what is common and frequent in a discourse, the genre perspective is concerned with what is typical and conventional. For example, a genre, like a prayer, a sonnet, or a solicitation for a donation, often has a specific rhetorical organization. These genres also have linguistic characteristics that are not necessarily overall pervasive, like the opening in a solicitation letter, the couplet in a Shakespearean sonnet, or the boundary marker "Amen" in a prayer. Both the rhetorical structure and such single features belonging to a genre are its typical characteristics. At the same time, texts of these genres can be equally studied from the register perspective, focusing on the linguistic features that are more frequent or pervasive in this type of text when compared to other registers: For example, most letters and prayers also contain many first- or second-person pronouns. Since registers differ by the extent to which grammatical features are used in them, and not in the single occurrence of a given feature, they have to be studied on the basis of a sufficient sample of discourse. Since the focus is on features that are pervasive, this analysis can also be based just on text excerpts, as from an electronic corpus, and not necessarily on complete texts. By contrast, genres need to be studied on the basis of complete texts. In reverse, this means that any genre, but not any register, can be looked at both from the register and from the genre perspective.

Genre being the term used for this chapter highlights that, in the following, we will explore types of texts in terms of characteristics that are either common (in the sense of frequent) *or* typical. We will start with a discussion of the principled distinction between spoken and written genres (Section 9.2) and then explore one genre and one register more thoroughly. In Section 9.3, we take a close look at a highly conventionalized genre that is well known by academics, which is scientific abstracts, and, in Section 9.4, we explore some characteristic features of **digital discourse**.

Having studied this chapter, you will be able to:

- identify key grammatical features of the registers of spoken and written genres and understand limitations that exist for applying that distinction;
- detect both genre and register features in a scientific abstract and discuss their discourse motivations;

- develop a research design for studying the nominal character of the register that is commonly used in abstracts and other types of academic writing;
- recognize and discuss features of online writing as linguistic innovation taking place in digital discourse.


### Concepts, Constructions, and Keywords

*agentivity,* because *X, CARS model, (phrasal/clausal) complexity, conceptually spoken vs. written language, digital discourse, hashtag, inanimate subject, linguistic innovation, mediality, netspeak, noun phrase, scientific abstract, textisms, Twitter*


## 9.2 Grammar and Medium: Written vs. Spoken Genres

The medium, or channel, is one of the most important parameters that motivates register and genre variation. When speaking, we have less time for planning what we are going to say, we cannot erase what we have said, and we are usually in more direct, often more personal, contact with our audience. Participants in spoken discourse are typically in face-to-face contact and therefore also rely on non-linguistic cues, such as gestures, facial expression, or intonation. By contrast, the written register typically has quite a delay between production and reception, which is why it is often more carefully planned or edited. In addition, the written register can make use of visual cues, such as spelling, punctuation, and layout.

This description of the spoken as opposed to the written register is a highly stereotypical one. It might mislead us to think that written discourse necessarily has linguistic characteristics opposite to speech. However, this view focuses not just on the channel of communication, but ultimately on a whole group of situational characteristics. For example, in most situations where we speak, we are less interested in communicating just information, but are also concerned with establishing and living our relations, expressing our attitudes and feelings. This is a distinction, not only of the medium, but one of the purpose, of the so-called "interpersonal" function of speech (Biber & Conrad 2019: 88). And it is true that, in most spoken registers, the social and emotional functions of language are more important than just informational ones. On the other hand, there are also texts that contain a lot of information and are therefore carefully planned, but will ultimately be spoken (sermons, or speeches in politics, for instance), or those that are written quite spontaneously and not addressed to a wider audience (text messages, for example).

A useful approach for disentangling these various aspects of speech as opposed to writing is to distinguish between *medially* and *conceptually* oral or written registers (Koch & Oesterreicher 1985). Following this approach, the spoken/written distinction is a true dichotomy only from the point of view of the medium. The spoken language uses the phonic code, while the written language is conveyed through the graphic code. Texts can easily change from one code into another: For example, important speeches usually start out in written form, to be read aloud, then they are delivered orally, and later they may be archived or shared in printed form. By contrast, the conceptual distinction between spoken and written discourse is not a simple dichotomy, but rather a continuum between idealized poles of typically written texts (texts that are not only written in a medial sense, but also carefully planned and highly edited) and typically oral texts (texts that are not only oral in the medial sense, but also produced spontaneously in a space shared by speaker and addressee). It refers to the communicative strategies that are employed, which involves planning, editing, and having a certain purpose in mind. Conversation, on the one hand, and written, published texts, on the other, are something like the idealized poles of this continuum of conceptually oral and written language, with many degrees being possible in between. For example, an oral presentation in a university classroom is conceptually less oral than a private conversation among students; and an academic lecture, which has been prepared by way of detailed lecture notes, is still conceptually less written than a printed, published text, since the communicative strategies during a lecture in most cases involve some interaction. Or think of an oral exam, which is probably situated somewhere in the middle of this continuum: It is carefully planned and highly informational, but the discourse situation nonetheless means that there is a lot of interaction. Summarizing these examples, take a look at Figure 9.1, which illustrates this continuum of conceptually oral and written language.

**Figure 9.1** University genres as conceptually spoken and written language

The idea of conceptually **spoken vs. written language** still does not capture all the situational characteristics of a genre with an effect on grammar. For example, as we discussed in Chapter 7, it is not easy to tell where to put digital registers on the oral–written continuum. As we discussed there, apart from the medium, the purpose of a discourse and the expected audience also play a crucial role. Distinctions such as the one between informational and non-informational registers, or the one between discourse for a specialist as opposed to a non-specialist audience, can be as powerful as the spoken–written distinction in triggering linguistic variation (Biber & Gray 2016).

From the point of view of concrete linguistic features, the spoken–written distinction is also not a very clear one. The research in this area justifies the overall position that the differences within speech or writing can generally be as great as the differences across the two modes. In fact, we cannot expect to find true linguistic markers of the phonic or graphic medium, since most elements of grammar can, in principle, occur in all media. Still, due to the circumstances under which we produce most oral speech (face-to-face contact, no time for planning), spoken discourse has overall less variation than written registers. As Biber & Conrad (2019: 261) note in their discussion of registers: "[A]n author can create almost any kind of text in writing, and so written texts can be highly similar to spoken texts, or they can be dramatically different. In contrast, all spoken texts are surprisingly similar linguistically, regardless of communicative purpose." This is why we want to take a brief look at some features of this one (idealized) pole of the spoken–written continuum before turning to written genres later in the chapter.

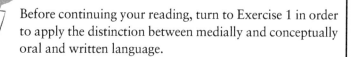

Before continuing your reading, turn to Exercise 1 in order to apply the distinction between medially and conceptually oral and written language.

Among the most typical grammatical features of the spoken mode described in reference grammars are incomplete clauses and overall shorter clauses, a higher density of verbs, a higher use of interrogative and imperative sentences and of coordination rather than subordination, more active verb forms, and the regular use of contractions and ellipsis. In addition to these features of grammar, there are also phenomena that directly result from the production of spoken language: in particular, its relative disfluency, which usually causes pausing, repetition, re-starts and re-formulations, as well as the insertion of discourse markers or parenthetical clauses. For example, in Chapter 7, we discussed the occurrence of elliptical clauses as a feature of spoken discourse, and in Chapter 8 we looked at discourse markers as different kinds of elements that are typically inserted within the clause in spoken discourse. For example, in the utterance in (1), which is taken from the *GSWE*, the clause contains a parenthetical clause (*I think*) as well as a re-start and re-formulation (*I don't think you sh-*).

(1)    Dad, I don't think you sh-, I think you should leave Chris home. (Biber
       et al. 2021: 1056)

In the corpus of conversations used for the *GSWE*, non-clausal units account for more than one-third (38.6 percent) of all units of conversations (Biber et al. 2021: 1065). The average length of these units in the corpus is only two words, which is all the more surprising since the units that were counted also include, for example, interjections (*oh*, *ah*), response forms (*mhm*, *okay*), or signals of hesitation (*uh*, *er*). Interjections, by their very nature, do not interact with other elements in the utterance, which is why we didn't deal with them as discourse markers in Chapter 8. You could find out more about them by studying the linguistic sub-discipline of Conversation Analysis, or by consulting the *GSWE*, which contains an entire chapter dedicated to the "grammar of conversation" (Biber et al. 2021: ch. 14; also see Further Reading at the end of this chapter).

For a corresponding view of the written mode, let us just note here that some typical features seem to be the opposite of the spoken mode features. For example, most written discourse contains twice as many nouns than verbs with considerably more embedding, both within the sentence as well as within the noun phrase itself (Biber et al. 2021; Biber & Gray 2010, 2016). In addition, we can expect most written discourse, if it is written to be printed and published, to contain complete rather than incomplete sentences and more varied syntactic structures. A higher complexity of sentences as well as a higher occurrence use of the passive voice are therefore among the classic grammatical characteristics that are usually referred to when describing the syntax of the written mode. However, when we think of writing that takes place online, it is obvious that these texts probably turn out to be more varied, or hybrid, in their use of such grammatical characteristics. In view of the overall larger variety of the written media and their genres, we'll take a closer look at a few selected genres in the remainder of the chapter.

Turn to Exercise 2 for identifying features of grammar that have been described in this section as being typical of the spoken and the written medium.

## 9.3 A Genre and Its Grammar: Research Article Abstracts

### *9.3.1 Typical of the Genre: The Handling of Agentivity*

Academic writing is an important part of every scholar's career and, as you perhaps know from Academic Writing courses, involves quite a few regularities and conventions. Among these, one that is often discussed concerns the role of the scientist being the agent both in the research process and in the written documentation when publishing the outcomes. As discussed in Chapter 4, the linguistic category of agent denotes an argument of the verb, referring to the willful and sentient initiator of an action. Since most scientific activity rests upon the observation and analysis of empirical evidence, clauses like the ones in (2) are statements of the kind most scientists make, in one way or another, in their writing: In both clauses, the scientist is the initiator of the activities that are expressed (*observe* and *argue*). However, you will find that clauses like the ones in (3) and (4) are usually more likely to occur in written discourse, since these are utterances that leave the scientist as the initiator of what is being reported implicit.

(2)  *I observed* that ... (Therefore) *I argue* that ...

(3)  Based on the comprehensive literature survey, *it is observed* that most of the research done so far is either sector-specific or consolidated by taking a sample of few companies irrespective of their sectorial belonging. (COCA, Academic, 2018)

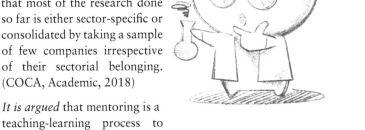

(4)  *It is argued* that mentoring is a teaching-learning process to which participants bring specific responsibilities. (COCA, Academic, 2013)

One core question about grammar as it is used in scientific texts thus has to do with the scientist being almost always the agent, and it is quite interesting to see how this role is expressed. As we discussed in Chapter 4, the agent role tends to be mapped to the grammatical subject, like in (2), but the passive voice as in (3) and (4) does not conform to that tendency. The expression of agentivity is a crucial area of genre-based syntactic variation, guided by the question of whether a scientific text will be more "author-centred" or more "object-centred" (Atkinson 1992).

One genre that is highly symptomatic of how these options are handled is the scientific abstract. An abstract accompanies many scientific publications, for example, book announcements, conference presentations, research reports, and, what we will look at here, articles from scientific journals. Abstracts can be described as a genre of "distillation" (Swales 2004), a property that highlights that abstracts contain a high condensation of information and are meant to be skimmed rather than read linearly (Gledhill 1995). As a result, the abstract is a genre that is highly likely to possess typical, that is, stand-alone, conventionalized features and, in addition, enables us to look at grammar in academic discourse based on complete texts, rather than text excerpts (compare Section 9.1).

As described above, a genre is often defined by its rhetorical organization, and one feature of the abstract is that its structure typically mirrors the conventionalized "packaging" of the research process that we also observe in many research article introductions (Atkinson 1992). One well-known model for describing an introduction is the **CARS model** (Swales 1990, 2004), named after the acronym for 'Creating A Research Space' and consisting of three so-called rhetorical "moves:" (1) establishing a research territory, where a scientist sets the context for the research, (2) establishing a niche, which is the space of knowledge to be filled through the new research, and (3) occupying this niche by announcing a research space that the publication is going to fill (Swales 1990: 141). Many abstracts have a similar organization and a corresponding typical pattern of syntactic variation.

Let us turn to an example and look at the abstract in (5) (a text you may be familiar with because it was shown in Exercise 6 of Chapter 2):

(5)    In this paper *we analyse* variable presence of the complementizer that, i.e. I think that/Ø this is interesting, in a large archive of British dialects. Situating this feature within its historical development and synchronic patterning, *we seek to understand* the mechanism underlying the choice between that and zero. *Our findings reveal* that, in contrast to the diachronic record, the zero option is predominant – 91 percent overall. *Statistical analyses of competing factors operating on this feature confirm* that grammaticalization processes and grammatical complexity play a role. (Tagliamonte & Smith, 2005)

As you can see, the abstract in (5) is structured closely in accordance with the CARS model. The text starts out by presenting the research topic (*variable presence of the complementizer* that), then turns to its research question (*the mechanism underlying the choice between that and zero*) and moves on to saying how this will be done, announcing *findings* and *analyses*. With that structure, (5) has what is currently the typical, conventional structure for the genre of abstracts.

What is also typical of the genre is the combination of presenting these moves with corresponding verbs of argumentation (*analyze, understand, confirm*). These verbs reflect an important property of modern science writing that can be described as "shaping" scientific knowledge, rather than just noting a discovery of findings (Bazerman

1988). What scientists nowadays do with their texts is both present their observations and provide an argument. While early science still had a focus on "facts over arguments" (Gross et al. 2002: 19), modern scientific texts are part of an ongoing scientific debate, which has a social component as well. The publication process and the genre are significant both for the scientist and for the discipline, a property that brought forth and certainly strengthened the role of the abstract as a genre.

You will have noted, though, that none of the three argumentative moves in (5) makes use of the passive voice. Considering the attention that the passive often gets both in style manuals and academic writing classes, this outcome may result from the fact that academics are typically criticized there for overusing the passive. But what are the alternatives? What we find in the abstract in (5) is the pattern that you saw in (1), the agented active (*I found, we see, I think, we argue*): It is used twice in the text (*we analyze, we seek to understand*). The abstract also contains a sentence in which an inanimate noun phrase is the grammatical subject of an active, agentive verb (*our findings reveal, our analyses confirm*). This sentence pattern makes the facts speak for themselves and moves the researcher more into the background. By contrast, the passive, as illustrated by (3) and (4), is not attested here. As discussed in Chapter 4, the passive would move the former object into the topic position (*the presence of . . . is analyzed*) or, alternatively, it could take *it* as a non-referential, "dummy" subject (*it is analyzed that . . .*). Both passive constructions would minimize the visibility of the researcher, turning them into an implicit agent (as explained in Section 4.3.1).

Table 9.1 provides a summary of the two active voice and the passive voice patterns available for dealing with the agent role of the scientist in a science text.

Table 9.1 *Three clause patterns of an argumentative utterance in scientific discourse*

| *I/we argue that . . .* | *It is argued that . . .* | *The findings/The paper . . . argue(s) that . . .* |
|---|---|---|
| agented active voice | passive voice with implicit agent | active voice with inanimate subject |

264 *Grammar and Genre*

Turning to abstracts with regard to this aspect of grammar, one finds that writers in science tend to use the strategy shown in the third column of Table 9.1, that is, they make use of the active voice, but often avoid direct reference to themselves as an explicit agent. For example, in a study that we carried out ourselves, we analyzed 160 abstracts from eight different disciplines (twenty abstracts per discipline) and looked at all clauses containing an argumentative verb (like *suggest, conclude, propose, argue, ...*). The most important finding was that, with a few rare exceptions, these verbs occurred in all of the abstracts. The other outcome was that the verbs were often used without a first-person subject (Dorgeloh & Wanner 2009). Figure 9.2 gives you the results in detail for four different academic disciplines. What is shown on the *y*-axis is the absolute number of argumentative events in the corpus with their different realizations (note that passives include both short and *by*-passives).

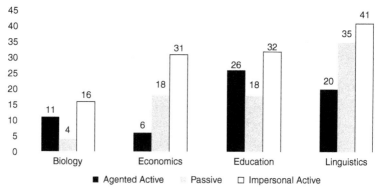

Figure 9.2 Scientific argumentation in abstracts from different disciplines
Data is from Dorgeloh & Wanner 2009.

Figure 9.2 illustrates that, within that corpus of abstracts, an active voice clause with an inanimate subject was more common than either an agented active clause or the passive voice. The data also shows that the use of these strategies varies to a certain extent across academic disciplines. Clauses for explicit argumentation are overall more common in the humanities and the social sciences (this is also in part due to the fact that the abstracts here are often longer), but they also have a stronger preference for an inanimate subject (the agented active accounts for 35.5 percent of all clauses in biology, but only for 10.9 percent in economics and 23.7 percent in linguistics). Another interesting finding from that study was that, in the humanities and the social sciences (such as linguistics, education, or economics), the inanimate subject was often a metatextual entity, something like *paper* or *article* (like in *this paper argues*, *this article analyzes*). By contrast, in an experiment-based science like biology, other types of inanimate subjects (*these/this data*, *these results*) prevailed.

Based on such findings, we learn that, for the expression of agentivity, the abstract as a genre allows for a considerable amount of syntactic variation within a text and, as we have seen, across disciplines. There are also sometimes preferences of individual authors or journals. Both the range of variation and the preference of a single author is what we find in the text in (6), which is from the same journal as (5), but in which the writer consistently uses the passive voice.

(6)  In this article various constructions of English with the form A + N *are considered*, with particular reference to stress patterns. *It is shown* that there are several such patterns, and that stress patterns do not correlate with fixed effects. *It is also argued* that a simple division between compound and phrase does not seem to provide a motivation for the patterns found. The patterns seem *to be determined* partly by factors *which are known* to influence stress patterns in N + N constructions, and partly by lexical class, though variability in which expression belongs to which class *is acknowledged*. *It is concluded* that this is an area of English grammar that needs further research. (Bauer 2020)

Despite this outcome on the range of variation, it can still be generalized that abstracts without any overt kind of argumentative statement are rare (Dorgeloh & Wanner 2003). Imagine the abstract above without reporting verbs; it could just as well be a Wikipedia entry. If the explicit argumentative moves are not present, the purpose and typical organization of the abstract are not established, that is, what is *typical* of the genre would be missing.

Exercise 3 provides an opportunity to identify the different strategies for dealing with agentivity in abstracts from different academic disciplines that we have just discussed.

## 9.3.2  *Noun Phrase and Phrasal Complexity*

Let us now turn to another widely discussed grammatical property of
the register we have to expect in an abstract. As discussed in Section
9.2, sentence complexity is a property which most people believe to
distinguish speech from writing and, in particular, expect to encounter
in academic texts. And while it is certainly true that we find many
written texts that contain long and complex sentences, at a closer
look, dependent clauses as such often turn out to be more common in
speech than in writing (Biber & Gray 2010). For example, we can note
that the first sentence of the abstract in (5), repeated below as (7),
contains no dependent clause at all, which could be reformulated as
in (8):

(7)   In this paper we analyze variable presence of the complementizer *that*,
      i.e. *I think that/Ø this is interesting*, in a large archive of British
      dialects.

(8)   We will analyze under which circumstances the complementizer *that* is
      present and will discuss to what extent its presence is variable, and we
      will look at data that comes from a large archive of British dialects.

Example (8) is a sentence with three embedded clauses whereas the
clause in (7) is, technically speaking, just a simple main clause. By
contrast, in (7) it is the noun phrase introducing the research topic
that is more complex: *variable presence of the complementizer that* is
both premodified (*variable*) and postmodified (*of the complementizer
that*), that is, it exemplifies complexity both within the noun phrase and
of a phrasal kind. By contrast, in (8), the noun phrases referring to the
topic (*the complementizer* that, *its presence*) are simple, that is, with no
embedded, modifying phrases. When exploring grammatical complexity as a feature of scientific texts, we therefore focus on complexity
within the noun phrase rather than within the clause.

  Embedding within the noun phrase is generally a characteristic of
highly informational and, in particular, scientific genres and registers.
Abstracts with their need for the distillation and condensation of
information (Section 9.2 above) are prone to making use of such
structures, resulting from syntactic compression rather than elaboration
(Biber & Gray 2010, 2011; see also Biber & Conrad 2019: ch. 6). For
example, (8) is more elaborate with finite, tensed verbs and explicit
clausal relations (*under which circumstances*, *to what extent*) while, in

(7), the information in the form of noun phrases is more compressed. It is packaged into phrases rather than clauses, with phrasal (rather than clausal) structures also within the phrase (e.g., *variable presence of the complementizer* being a phrase *and* one with a prepositional phrase as modifier). Complex noun phrases of that type can be expected to be common in abstracts since they are part of the register in which those are written.

What would be the research design for exploring that assumption more closely? Since there is no simple syntactic or lexical marker corresponding to complexity, we will have to look at different patterns that make a noun phrase more complex. We therefore first need to refer to the overall structure of the noun phrase. A noun phrase is defined by its nominal head and, in case this head is a lexical noun, not a pronoun, has four major components. Two of these components are optional, functioning as modifier or complement to the head noun. The examples in Table 9.2 illustrate these four components.

Table 9.2 *Components of noun phrase structure*

| Class | Determiner | Premodifier | Head | Postmodifier | Example |
|---|---|---|---|---|---|
| 1 | + | | + | | *these implications* |
| 2 | + | + | + | | *these important physical implications* |
| 3 | + | | + | + | *the implications of Miller's famous formula* |
| 4 | + | + | + | + | *the full implications of Darwin's revolution* |

Table 9.2 gives us a system for analyzing and classifying noun phrase complexity, which is also applied in other studies (Schaub 2016; Schilk & Schaub 2016). According to this system, Class 1 noun phrases are NPs with no modification, including pronouns and proper nouns, Class 2 are premodified NPs, Class 3 are postmodified NPs, and, finally, class 4 includes all NPs that are both pre- and postmodified. Before returning

to the genre of abstracts, let us take a short look at the occurrence of these noun phrase types in the academic register in general.

Figure 9.3 is based on a study by Schaub (2016), who sampled 8,000 noun phrases from academic texts in the humanities and three other registers. Note that the data is not based on US American or British English, but that the texts came from different regional varieties of English (Canadian, Indian, Jamaican, Hong Kong, and Singapore English). The chart shows the complexity of noun phrases in the proportions of the four classes that we derived from Table 9.2. For a more precise description of the method of collecting noun phrases for such an analysis, see the toolbox below.

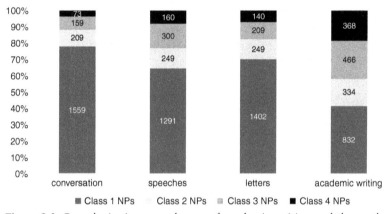

**Figure 9.3** Complexity in noun phrases of academic writing and three other registers
The chart represents the distribution of 8,000 NPs classified by the system in Table 9.2; data is from Schaub 2016.

Figure 9.3 shows that only around 40 percent of the noun phrases in academic writing are simple noun phrases and that around 60 percent contain at least one modifier. It also shows that, in the academic register, about 20 percent of all the noun phrases belong to Class 4, that is, are both premodified and postmodified. This outcome is in clear contrast to all the other registers, which all have more than 50 percent simple, that is, unmodified, noun phrases. We can conclude that complex, in the sense of more modified, noun phrases are clearly more common in the academic register (in the varieties that were examined).

Studying Noun Phrase Complexity Based on a Sample
of Attestations

It is usually not possible to extract all noun phrases from an
(unparsed) corpus, which is why the data we discuss in this box
result from a different procedure (Schilk & Schaub 2016). The data
shown in Figure 9.3 is based on a given *sample* of noun phrases as it
was found in a corpus of texts, and not on the occurrence of different noun phrase types per register (which would be their text-
linguistic variation). Here, with the same amount of noun phrases
from each register, the researcher is able to determine the different
proportions of the types of noun phrases as presented in Table 9.2.

When producing the database for such an analysis, there are a few
important steps to be followed. First, you need to compile a corpus
with a given number of (randomly chosen) texts of one or several
genres (several texts are needed because it is necessary to represent a
genre as fully as possible). Next, in each text you now search
manually for a given number of the first (for example, 400) NPs, a
procedure leading you to your preliminary database. Since you
should also minimize the possible effect of different text sections,
in which noun phrase complexity may not be distributed evenly, you
then produce a random sample of *x* (for example, 150) NPs out of
that initial collection, giving you your final database. These NPs
then have to be categorized according to the four classes provided by
Table 9.2. You will have the opportunity to practice this method in
Exercise 9 (Level 2).

With Figure 9.3, we have looked at the pattern of syntactic variation
within the noun phrase as depending on the register. The pattern we
have discerned is that noun phrases are clearly more complex in academic writing (and, with that, in all likelihood also in abstracts) when
compared to other registers.

Since, with the procedure we have described, we look at percentages
based on a given set of noun phrases, let us emphasize again that the
resulting observations are not directly about a case of text-linguistic
variation. As explained in Section 2.5 and at several points throughout
this book, a proper look at register variation would have to be based on

the actual frequencies of different noun phrase types in a corpus, for example, the frequency of simple versus modified noun phrases, or of phrasal compared to clausal modifiers. For example, in that text-linguistic tradition, it has been found that the average (i.e., normalized) frequency of premodifying nouns and adjectives and of postmodifying prepositional phrases is considerably higher than the one of clausal modifiers, that is, relative clauses (Biber & Gray 2010: 8). Also, it has been observed that especially the relative density of NN-strings, that is, the use of nouns as modifiers (e.g., in (6) *stress patterns*, rather than *patterns of stress*), has steadily increased in the development of academic genres (Biber & Gray 2011, 2016). While this section has introduced you to the method of studying noun phrase complexity based on sampled noun phrases, there is also a wealth of data available on the text-linguistic variation in this area. This data could provide you with the different rates of usage of the different aspects of noun phrase structure and would enable you to look at their frequency relative to the length of the text or corpus. For publications in this area, see Further Reading at the end of this chapter.

Turn to Exercises 4 and 5 for classifying noun phrases and observing the different types of noun phrase complexity in texts. Exercise 9 (Level 2) asks you to produce your own sample of noun phrases for a comparison of noun phrase complexity across genres.

## 9.4  Register Features of Digital Discourse

### 9.4.1  *Digital Discourse as an Environment for Linguistic Innovation*

In Section 9.2 we discussed the distinction between spoken and written language from a medial as well as a conceptual perspective, building on a distinction by Koch & Oesterreicher (1985). Little could Koch and Oesterreicher have known at the time how much the boundaries between spoken and written language would be blurred by the rapid success of what was called "the new media." It may be hard to imagine now, but in

1985, business communication did not happen through e-mail or Slack channels. Nobody carried a cell phone or began their day by checking their social media accounts, and the word *text* was mostly used as a noun. People who wanted to buy a toaster or book a hotel could not easily read reviews written by other customers. Families did not communicate in WhatsApp groups, customer service representatives did not communicate via online chats, and politicians did not announce campaign events on Twitter. What all these forms of communication have in common is that they use medially written language in a way that often reminds us more of spoken discourse (in a 2013 TED talk, linguist John McWhorter memorably referred to texting as "fingered speech;" McWhorter 2013). Text messages, tweets, and chat messages are often produced without much planning or editing; online discourse is transient, has interpersonal functions, and shows grammatical characteristics of spoken language, such as the use of sentence fragments, first- and second-person pronouns, and frequent turn-taking. Medially, however, the language used in digital discourses, also known as "computer-mediated communication," is written, which is a setting normally associated with more formal language. From the get-go, linguists who studied the language of digital registers discussed if computer-mediated communication has brought about linguistic formats that are truly new and could only exist in the digital environment, and how these formats use existing mechanisms in new patterns. Linguists have also addressed the perception that the spread of digital writing leads to a loss of grammatical abilities, especially in young people (for details, see our Good to Know box at the end of Section 9.4.3).

In his book *Language and the Internet*, first published in 2007 (the year the first iPhone was released and one year after Twitter was founded), David Crystal coined the term "netspeak" for the kind of language used in digital discourse. The term suggests that digital discourse is truly of its own kind – not spoken, not written, but merging characteristics of both spoken and written language, "a genuine third medium" (Crystal 2007: 52). This line of thinking has shifted toward a consensus that the language used in digital discourse is as heterogeneous as the language of conventionally spoken or written discourse, and research questions around digital discourse have moved from cataloguing digital genres and their linguistic characteristics to questions about the impact of digital communication on language development (Squires 2016) and the nature of human interaction (Turkle 2015).

In this section, we want to focus on two innovations brought about or sped up by digital registers: **hashtags** as an innovation resulting from the technological affordances of the digital medium and the *because* X construction as an innovation based on an existing grammatical element (*because* as a syntactic subordinator and preposition with limited complementation). Hashtags can be seen in the tradition of digital registers to use spelling and punctuation creatively to set a "typographical tone of voice" (McCulloch 2019: 109). These typographical choices include the omission of letters (*tmrw*, "tomorrow") simply to shorten words, the lengthening of words (*yesssssss*) to add emphasis, as well as the creative use of punctuation marks. Sometimes the extra message lies in the absence of a feature rather than in its presence. In short text messages, it is common not to put a period at the end of the utterance. Ending a sentence with a period in this type of discourse sends a message beyond just signaling the end of a syntactic unit. Often, the use of a period at the end of a text is interpreted as a somewhat aggressive declaration that the speaker is done with engaging. To check if this interpretation holds across registers or is tied specifically to digital discourse, Gunraj et al. (2016) compared the use of periods at the end of utterances in texts and handwritten notes. They presented participants with one-line text messages and handwritten notes (*Wanna come?*) and answers that either included or didn't include a period (*Sure./Sure*). They found that the presence of a period led to the perception of the message as less sincere in texts (but not in handwritten notes) and concluded that in digital discourse standard punctuation marks are indeed used in innovative, pragmatically meaningful ways.

### 9.4.2 *Hashtags: #informationpackaging #coolstuff*

Unlike the period or exclamation mark, hashtags have their origin in digital discourse. They were originally developed to tag the general topic of a message on microblogging platforms and to facilitate the organizing of groups on Twitter (former Google employee Chris Messina is usually credited as the person who introduced the hashtag to Twitter in 2007). The hashtag consists of the pound sign (#) – also known as the number sign outside the US – followed by linguistic material. Hashtags can be individual words, acronyms, phrases, or full sentences. They may or may not be integrated into the syntax of the message. Depending on the platform, the number of hashtags per message can be limited. This sounds as if there is not a lot of order around hashtags, but linguists have identified several distinct functions performed by hashtags. Based on a study of a 100-million-word Twitter corpus, Zappavigna (2015) recognizes three main functions of hashtags: textual, experiential, and interpersonal. The textual function is to organize a post and to convey metadata status to a word or phrase, that is, to make the word or phrase searchable. At the typographical level, this happens through using the # symbol, which Zappavigna considers a form of punctuation. The hashtag may be integrated into the syntax of the post, as in (9), or it may be added at the beginning or end, as in (10). Using textual hashtags is built on the assumption that other people might search for posts on a specific topic and might use the same hashtags.

(9)    Myself and #GeorgeClooney on set @Nespresso commercial!!!
       (Twitter, @NickyWhelan, 2015)

(10)   #sandiegofire 300,000 people evacuated in San Diego County now
       (Twitter, @nateritter, 2007)

The experiential function of a hashtag is to say what the post is about, which is another way of saying that hashtags can serve the same function as verbal topic markers and topic-marking constructions, such as topicalization and left-dislocation (as discussed in Chapter 3). What we see here, then, is that a tool afforded by the digital environment provides an innovative way to package the information in a text. Crucially, the hashtag does not only serve the function to establish the topic of the discourse, it also helps create "searchable talk" as a way to enact "ambient community" (Zappavigna 2015: 280) – it enables individuals to affiliate with other people on Twitter who are interested in the same things they are. This function of hashtags also plays an important role in marketing campaigns, like *#ShareACoke* by Coca Cola. Finally, the interpersonal function of hashtags is to add stance to a post and thus enact a relationship with the ambient audience, as in (11).

(11)   @easyJet so I gather my flight tomorrow is cancelled for tomorrow to
       Sharm. No email yet or message sent #madashell (Twitter,
       @NickyUser, 2015)

Here, the hashtag *#madashell* does not have the function to identify the post as one about the topic "mad as hell," rather, it is a concise way (only ten characters) to add a level of commentary (namely that the writer is "mad as hell") to the post about a delayed flight. Zappavigna notes that interpersonal hashtags often are very long and specific *(#SocialMediaIsNotAsImportantAsYouThinkItIsKyle)* and can thus counteract the original aggregating function of hashtags.

The popularity of hashtags is reflected in the election of the word *hashtag* as Word of the Year 2014 by the American Dialect Society and in the election of the hashtag *#blacklivesmatter* as Word of the Year

two years later. Ben Zimmer, chair of the ADS New Words Committee, conceded at the time that "#blacklivesmatter may not fit the traditional definition of a word," but he argued that the hashtag deserved to be considered because it was a forceful example of linguistic innovation (American Dialect Society 2015).

And forceful hashtags certainly are: They have spread not only beyond the borders of Twitter, but also beyond the context of digital media and even medially written registers. As stated above, they are used in marketing campaigns, not only on social media, but also in print, as well as in spoken discourse, where they cannot have the same range of functions as in digital formats.

Using the word *hashtag* in spoken discourse to perform the textual function of actual hashtags can easily come across as comical, as in the following excerpt in (12), taken from the award-winning Canadian comedy show *Schitt's Creek* (Season 6, Episode 2, first aired in 2020). Moira Rose, a soap opera actress trying to revive her career via connecting with fans on social media, is entering a store that is co-owned by her son David Rose and his fiancé, Patrick, who gently points out to her that she is not using the word *hashtag* correctly.

(12)  MOIRA (holding up her      Bongiorno, boys!
       cell phone, recording):
       DAVID:                   Oh no!
       MOIRA:                   Say hello to all my hashtag "frands!" It's a
                                little word I assembled to consecrate my
                                fans, who are also my friends.

| | |
|---|---|
| DAVID: | Okay, "frands" doesn't sound nice. |
| MOIRA: | To all of you asking "What is this little mercantile establishment with the almost gallery-like austerity?" Well, it so happens it's also owned by my son, David Rose. Say hi, David . . . |
| DAVID: | Okay, I would rather not, thanks. |
| MOIRA: | . . . and his hashtag fiancé, Patrick. |
| PATRICK: | I don't think you have to say "hashtag" when you're just talking, Mrs. Rose. |

(Schitt's Creek 2020)

Overall, we see that hashtags are a linguistic innovation that has been brought about by the digital medium. They serve a range of functions, some of them inherent to the medium, others of a more general kind, like packaging information.

> You should now be able to address Exercise 6, which asks you to consider different types of hashtags.

## 9.4.3 Because X: *A New Chapter in a Preposition's Life*

While hashtags are a linguistic innovation that could only have started in digital discourse, due to the embedded technology, digital registers also contribute to the spread of constructions that align with patterns of language change which are not contingent on a particular register, but which may be favored by the situational settings of digital discourse. One such construction is the spread of a new(-ish) complementation pattern after *because*. The "old" *because* falls into one of the following two classes: Either it is a conjunction that introduces a finite clause, as in (13) and (14), or it behaves as a preposition that must be followed by another PP, introduced by *of*, as in (15). (Alternatively, one might analyze the sequence *because of* as a complex preposition. For our discussion here it does not really matter which analysis is applied.)

(13)    Neal, are you here tomorrow? *Because* we're making a Costco run. (COCA, TV, 2014)

(14)    We picked this postcard out for you *because* you look like Pluto.
        (COCA, Spoken, 1992)

(15)    Austen's Mrs. Bennet can be seen as a woman given over to frivolity
        partly *because of* her husband's lack of interest in her character.
        (COCA, Academic, 1993)

The "new" *because*, or, more precisely, the new use of *because*, differs
from these uses in that it can be followed by a noun phrase (or even a
bare noun), as in (16a)–(16c), an adjective or adjective phrase, as in
(17), or an interjection, as in (18). The following examples are all from
Twitter:

(16)    a.  I had my FB disabled *because reasons* (@AmbuloKing, 2021)
        b.  I just ordered lots of Chinese dumplings, *because NYC!!*
            (@AnitaTimeOut, 2021)
        c.  Ok minirant. Been travelling since the last 2 days. First of all, I cant
            stop to eat *because* covid (@honey_crypt, 2021)

(17)    Then I make plans and cancel .... *because tired* (@CupidsAaro, 2021)

(18)    Wow. The arrogance. The selfishness. The greed. The sheer audacity.
        Millions of people either haven't gotten vaccinated yet or don't plan
        to at all but yes let's rush back to normal *because yay!*
        (@FierceAssSistah, 2021)

Because of the syntactic variability of the linguistic material after
*because*, Bohmann (2016), whose corpus-based study we explain in
more detail below, refers to examples like (16)–(18) as the *because X*
complementation. What all *because X* instances have in common is
that they are shorter than the more traditional uses of *because*. In many
cases, as in the examples above, X in *because X* consists of only one
word (*because reasons, because tired, because yay*). In this way,
*because X* is a form of complementation that aligns with several
language change trends that have been identified for the development
of Modern English well before the arrival of Twitter (Leech et al. 2009):
(a) densification (using fewer words or fewer characters to express the
same thing – think *delish* and *natch* instead of *delicious* and *naturally*);
(b) a shift of written language to incorporating constructions more
characteristic of spoken language (shorter constructions, for example,
fewer modifiers, fewer passive constructions, and more ellipsis); and (c)
a spread of constructions identified as Americanisms, such as the

spread of the mandative subjunctive (*They demanded that he leave*). With these trends in mind, it makes sense to expect that posts on Twitter, with its limitations on number of characters, its high frequency of non-standard spellings and punctuation that is so characteristic of digital discourse, and its high number of users from the United States are a fertile ground for the spread of *because X*. In a variationist study based on about 12,000 tweets containing the word *because,* Bohmann (2016) found that *because X* occurred almost as often as *because of* (6.3 percent vs. 7.7 percent of all tokens), but both occurred much more rarely than *because* as a conjunction, see Figure 9.4.

In 38.8 percent of *because X* cases (*because reasons*), X was a noun *(because reasons)*, in 9.8 percent an adjective (*because tired*). The remainder was made up of interjections, clause fragments, hashtags, hyperlinks, adverbs, and emoji. For a second step in his analysis, however, Bohmann decided to conceptualize the use of *because X* as a binary choice between the traditional use of *because* (*because* + clause, *because* + *of*) and the new use of *because*.

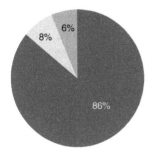

■ clause    because of   ■ because X

**Figure 9.4** *Because* complementation
Data is from Bohmann 2016.

In this second step Bohmann examined if there was any correlation between the choice of *because X* (over one of the traditional uses of *because*) and high scores in terms of linguistic density, colloquialness, proficiency as Twitter user (based on metrics such as use of hashtags, @-mentions, number of followers, frequency of postings), and geo-graphical origin of tweets. In order to do this, he had to operationalize linguistic density and colloquialness, which is tricky because some of the relevant linguistic markers cannot easily be parsed automatically. For density, he relied on factors like the shortening of the word *because,* length of the tweet, mean word length, and noun-verb ratio (a higher noun-verb ratio contributes to a denser text); for colloquialness, he used an established formula for measuring how context-dependent a text is, as measured through part-of-speech frequencies as well as the non-standard spelling of *because* (*coz, cos, bc*), which mimics the low degree of formality characteristic of spoken language. The home country of the user was established by checking the user's Twitter profile. The expectation was that one would see the central position American English holds in the development of written English would be reflected in higher numbers of *because X* used by speakers from the US.

What Bohmann found was that the three most significant predictors for *because X* all related to density: length of tweet, mean word length, choice of *coz/cos/bc* over the longer form *because* (obviously, all shortened forms of *because* are also non-standard forms of *because*). A discourse that favors short, compact utterances is an environment that favors the choice of *because X*, although not to the extent that *because X* becomes the dominant form. Bohmann did not find a clear correlation between a low formality score and a preference for *because X* (less formal tweets actually showed a preference for a clausal complementation pattern). With regard to digital discourse proficiency, he found that the metrics he included to determine a proficiency score did not uniformly behave as predictors for the use of *because X*. Lastly, he did not find confirmation for the hypothesis that *because X* is most popular in the US. He concluded that Twitter as an "inherently dense format" is "an ideal environment for a newly emerging, metalinguistically salient, and economical construction like *because X*" (Bohmann 2016: 170 f.). Unlike the hashtag, *because X* is not contingent on the digital medium, but the settings of the digital discourse favor its use.

There is a lot, of course, that this study did not address. For example, Bohmann only looked at the shortening of *because*, since this was a word that occurred in all tweets under examination. He did not look at other shortened words, mainly because this would require extensive manual coding (for example, someone might spell *tomorrow* as *tmrw* or *tw*, but how would the software know that, considering that shortened forms could be idiosyncratic). There is also no consideration of linguistic markers beyond parts of speech that are characteristic of informal language. For example, it might be interesting to look at whether or not tweets that use *because* X contain fewer passives and fewer modifiers than tweets that use *because of*. Referring back to the distinction we have used throughout this book, Bohmann's study took a variationist perspective, that is, he looked at the impact of the discourse medium on the choice of *because* variant. We should note that this does not necessarily mean that *because* X is more pervasive in the register he studied than in others, that is, his results do not reflect a text-linguistic perspective.

As with any empirical study, one always has to balance out the desire for a broad data basis with the feasibility of the analysis. This is something that by now you will have seen in your own empirical projects. Still, what we can observe is how digital registers, especially those that put limits on the length of texts, can amplify existing trends toward compact expressions, even at the level of complementation after a functional category such as a preposition – not normally the most fertile ground for linguistic innovation. In January 2014 the American Dialect Society crowned the new *because* Word of the Year 2013 – because useful!

You should now be able to handle Exercise 7, which asks you to retrieve *because* X constructions from a corpus (which is harder than it sounds).

Good to Know: Texting Doesn't Ruin Your Grammar!

Many people are concerned that extensive texting – with its characteristic truncated syntax, acronyms, and alternative spellings, also known as "textisms" – has a negative impact on children's ability to use standard syntax and spelling and to express complex ideas. In 2006, many politicians and pundits ridiculed a decision by the Scottish Qualifications Authority not to penalize students for using elements of texting language in their English high school exams, which had made waves internationally. Others, including the British national newspaper *The Guardian,* praised the SQA as "champions of reason."

Is there any way to determine who is right? In 2016, a team of Dutch linguists and child development specialists (van Dijk et al. 2016) attempted just that. They set out to test empirically if heavy use of texting influenced children's grammar performance as well as their executive functions in general (for example, the ability to disregard irrelevant or distracting information). In their experimental study, they elicited text messages from fifty-five Dutch 5th and 6th graders and also collected text messages produced by the students in a natural setting. They then looked at the number of "textisms" used (including unconventional spelling and words borrowed from English) as well as the number of omitted words. In order to determine children's grammar abilities, participants underwent a standardized vocabulary test (they had to point to a picture that corresponded to the word said by the experimenter) as well as a sentence repetition task. You may think that just repeating a sentence tells you more about someone's memory than their grammar abilities, but psycholinguistic research has established that in order to repeat utterances longer than one or two words, speakers must use their syntactic knowledge to parse the sentence before they repeat it. The Dutch team found that there was a clear relationship between the frequency of using word omission and participants' grammar abilities – in a positive way. The more the students utilized word omission in their texts, the better they performed in the repetition task. The researchers interpreted this result as a sign that omitting the right kind of word in a text requires syntactic knowledge and that heavy users of texting constantly train their grammar system in ways that other people don't. (The relationship between use of other linguistic features related to texting language – alternative spelling etc. – and grammar abilities was less clear.)

The study was carried out based on data from Dutch, but there is no reason to believe that the results are language specific. We can think of *textese* as a genre-based language variety – and the more often speakers have to switch from one variety to another, the more they train their grammar awareness. In other words, texting does not ruin your grammar, it sharpens your sense of it.

## 9.5 Summary

In this chapter, we have introduced you to grammatical patterns in discourse that are tied to the situational settings as well as the conventions of a particular genre. Such patterns may be either pervasive (such as the use of passive voice in scientific abstracts) or typical (such as the use of hashtags in tweets). We saw that some of these patterns can be explained by considering the modality of the discourse situation. Writing often, but not exclusively, happens in situations that allow for planning and editing, speaking is often, but not exclusively, linked to situations in which utterances are produced spontaneously, in turns, and without much planning. As a prototypical written genre, we discussed the scientific abstract and specifically looked at the linguistic representation of agentivity. We saw that the needs of a discipline to background the involvement of human agents in experiments can lead to innovative constructions, such as the active voice with impersonal, metatextual subjects (*this paper argues* ...). We also examined the way in which scientific genres handle the need to condense information without losing precision, namely through syntactic compression in noun phrases rather than through elaboration in subordinate clauses. We then turned to a discussion of where digital genres fit on the continuum of conceptually spoken vs. written language and which linguistic features may be brought about or favored by the register of digital discourses. Specifically, we discussed how hashtags combine both innovative and traditional functions of structuring the discourse and that social media platforms with character limits are a particularly fertile ground for densifications like the *because* X construction. In this way, we showed that digital genres, while opening new avenues for the features of a register, are not of a completely different kind and fit the overall pattern of language variation to serve the needs of the discourse.

## 9.6 Exercises

### *Level 1: Classification and Application*

1. Classify the following situations in which discourse is produced making use of the distinction between medially and conceptually oral or written language.

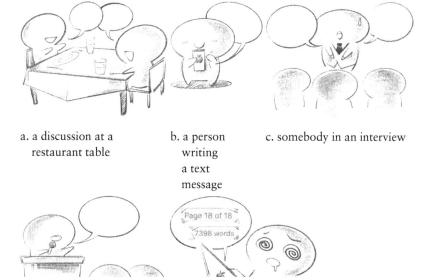

a. a discussion at a     b. a person         c. somebody in an interview
   restaurant table         writing
                            a text
                            message

d. a person delivering    e. somebody writing and carefully editing a text
   a speech

2. Classify the two text excerpts below, both taken from discourse that was published online (the excerpts are from the CORE corpus). Identify grammatical features that we discussed in Section 9.2 as typically occurring in speech or in writing. Discuss your findings in the light of the role of the medium as determining a register. Which features have more to do with other aspects of the discourse situation, such as the purpose of the text, or the expected audience?

A. Hello all, I hope some can offer me some advice? Sorry if this is a long post but really don't know where to turn. I have a dog called Frankie, who is 5.5 years old. He came to live with me when he was 1, after his original owners (who I knew through work) had twins and said they couldn't give him the attention he needed. It now turns out they lied and he didn't like the babies, strangers or other dogs but chose not to tell me. He is a Jack Russell cross with some other small dog, not sure what! Frankie has always had anxiety/ aggression issues . . .. (CORE, Interactive Discussion, 2012)

B. Frank claims he has a nice apartment. Was brought up to believe the two most important things in life are family and friends. He goes to the track 3–4 times a year. He has never seen a shrink, does not have a drinking problem nor has he taken any drugs. Likes milk and sugar in his coffee. Was 25 years old at the time of the first season. Can breakdance. Has a grandmother. Hangs out a Panama Joes alot – to see twins. He once got bitten by a dog. He gets sick by meat factories. If he ever has a kid, he will name it Eddie. Disgusted by the sport of boxing. Uses Sprat deodorant. He has not given any thought about his own funeral arrangements. His stomach has coreners. Is crazy about Lana Turner. Was a good student, always did his homework. He likes dogs. Played High School hockey. Alleges his sisters name is Jenny (but in another episode he claims he has no sister). (CORE, Description of a person, undated)

3. In Section 9.3, we discuss three different strategies for dealing with the expression of agentivity in scientific abstracts. Analyze the three abstracts below for the occurrence of these strategies. Which ones do you find, and how much variation is there within each text? Do you find a difference that may be related to the last abstract coming from a different discipline?

C. This article introduces a quantitative method for identifying newly emerging word forms in large time-stamped corpora of natural language and then describes an analysis of lexical emergence in American social media using this method, based on a multi-billion-word corpus of Tweets collected between October 2013 and November 2014. In total 29 emerging word forms, which represent various semantic classes, grammatical parts-of-speech and word formation processes, were identified through this analysis. These 29 forms are then examined from various perspectives in order to begin to better understand the process of lexical emergence. (Grieve et al. 2017)

D.  In this paper we analyse variable presence of the complement-izer *that*, i.e. *I think that/Øthis is interesting*, in a large archive of British dialects. Situating this feature within its historical development and synchronic patterning, we seek to understand the mechanism underlying the choice between *that* and zero. Our findings reveal that, in contrast to the diachronic record, the zero option is predominant – 91 percent overall. Statistical analyses of competing factors operating on this feature confirm that grammaticalization processes and grammatical complexity play a role. However, the linguistic characteristics of a previously grammaticalized collocation, I think, exerts a greater effect. Its imprint is visible in multiple internal factors which constrain the zero option in the other contexts. We argue that this recurrent pattern in discourse propels the zero option through the grammar. These findings contribute to research arguing for a strong relationship between frequency and reanalysis in linguistic change. (Tagliamonte & Smith 2005)

E.  From 1932 to 1973, Chicago women who wanted to avoid the high costs and impersonal treatment of the city's maternity wards had another option: they could choose to give birth at home, attended by obstetricians and nurses of the Chicago Maternity Center (CMC). As the rest of the nation moved toward the hospital as the normalized place of delivery, low-income white women and women of color in Chicago continued

> to assert not only their preference for home birth but also their demand for affordable, dignified, and family-centered care. When the CMC was threatened with closure, women from diverse backgrounds joined together to save this alternative maternity option. This article explores how these Chicago mothers resisted hospitalization and asserted their right to choose home birth years before the women's health movement offered a similar critique. (Lewis 2018)

4. The noun phrases below were retrieved from texts written by academic authors in the natural sciences. Classify the noun phrases using the classification scheme we introduced in Section 9.3.2 for the different degrees of noun phrase complexity (simple, premodified, postmodified, pre- and postmodified). Which noun phrases have other noun phrases embedded within them and could therefore be analyzed further for noun phrase complexity?

| Attested noun phrase | Type of NP |
| --- | --- |
| *a large number of experimental and theoretical studies* | |
| *actual experimental applications* | |
| *the general theory of magnetic resonance line shape* | |
| *the theory* | |
| *the density matrix for the system at a temperature T* | |
| *the efficiency of energy transfer* | |
| *the expansion* | |
| *the strong interaction* | |
| *the extra energy in its electric field* | |
| *strong interaction effects in our experiments* | |
| *the magnetic field dependence of the rate at which energy is absorbed from the electromagnetic field by a spin system* | |
| *a manner that efficiently meshes with our F-flatness constraints* | |

5. Using the same classification scheme for noun phrase complexity as in Exercise 4, analyze the abstracts from Exercise 3 as a text corpus. Collect a sample of thirty noun phrases and determine the proportions of the four different classes. Note: You should only analyze first-level noun phrases, i.e., no noun phrases that are embedded in another noun phrase (for instance, if *a quantitative method for identifying newly emerging word forms* is the second NP in text C., *newly emerging word forms* should not be taken as a separate NP).

6. In Section 9.4.2 we discussed different functions that hashtags can take. Apply the three functions that were introduced to the tweets below while also paying attention to the position of the hashtag in the tweet. Is there any relationship between the two?

Tweet 1: On this World Health Day, let's pledge that we'll prioritize our health above all – be it Mental or Physical Health. And we'll make this world a healthier and happier place. #WorldHealthDay #HealthForAll #MentalHealthMatters

Tweet 2: I know it's a #FirstWorldProblem but I'm angry that my 2021 #Toyota Camry is spending the weekend in the shop because of a bad O2 sensor. I bought a new car because I don't have time for car problems. #disappointed

Tweet 3: Can't flip over a vault and stick a perfect landing but hey, still proud to show off my #vaccine card. #FullyVaccinated

Tweet 4: #BREAKING: The #CDS on Thursday will ease indoor #mask guidance for fully vaccinated people, allowing them to safely stop wearing masks inside in most places, a government source told the AP. #pandemic #covid19 #safety

7. Applying the lexical shortcut route we introduced in Chapter 3, let's study the use of *because X* based on specific lexical items. Two nouns that occur with some frequency in the *because X* construction are *reasons (because reasons)* and *science (because science)*. Do a search for these in the Corpus of Global Web-Based English (GloWbE). What do you find? Is there any indication that the construction is more popular in American English than elsewhere? Are there any false positives you have to rule out?

## Level 2: Interpretation and Research Design

8. Scientific podcasts are a well-established genre, but there is not a lot of research on them. Pick a scientific podcast that makes transcripts available (such as the podcast published by the journal *Science*), download four or five transcripts, and assess, based on the grammatical features we discussed in Section 9.2, if their linguistic profile is closer to prototypically written or prototypically spoken language. (Obviously, your analysis will be based on a very small sample.) Explain your choice of linguistic variable(s).

9. Using the sampling method described in the toolbox of Section 9.3.2, analyze two written genres for their preferred type of noun phrase. You should come up with a sample of fifty noun phrases from each text type. How many noun phrases will you first have to collect (approximately)?

10. Bohmann's study of *because X* was published in 2016 and the data comes from Twitter. How would one go about it if one wanted to know if *because X* has spread since then? Which genre(s) might be good candidates to look at? What might be challenges for a corpus linguistic approach? Might there be different ways to assess if *because X* has spread? Develop a research design, starting with a testable hypothesis.

## Further Reading

- A comprehensive overview of the grammatical features of spoken English can be found in chapter 14 of the *Grammar of Spoken and Written English* (Biber et al. 2021). A detailed analysis of the bundles of linguistic features in which speech and writing differ is the study of Biber (1988). For an introduction to Conversation Analysis, see, for example, Clift (2016). On the hybrid nature of online registers with regard to features of the spoken and written mode, see Biber & Egbert (2018).

- A detailed description of the noun phrase in English is given in Berlage (2014). The development of written English toward more compressed sentence structures is described, for example, in Mair (2006), Leech et al. (2009), and Biber & Gray (2011). A wealth of data on the frequency and types of pre- and postmodifiers within the complex noun phrase is also provided by the *GSWE* (Biber et al.

2021: ch. 8). Data on the occurrence of categories reflecting a phrasal or clausal discourse style in the academic as opposed to other registers is contained, for example, in Biber & Gray (2016: ch. 3).

- For an overview of trends and topics in the analysis of computer-mediated communication since its beginnings, see Herring (2019). Herring describes how earlier scholarship focused on textual features of digital genres, but now includes the analysis of multimodal discourses. If you are mostly interested in how language development on the Internet fits with language change in general, check out McCulloch (2019), written for a non-academic audience, and the articles in Squires (2016). If you would like to learn more about different strands of research on hashtags, see Heyd & Puschmann (2017), who compare hashtags in social media to hashtag graffiti in public spaces. If you want to learn more about ongoing trends in the syntactic development of English, especially with regard to colloquialization and density, the overview chapter by Mair & Leech (2020) is a good start. For an overview of trends in the analysis of syntax and genre in the digital domain, see Dorgeloh & Wanner (2020).

# Glossary

**adjunct** Adjunct (or adverbial) is the function of a clausal modifier. Adjuncts are not arguments, i.e., verbal complements, because they are non-obligatory sentence elements. They occur in initial position as well as in mid- and end-position. Their semantic contribution is to add information to the semantics of the core clause (circumstance adverbials/adjuncts), on the attitude of the speaker toward it (stance adverbials/adjuncts), or to connect sentences (linking/connective adverbials/adjuncts). Syntactically, an adjunct can be realized by a phrase or a clause (traditionally referred to as an "adverbial clause").

**agent** The semantic role associated with an entity in the clause that willfully brings about an event or change of state is referred to as the "agent." Syntactically, an agent is usually realized in the subject position, but not every verb requires an agent (think of verbs like *be, happen, fall*). In the passive construction, the agent of the verb shows up in a *by*-phrase or remains implicit.

**animacy** A noun phrase referring to a living entity is called "animate." Animacy is a semantic concept with syntactic ramifications. For example, for an animate possessor, the *'s*-genitive is preferred over the *of*-genitive (*the Queen's house* vs. *the house of the Queen*).

**argument** Arguments are phrases required by the verb to express the verb's meaning in syntax. They are typically realized in subject and object position and can be categorized by their semantic roles, such as agent, theme, or goal.

***because* X** In the "*because* X" construction, the word *because* is followed by a minimal phrase, most often a noun phrase consisting of just one word (*"because rules"*). *Because* in this construction is sometimes referred to as the "new *because*."

**bracketing** Discourse markers are defined by their bracketing function because they are used to connect or mark a boundary within ongoing speech.

**canonical sentence** The canonical sentence in English follows the pattern subject–verb–complement, with the agent argument of the verb realized as the subject. Non-canonical sentences are derivations from this more basic pattern, for example through movement operations. They are often motivated by the discourse environment.

**CARS model** CARS (Creating a Research Space) is an acronym for a pattern of three rhetorical moves characteristic of the research article: establishing a territory, identifying a niche or space, and occupying that space.

**clefting** A cleft construction divides a single clause into two parts in order for one part to become foregrounded. The foregrounded element becomes the complement of a main clause, while the rest of the sentence is turned into a subordinate clause and thereby backgrounded. In *it*-clefting, the pronoun *it* becomes the subject of the matrix clause that has the foregrounded part as its complement, and the backgrounded material appears as a relative clause (*It's the cake there that I like*).

**coherence** The meaningfulness of a text not only results from its cohesion, but also relies on implicit assumptions and background knowledge. Coherence results from processes of interpretation, for example, of pronouns or discourse connections.

**cohesion** Cohesion is the cover term for all explicit ties within a text, i.e., for all lexical and grammatical connections. Grammatical cohesion is a synonym for the grammar *of* discourse.

**comment clause** Clauses which function as discourse markers, rather than a true matrix clause (*I mean, you know, I think, you see*), are also described as a parenthetical or "comment clause."

**complement clause** A complement clause is a clause required by verbs like *say, think, promise,* usually taking on the role of direct object. Finite complement clauses are typically introduced by the complementizer *that*, which can also be left out (→ *that*-omission). Nouns and adjectives can also be followed by complement clauses, but clauses after nouns and adjectives are always optional.

**complementizer** In the narrow sense, a complementizer is a subordinating conjunction that introduces a complement clause (such as *that, if, whether*). Some linguists also use the term for all subordinating conjunctions, including those that introduce adverbial clauses, such as *before, after, because*.

**conjunction** When dealing with the grammar of discourse, conjunction is not a word class, but the superordinate term for the different kinds of relationships between sentences within discourse. Conjunction is one area of grammar that creates cohesion in a text.

**connectives** Elements that connect sentences or other parts of a discourse (paragraphs, sections) are called sentence or discourse connectives. Connectives can be coordinators, like *and* or *but*, or connective adjuncts, such as *next, in addition*, or *however*. Connectives are classified by their semantics as expressing an additive, temporal, causative, or adversative relation, and into "pure" and "impure" connectives by the amount of information included.

**context** (or **discourse context**) The context of an utterance consists of situational context and the surrounding text, which is also called "co-text." Non-linguistic properties determining the context are the channel or medium, the relationship between speaker and hearer, the setting, a specific topic or purpose, the formality of the situation, and the like.

**coordination** Coordination is the syntactic connection of elements that have an equal syntactic status. In phrasal coordination phrases of the same type are connected, while clausal coordination expands a simple sentence into a compound, or coordinate, sentence. Within discourse, the coordination of utterances without a connective is called "zero" coordination.

**coordinator** Coordinators, or coordinating conjunctions, connect phrases or clauses of an equal syntactic status. This means that none of the two elements connected by a coordinator is a dependent element. Coordinators with a function within discourse, not within the sentence, are called sentence or discourse connectives.

**core clause** The core clause tells us who did what to whom and reaches from the subject to the complement position. The area before or after the core clause is referred to as → **sentence periphery**.

**corpus** In principle, any collection of utterances from real language use, but typically a searchable electronic database of written and/or spoken discourse. A corpus can be a collection of full texts, but more often it is comprised of randomly selected text excerpts. A popular collection of freely available corpora can be found at the website English-corpora.org.

**co-text** The co-text is the concrete surrounding, i.e., preceding and subsequent, text in which a sentence is situated.

**data cleaning** Results from a corpus search need to be checked for precision. Minimally, false positives need to be removed before you proceed with analyzing the data set. This kind of check is referred to as "data cleaning."

**digital discourse** In this book, we are using the label "digital discourse" to refer to discourse that is constituted by and makes use of features associated with digital media, such as using links, hashtags, and → **textism**. Digital discourse is typically medially written, but conceptually oral. Genres of digital discourse include tweets, text messages, email, and online chats.

**discourse marker** Discourse markers are elements that do not belong to the core clause but occur parenthetically at the beginning, within, or at the end of an utterance (elements such as *and*, *now*, *so*, or *well*, *you know*, or *I mean*). They bracket the ongoing discourse or provide some kind of cue for the interaction going on between speaker and listener. In addition to discourse markers that typically occur as parentheticals, "freestanding" discourse markers are elements that can also occur just on their own (e.g., *oh*, *ok*).

**discourse type** There are many different discourse types, resulting from various kinds of discourse classification. A discourse type can be a very general, supposedly universal category (such as narration, or argumentation), but more often it is identical with a → **genre** (such as textbook, short story, or telephone call).

**ellipsis** In the general sense, ellipsis means the absence of one or several obligatory grammatical elements in a sentence. The missing information is to be recovered from the surrounding discourse or the discourse situation. A common type of ellipsis, on which we also focus in this book, is subject ellipsis, i.e., the omission of the grammatical subject in a sentence (*Didn't manage to do my homework*).

**endophoric reference** Pronouns that have a referential relation located within the text express endophoric reference. Anaphoric pronouns point backward for their resolution, cataphoric pronouns point forward in the text.

**existential construction** In an existential construction, the subject is placed later in the clause, and is replaced by *there* as an empty ("dummy") subject (*There's a free table over there*). The construction serves information packaging and usually occurs with an NP as a subject that contains new information.

**exophoric reference** Pronouns that point to an entity in the situational context, and not in the preceding or subsequent text, are used as exophoric pronouns. Typically, first- and second-person pronouns as well as demonstrative pronouns have exophoric reference.

**extended reference** Pronouns have extended reference when they refer to an entire proposition, and not to another nominal entity within the surrounding text or the discourse situation. Both the pronoun *it* and the demonstrative pronouns (*this, that, these*) can be expressions of extended reference, but speakers have a preference for interpreting *it* as referring to an entity and *this* as referring to a proposition (*I visited my mom yesterday. It/This seems to have done her a lot of good*).

**extraposition** Extraposition, or, more precisely, *it*-extraposition, is a construction that moves a subordinate clause with the syntactic function of subject into the sentence-final position. The position of the subject is filled by the pronoun *it* (*It is too bad that you won't be able to come*). Complex sentences in which extraposition could occur, but the subject clause remains in the original position, are described as cases of non-extraposition (*That you won't be able to come is too bad*).

**focus** Generally speaking, the focus of a sentence is what the speaker wants to highlight as its most important part. The focus can be marked through stress, positioning, and/or lexical choices. Focused information is not necessarily new, the importance can also result from a contrast (contrastive focus). The normal position for the focus is sentence-final (end-focus), while focus-marking (or a marked focus) is realized by a range of non-canonical constructions.

**foregrounding** The highlighting of one sentence element by way of a cleft construction can be described as foregrounding this particular element. In that an *it*-cleft makes one sentence element the complement of a new matrix clause, turning the remainder of the sentence into a subordinate clause, the original clause is split into foregrounded and background information.

**functional linguistics** Functional linguistics is often used as a cover term for all linguistic concepts and theories aiming at the description of grammar from the point of view of language use. More specifically, a functional perspective on syntax focuses on aspects of information structure, topic, and focus.

**genre** In this book, we are focusing on genre as a situational determinant of linguistic variation. For example, the genre of research articles is characterized by a high number of inanimate subjects because the discourse is typically not about who did what to whom. A genre analysis approach to syntactic usage patterns typically considers the text as a whole and examines both pervasive features and typical features of the text that can be explained through the factors anchored in the discourse situation.

*get*-**passive** The *get*-passive is a non-canonical passive in English. It is formed with *get,* rather than *be*, and is used more often in informal contexts than the *be*-passive (*He got fired*). Syntactically, *get* in the *get*-passive does not behave like an auxiliary verb ( *\*He gotn't fired*).

**given and new information** Given information generally describes information that has been mentioned in previous discourse and is therefore, or for some other reason, known to the reader or listener. Givenness may result from mere repetition, or from information being evoked by the discourse, inferable, or otherwise anchored to some previously mentioned element. New information is information that is not known or accessible to the reader or listener at the moment of an utterance.

**grammaticalization** Developments in language whereby lexical expressions come to serve grammatical functions and often continue to develop new functions are generally described as "grammaticalization."

Grammaticalization typically goes along with the loss of meaning and categorial restrictions and is a common process through which discourse markers come about.

**hashtag** Hashtags consist of a pound sign (#) followed by linguistic material and are used in digital discourse to establish the discourse topic (#discoursesyntax) or to express stance (#cantdeal). They may or may not be integrated into the syntax of an utterance.

**inference** An inference is a pragmatic kind of meaning, i.e., meaning that is not encoded literally, but needs to be "inferred" by the reader or listener based on world knowledge and/or pragmatic plausibility.

**information packaging** The principle that given information tends to precede new information in an utterance is known as "information packaging." Constructions that arise from the need to follow this principle (such as inversion or the passive) are said to serve an "information-packaging" function.

**information status** → **Given and new information**

**inversion** Inversion describes the positioning of the entire verb phrase in front of the grammatical subject of the clause. Full inversion contrasts with subject–auxiliary inversion (such as in interrogatives) and results from the fronting of a PP, NP, AdjP, VP, or AdvP, which often have locative or directional meaning (*Into his life came a new taste*). Locative inversion is the most common semantic type of inversion, while non-locative inversion also occurs, usually with a fronted AdjP or NP (*More important/Another important issue is the following* ...).

**left-dislocation** Left-dislocation is a construction that results from moving an NP of the core clause to the clausal beginning, with a pronoun filling the gap that is created by this movement (*Lentils, I can't stand them*). Left-dislocation differs from topicalization, i.e. mere NP-fronting, in that it has the general function of identifying the referent of the fronted NP from the ground of knowledge established by the discourse. Left-dislocation does not require the referent of the NP to be directly recoverable from the text, but strengthens its role as the topic for the following discourse.

**matrix clause** A matrix clause is the main clause of a complex sentence, i.e., it has a subordinate clause as one of its sentence constituents.

**narrative mode** There are many views on the defining properties of narrative discourse, but a narrative "mode" is more straightforward than these. It is present in a text that has a structure based on chronology, i.e., texts in a narrative mode, with a narrative syntax, put the sequence of events they report into a corresponding sequence of two (or more) sentences.

**particle shift** The word order pattern in which a verb is separated from its particle is known as "particle shift," as in *look it up*. While the term implies that this word order results from moving the particle, there are also analyses that propose that it is the noun phrase that has been moved away.

**passive construction** In a passive construction, the semantic object (the entity undergoing a change or targeted by the action expressed by the verb) becomes the subject of the clause, and the agent argument, normally the subject of a clause, can remain unexpressed (short passive) or is realized inside a PP (long passive). In English, the canonical passive is formed with a form of *be* and the past participle of the lexical verb (*The horse was kicked [by the cow]*).

**premodifier/postmodifier** Pre- and postmodifiers are optional elements within a noun phrase, i.e., phrasal elements that are added to and semantically modify the head noun. The premodifying element is usually an adjective or noun (phrase), whereas postmodifying elements can be a relative clause, a prepositional phrase, or an adverb or adjective (phrase).

**preposition stranding** Preposition stranding – ending a clause on a preposition – results from moving a noun phrase that is the object of a preposition to the beginning of a sentence, which regularly happens in English in question formation (*Who did you buy this for __?*), passivization (*He was laughed at __ in school*), and relative clause formation (*He is a person I just can't see eye to eye with__*). The syntactic alternative to preposition stranding is pied piping, which fronts the whole prepositional phrase (*For whom did you buy this?*), but most speakers prefer preposition stranding, especially in informal contexts.

**presupposition** A presupposition, or presupposed information, is information that does not constitute truly given information for the reader or listener, but is presented *as if* already known. An *it*-cleft can have the function of evoking a presupposition, through placing new information into the subordinate clause and thus backgrounding it, which creates the impression that the information could still be known.

**Principle of End-Weight** The Principle of End-Weight refers to the preference for presenting short phrases before long phrases, all things being equal. It is one of the motivating factors for extraposition (over a clausal subject) and the use of *by*-phrases in the passive.

**pronoun** Pronouns constitute a category of lexemes that are used instead of a noun phrase when the entity they are referring to is identifiable by the reader or listener. Personal pronouns refer to the speaker, the listener, or some other entity, while demonstrative pronouns refer to entities within the local or temporal discourse situation or within the preceding or upcoming text. Hearers interpret pronouns following both semantic, grammar-based principles, and pragmatic, coherence-based plausibility.

**proposition** In simple terms, the term "proposition" refers to the semantic content of a sentence. Sentences that are variants of each other express the same propositional content, i.e., they underlie the same truth conditions. For example, if the sentence *Sally switched off the radio* is true, the sentence *Sally switched the radio off* is also true. Both sentences have the same propositional content.

**rate of occurrence** When interpreting frequencies gathered from a corpus, the rate of occurrence is a normalized count of a given feature of grammar, its frequency computed as a rate per a certain number of words. The formula for calculating a rate of occurrence is:

(raw count ÷ total word count) × reference size in number of words

Rates of occurrence are used to compare frequencies from corpora or sub-corpora that differ in length.

**recoverability** If a discourse entity is fully accessible by the reader or listener, this means that it is recoverable. Recoverability is a necessary condition for an elliptical reference (→ **ellipsis**) and means that the entity is either anaphorically recoverable from the preceding text, or situationally recoverable if the referent can be retrieved from the surrounding context.

**reference** Reference describes the relation between a linguistic form and the entity or situation the speaker or writer is dealing with (the referent). Reference can be expressed by a full NP or by a pronoun.

**reference grammar** A reference grammar is a comprehensive description of the grammar of a language, written from a linguistic perspective. It is different from a pedagogical grammar designed for language learners and a style manual providing guidance on language use in specific situations. For this book, we have chosen the *Cambridge Grammar of the English Language* as our main point of reference (Huddleston & Pullum 2002).

**register** Registers are functional language varieties, which are described and systematically analyzed from the perspective of the discourse situation. A register analysis identifies features of grammar as register features if they are more pervasive in a target register than in other kinds of texts. It can take place at different levels of specificity, so that registers range from widely studied varieties such as conversation or academic writing to sub-registers like article introductions or office-hour consultations. Register analysis thus combines the identification of register features with their explanation in the light of the situational context.

**retrievability** Information is understood as retrievable if it is either mentioned in the preceding discourse or inferable from the discourse situation.

**semiotic triangle** The semiotic triangle highlights that the meaning of a linguistic expression does not have a direct relation to an object or other aspect of the outside world, but that this relation exists via a learned mental representation (the concept). In this way, the model explains that the same referent can be covered in discourse by using different linguistic expressions (e.g., noun phrases or pronouns).

**sentence periphery** The sentence periphery is what precedes the subject and follows the complement. A syntactic construction that targets the left sentence periphery is → **topicalization**.

**spoken vs. written language** → **written vs. spoken language**

**syntactic complexity** At the sentence level, syntactic complexity is measured through the number of embedded clauses inside a sentence. A sentence with no embedded clauses is, in this sense, not complex. At the level of phrases, syntactic complexity is measured through phrasal length and depth (the level of embedding). High phrasal complexity is a marker of written language.

**syntactic variation** The concept of syntactic variation relates to the fact that the same propositional meaning can be expressed in different ways. For example, the two sentences *The horse kicked the cow* and *The cow was kicked by the horse* are true under exactly the same truth conditions and can be considered variants of each other. Like linguistic variation in other domains (e.g., phonology), syntactic variation is highly systematic.

**textism** Textisms are instances of non-standard written language associated with the register of texting, such as abbreviations, number homophones (*l8* for *late*), and emoticons. The language associated with the register of texting is sometimes referred to as "textese."

**text-linguistic approach** In a text-linguistic study, the objects of analysis are the linguistic properties of a specific discourse type or register. For example, one might look at why conversations, relatively speaking, use more pronouns than other registers.

***that*-omission** In complement clauses after verbs, the complementizer *that* may be realized or omitted. The two versions (with and without *that*) are considered to be an example of syntactic variation.

**theme/patient** The semantic role associated with the argument of the verb that undergoes the action or a change of state is referred to as the "theme" or, less often, the "patient." In canonical sentences, the theme argument is realized as the direct object.

**topic** The concept of topic has several facets, the most straightforward one being the entity that a sentence is "about" (usually its subject). Topic also refers to what the discourse is about, i.e., to its current focus of interest. Entities that are the topic of one or several utterances in discourse possess topicality, reflected by their topic continuity, or topic persistence (which can be measured, for example, by the number of times an entity recurs in a sequence of sentences).

**topicalization** In topicalization, or NP-fronting, a noun phrase that normally belongs somewhere later in the clause is moved to the beginning of the sentence (in front of the grammatical subject) (*Lentils I hate*). This movement adds extra emphasis to the constituent and often turns it into the sentence focus. The construction has a close link to the preceding text: The referent of the NP must be given or at least inferable (*What about having lentil soup? Lentils I hate*).

**transitivity** The property of verbs and prepositions to require a noun phrase as complement is referred to as *transitivity*. Intransitive verbs like *sleep* or *frown* are not followed by a noun phrase, ditransitive verbs are followed by two noun phrases (*give John an apple*). Whether or not a verb is transitive depends on the verb's semantics. There are also linguists who consider transitivity a property ascribed to sentences, rather than verbs, but that is not the definition we are working with in this book.

**utterance** An utterance is a sentence or other linguistic unit together with its context of occurrence. A sentence becomes an utterance if it is looked at as bound to the situation in which it is used, which is why the same sentence, repeated or used under new conditions, easily gives rise to many utterances.

**variable** In a research design, a variable is what takes on different values and is used to predict an effect. Discourse syntax typically works with properties of the discourse situation and with genres as the "predictor" variable, while a pattern of syntactic variation or the occurrence of certain grammatical features is the "dependent," or "outcome" variable.

**variationist approach** In a variationist research design, the objects of analysis are a specific pattern of syntactic variation and the reasons why one might choose one variant over the other in a given speech situation. For example, one might look at the choice of passive voice over active voice or at complement sentences without *that* over complement sentences with *that*.

**verb-particle construction** In the verb-particle construction a verb forms a semantic unit with a particle that is often semantically opaque (*eat up, put off, give up*). The verb-particle construction allows two word order sequences: In the continuous pattern, the verb is followed immediately by the particle (*give up an idea*); in the discontinuous or split pattern, the verb is separated from the particle by an intervening noun phrase or pronouns (*give it up*). The latter pattern is also referred to as → **particle shift**.

**voice** The grammatical category "voice" refers to the mapping of arguments to syntactic positions. In active voice, the agent becomes the subject of the clause, and in passive voice, the semantic object becomes the subject of the clause. Usually, voice is also marked morphologically on the verb (→ **passive construction**).

**world knowledge** World knowledge is one part of the background knowledge that speakers use when creating and interpreting discourse. Apart from their world knowledge, speakers also use knowledge of the discourse situation when looking out for the coherence of a text (for example, when interpreting a relation among sentences, or retrieving the referent of a pronoun).

**written vs. spoken language** The distinction between written vs. spoken language is both medial (written language has visual output, spoken language has phonetic output) and conceptual (written language tends to be planned and more formal, spoken language tends to be less formal and more spontaneous). The arrival of → **digital discourse** has challenged this dichotomy.

# References

Aijmer, Karin. 2011. Well I'm not sure I think . . . The use of *well* by non-native speakers. *International Journal of Corpus Linguistics*, 16(2), 231–54.

Aijmer, Karin. 2013. *Understanding Pragmatic Markers in English: A Variational Pragmatic Approach*. Edinburgh: Edinburgh University Press.

Allen, Cynthia. 2016. Typological change: Investigating loss of inflection in early English. In Merja Kytö & Päivi Pahta, eds., *The Cambridge Handbook of English Historical Linguistics*. Cambridge: Cambridge University Press, pp. 444–59.

Ameka, Felix A., Alan Dench & Nicholas Evans. 2006. *Catching Language: The Standing Challenge of Grammar Writing*. Berlin and New York: De Gruyter Mouton.

American Dialect Society. 2014. *"Because" is the 2013 word of the year*. Online. Accessed August 8, 2021. https://bit.ly/because_2013wordoftheyear

American Dialect Society. 2015. *2014 Word of the year is "#blacklivesmatter"*. Online. https://bit.ly/blm_2014wordoftheyear

American Dialect Society. 2020. *2019 Word of the year is "(My) Pronouns," Word of the decade is singular "they"*. Online. https://bit.ly/they_2019 wordoftheyear

Andersen, Gisle. 2001. *Pragmatic Markers and Sociolinguistic Variation: A Relevance-theoretic Approach to the Language of Adolescents*. Amsterdam and Philadelphia: John Benjamins.

Aravind, Athulya, Martin Hackl & Ken Wexler. 2018. Syntactic and pragmatic factors in children's comprehension of cleft constructions. *Language Acquisition*, 25(3), 284–314.

Ariel, Mira. 1988. Referring and accessibility. *Journal of Linguistics*, 24(1), 65–87.

Ariel, Mira. 2001. Accessibility theory: An overview. In Joost Schilperoord, Ted Sanders & Wilbert Spooren, eds., *Text Representation: Linguistic and Psycholinguistic Aspects*. Amsterdam and Philadelphia: John Benjamins, pp. 29–87.

Ariel, Mira. 2013. Centering, accessibility and the next mention. *Theoretical Linguistics*, 39(1–2), 39–58.

Arnold, Jennifer E. & Michael K. Tanenhaus. 2011. Disfluency effects in comprehension: How new information can become accessible. In Edward Gibson & Neal J. Pearlmutter, eds., *The Processing and Acquisition of Reference*. Cambridge, MA: MIT Press, pp. 197–218.

Atkinson, Dwight. 1992. The evolution of medical research writing from 1735 to 1985: The case of the Edinburgh Medical Journal. *Applied Linguistics* 13(4), 337–74.

Bazerman, Charles. 1988. *Shaping Written Knowledge: The Genre and Activity of the Experimental Article in Science*. Madison: University of Wisconsin Press.

Beeching, Kate. 2016. *Pragmatic Markers in British English: Meaning in Social Interaction*. Cambridge: Cambridge University Press.

Behaghel, Otto. 1909. Beziehungen zwischen Umfang und Reihenfolge von Satzgliedern. In Wilhelm Streitberg, ed., *Indogermanische Forschungen: Zeitschrift für Indogermanistik und Allgemeine Sprachwissenschaft*. Strasbourg: Karl J. Truebner, pp. 110–42.

Bell, David M. 2007. Sentence-initial *And* and *But* in academic writing. *Pragmatics*, 17(2), 183–201.

Berlage, Eva. 2014. *Noun Phrase Complexity in English*. Cambridge: Cambridge University Press.

Biber, Douglas. 1988. *Variation across Speech and Writing*. Cambridge: Cambridge University Press.

Biber, Douglas. 1992. Using computer-based corpora to analyze the referential strategies of spoken and written texts. In Jan Svartvik, ed., *Directions in Corpus Linguistics: Proceedings of Nobel Symposium 82 Stockholm, 4–8 August 1991*. Berlin and New York: De Gruyter Mouton, pp. 213–52.

Biber, Douglas. 2006. *University Language: A Corpus-based Study of Spoken and Written Registers*. Amsterdam and Philadelphia: John Benjamins.

Biber, Douglas. 2012. Register as a predictor of linguistic variation. *Corpus Linguistics and Linguistic Theory*, 8(1), 9–37.

Biber, Douglas & Susan Conrad. 2019. *Register, Genre, and Style*, 2nd edn. Cambridge: Cambridge University Press.

Biber, Douglas & Jesse Egbert. 2018. *Register Variation Online*. Cambridge: Cambridge University Press.

Biber, Douglas & Bethany Gray. 2010. Challenging stereotypes about academic writing: Complexity, elaboration, explicitness. *Journal of English for Academic Purposes*, 9(1), 2–20.

Biber, Douglas & Bethany Gray. 2011. Grammatical change in the noun phrase: The influence of written language use. *English Language and Linguistics*, 15(2), 223–50.

Biber, Douglas & Bethany Gray. 2016. *Grammatical Complexity in Academic English: Linguistic Change in Writing*. Cambridge: Cambridge University Press.

Biber, Douglas, Susan Conrad & Geoffrey Leech. 2002. *Longman Student Grammar of Spoken and Written English*. Harlow: Longman.

Biber, Douglas, Susan Conrad, Edward Finegan, Stig Johansson & Geoffrey Leech. 1999. *Longman Grammar of Spoken and Written English*. Harlow: Longman.

Biber, Douglas, Stig Johansson, Geoffrey Leech, Susan Conrad & Edward Finegan. 2021. *Grammar of Spoken and Written English*. Amsterdam and Philadelphia: John Benjamins.

Birner, Betty J. 1994. Information status and word order: An analysis of English inversion. *Language*, 70(2), 233–59.

Birner, Betty J. & Gregory Ward. 1998. *Information Status and Noncanonical Word Order in English*. Amsterdam and Philadelphia: John Benjamins.

Bloom, Lois, Jeremie Hafitz & Karin Lifter. 1980. Semantics of verbs and the development of verb inflection in child language. *Language*, 56(2), 386–412.

Bohmann, Axel. 2016. Grammatical change because Twitter? Factors motivating innovative uses of because across the English-speaking Twittersphere. In Lauren Squires, ed., *English in Computer-Mediated Communication: Variation, Representation, and Change*. Berlin and Boston: De Gruyter Mouton, pp. 149–78.

Borer, Hagit & Kenneth Wexler. 1987. The maturation of syntax. In Thomas Roeper & Edwin Williams, eds., *Parameter Setting*. Dordrecht: Springer Netherlands, pp. 123–72.

Borer, Hagit & Kenneth Wexler. 1992. Bi-unique relations and the maturation of grammatical principles. *Natural Language and Linguistic Theory*, 10(2), 147–89.

Bosch, Peter. 1983. *Agreement and Anaphora: A Study of the Role of Pronouns in Syntax and Discourse*. London: Academic Press.

Bowie, Jill & Gergana Popova. 2020. Grammar and discourse. In Bas Aarts, Jill Bowie & Gergana Popova, eds., *The Oxford Handbook of English Grammar*, 1st edn. Oxford: Oxford University Press, pp. 554–80.

Branco, António, Tony McEnery & Ruslan Mitkov, eds. 2005. *Anaphora Processing: Linguistic, Cognitive and Computational Modelling*. Amsterdam and Philadelphia: John Benjamins.

Brezina, Vaclav. 2018. *Statistics in Corpus Linguistics: A Practical Guide*. Cambridge: Cambridge University Press.

Brinton, Laurel J. 1996. *Pragmatic Markers in English: Grammaticalization and Discourse Functions*. Berlin and New York: De Gruyter Mouton.

Brinton, Laurel J. 2010. Discourse markers. In Andreas H. Jucker & Irma Taavitsainen, eds., *Historical Pragmatics*, Berlin and New York: De Gruyter Mouton, pp. 285–314.

Brinton, Laurel J. 2011. *The Comment Clause in English: Syntactic Origins and Pragmatic Development*. Cambridge: Cambridge University Press.

Brinton, Laurel J., ed. 2017. *English Historical Linguistics: Approaches and Perspectives*. Cambridge: Cambridge University Press.

Burridge, Kate. 2014. *Cos* – a new discourse marker for Australian English? *Australian Journal of Linguistics*, 34(4), 524–48.

Buysse, Lieven. 2012. *So* as a multifunctional discourse marker in native and learner speech. *Journal of Pragmatics*, 44(13), 1764–82.

Buysse, Lieven. 2015. 'Well it's not very ideal . . .' The pragmatic marker *well* in learner English. *Intercultural Pragmatics*, 12(1), 59–89.

Buysse, Lieven. 2020. 'It was a bit stressy as well actually'. The pragmatic markers *actually* and *in fact* in spoken learner English. *Journal of Pragmatics*, 156, 28–40.

Carusillo, Claire. 2014. "Actually" is the most futile, overused word on the internet. *The New Republic*. March 17. Online. https://bit.ly/carusillo_nr

Chambers, Craig G. & Ron Smyth. 1998. Structural parallelism and discourse coherence: A test of centering theory. *Journal of Memory and Language*, 39(4), 593–608.

Clift, Rebecca. 2001. Meaning in interaction: The case of *actually*. *Language*, 77(2), 245–91.

Clift, Rebecca. 2016. *Conversation Analysis*. Cambridge: Cambridge University Press.

Çokal, Derya, Patrick Sturt & Fernanda Ferreira. 2018. Processing of *it* and *this* in written narrative discourse. *Discourse Processes*, 55(3), 272–89.

Cooper, William E. and John R. Ross. 1975. World order. In Robin E. Grossman, L. James San and Timothy J. Vance, eds., *Papers from the Parasession on Functionalism*. Chicago: Chicago Linguistic Society, pp. 63–111.

Cowles, Wind H. & Alan Garnham. 2011. Noun-phrase anaphor resolution: Antecedent focus, semantic overlap, and the Informational Load Hypothesis. In Edward Gibson & Neal J. Pearlmutter, eds., *The Processing and Acquisition of Reference*. Cambridge, MA: MIT Press, pp. 297–322.

Crompton, Peter. 2006. The effect of position on the discourse scope of adverbials. *Text & Talk*, 26(3), 245–79.

Crystal, David. 1995. *The Cambridge Encyclopedia of the English Language*. Cambridge: Cambridge University Press.

Crystal, David. 2007. *Language and the Internet*. Cambridge: Cambridge University Press.

Cuenca, Maria J. & Ludivine Crible. 2019. Co-occurrence of discourse markers in English: From juxtaposition to composition. *Journal of Pragmatics*, 140, 171–84.

Dalrymple, Mary & Irina Nikolaeva. 2011. *Objects and Information Structure*. Cambridge: Cambridge University Press.

Dant, Doris. 2012. Using COCA to evaluate the Chicago Manual of Style's usage prescriptions. In Joybrato Mukherjee & Magnus Huber, eds., *Corpus Linguistics and Variation in English: Theory and Description*. Amsterdam: Rodopi, pp. 29–39.

D'Arcy, Alexandra. 2007. *Like* and language ideology: Disentangling fact from fiction. *American Speech*, 82(4), 386–419.

D'Arcy, Alexandra. 2017. *Discourse-Pragmatic Variation in Context: Eight Hundred Years of LIKE*. Amsterdam and Philadelphia: John Benjamins.

Dehé, Nicole. 2002. *Particle Verbs in English: Syntax, Information Structure, and Intonation*. Amsterdam and Philadelphia: John Benjamins.

Diessel, Holger. 2004. *The Acquisition of Complex Sentences*. Cambridge: Cambridge University Press.

Diessel, Holger. 2005. Competing motivations for the ordering of main and adverbial clauses. *Linguistics*, 43(3), 449–70.

Diessel, Holger & Michael Tomasello. 2005. Particle placement in early child language: A multifactorial analysis. *Corpus Linguistics and Linguistic Theory*, 1(1), 89–112.

Diewald, Gabriele. 2011. Grammaticalization and pragmaticalization. In Bernd Heine & Heiko Narrog, eds., *The Oxford Handbook of Grammaticalization*. Oxford: Oxford University Press, pp. 450–61.

Dik, Simon C. 1997. *The Theory of Functional Grammar, Part 2: Complex and Derived Constructions*. Berlin and New York: Mouton de Gruyter.

Dorgeloh, Heidrun. 1997. *Inversion in Modern English: Form and Function*. Amsterdam and Philadelphia: John Benjamins.

Dorgeloh, Heidrun. 2005. Patterns of agentivity and narrativity in early science discourse. In Janne Skaffari, Matti Peikola, Ruth Carroll, Risto Hiltunen & Brita Wårvik, eds., *Opening Windows in Discourse and Texts from the Past*, Amsterdam and Philadelphia: John Benjamins, pp. 83–94.

Dorgeloh, Heidrun. 2006. Inversion in descriptive and narrative discourse: A text-typological account following functional principles. *Cahiers de Recherche*, 9, 101–14.

Dorgeloh, Heidrun & Gero Kunter. 2015. Modelling adjective phrase inversion as an instance of functional specialization in non-locative inversion. In Christina Sanchez-Stockhammer, ed., *Building Bridges into the Future: Can We Predict Linguistic Change?* Studies in Variation, Contacts and Change in English, Vol. 16. https://varieng.helsinki.fi/series/volumes/16/dorgeloh_kunter/.

Dorgeloh, Heidrun & Anja Wanner. 2003. Too abstract for agents? The syntax and semantics of agentivity in abstracts of English research articles. In Holden Härtl & Heike Tappe, eds., *Mediating between Concepts and Grammar*, Berlin and New York: Mouton de Gruyter, 433–56.

Dorgeloh, Heidrun & Anja Wanner. 2009. Formulaic argumentation in scientific discourse. In Roberta Corrigan, Edith A. Moravcsik, Hamid Ouli and Kathleen M. Wheatley, eds., *Formulaic Language. Vol. 2: Acquisition, Loss, Psychological Reality, and Functional Explanations.* Typological Studies in Language 83. Amsterdam and Philadelphia: John Benjamins. 523–44.

Dorgeloh, Heidrun & Anja Wanner. 2020. Genre variation. In Bas Aarts, Jill Bowie & Gergana Popova, eds., *The Oxford Handbook of English Grammar*, Oxford: Oxford University Press, pp. 654–72.

Dupont, Maïté. 2021. *Conjunctive Markers of Contrast in English and French: From Syntax to Lexis and Discourse.* Amsterdam and Philadelphia: John Benjamins.

Ehrlich, Kate. 1980. Comprehension of pronouns. *Quarterly Journal of Experimental Psychology*, 32(2), 247–55.

Erteschik, Nomi & Shalom Lappin. 1979. Dominance and the functional explanation of island phenomena. *Theoretical Linguistics*, 6(1–3), 41–86.

Fischer, Kerstin, ed. 2006. *Approaches to Discourse Particles.* Amsterdam: Elsevier.

Fontaine, Lise. 2013. *Analysing English Grammar: A Systemic-Functional Introduction.* Cambridge: Cambridge University Press.

Forster, Edward M. 1927. *Aspects of the Novel.* New York: Harcourt, Brace & Co.

Fox, Barbara A. 1986. Local patterns and general principles in cognitive processes: Anaphora in written and conversational English. *Text – Interdisciplinary Journal for the Study of Discourse*, 6(1), 25–52.

Fox, Barbara A. 1987. Anaphora in popular written English narratives. In Russel S. Tomlin, ed., *Coherence and Grounding in Discourse: Outcome of a Symposium, Eugene, Oregon, June 1984.* Amsterdam and Philadelphia: John Benjamins, pp. 157–73.

Fox, Barbara A., ed. 1996. *Studies in Anaphora.* Amsterdam and Philadelphia: John Benjamins.

Fox Tree, Jean E. 2015. Discourse markers in writing. *Discourse Studies*, 17 (1), 64–82.

Fox Tree, Jean E. & Josef C. Schrock. 2002. Basic meanings of *you know* and *I mean. Journal of Pragmatics*, 34(6), 727–47.

Fraser, Bruce. 2006. Towards a theory of discourse markers. In Kerstin Fischer, ed., *Approaches to Discourse Particles*. Amsterdam: Elsevier, pp. 189–204.

Fraser, Bruce. 2009. An account of discourse markers. *International Review of Pragmatics*, 1(2), 293–320.

Gao, Xia. 2016. A cross-disciplinary corpus-based study on English and Chinese native speakers' use of linking adverbials in academic writing. *Journal of English for Academic Purposes*, 24, 14–28.

Gardelle, Laure & Sandrine Sorlin, eds. 2015. *The Pragmatics of Personal Pronouns*. Amsterdam and Philadelphia: John Benjamins.

Geluykens, Ronald. 1992. *From Discourse Process to Grammatical Construction*. Amsterdam and Philadelphia: John Benjamins.

Gerrig, Richard J., William S. Horton & Amanda Stent. 2011. Production and comprehension of unheralded pronouns: A corpus analysis. *Discourse Processes*, 48(3), 161–82.

Gibbons, Alison & Andrea Macrae, eds. 2018. *Pronouns in Literature: Positions and Perspectives in Language*. London: Palgrave Macmillan.

Gledhill, Chris. 1995. Collocation and genre analysis. *Zeitschrift für Anglistik und Amerikanistik*, 43(1/1), 11–35.

Gregory, Michelle L. & Laura A. Michaelis. 2001. Topicalization and left-dislocation: A functional opposition revisited. *Journal of Pragmatics*, 33(11), 1665–706.

Gries, Stefan T. 2003. *Multifactorial Analysis in Corpus Linguistics: A Study of Particle Placement*. New York: Continuum.

Gross, Alan G., Joseph Harmon & Michael Reidy. 2002. *Communicating Science: The Scientific Article From the 17th Century to the Present*. New York: Oxford University Press.

Grosz, Barbara, Aravind Joshi & Scott Weinstein. 1995. Centering: A framework for modeling the local coherence of discourse. *Computational Linguistics*, 21, 202–25.

Gundel, Jeanette K., Nancy Hedberg & Ron Zacharski. 1993. Cognitive status and the form of referring expressions in discourse. *Language*, 69(2), 274–307.

Gundel, Jeanette K., Nancy Hedberg & Ron Zacharski. 2001. Definite descriptions and cognitive status in English: Why accommodation is unnecessary. *English Language and Linguistics*, 5(2), 273–95.

Gunraj, Danielle N., April M. Drumm-Hewitt, Erica M. Dashow, Sri S. N. Upadhyay & Celia M. Klin. 2016. Texting insincerely: The role of the period in text messaging. *Computers in Human Behavior*, 55, 1067–75.

Haegeman, Liliane. 1985. The *get*-passive and Burzio's generalization. *Lingua*, 66(1), 53–77.

Haegeman, Liliane & Tabea Ihsane. 1999. Subject ellipsis in embedded clauses in English. *English Language and Linguistics*, 3(1), 117–45.

Halliday, Michael A. K. & Ruqaiya Hasan. 1976. *Cohesion in English*. London: Longman.

Haselow, Alexander. 2011. Discourse marker and modal particle: The functions of utterance-final *then* in spoken English. *Journal of Pragmatics*, 43, 3603–23.

Haselow, Alexander. 2012. Subjectivity, intersubjectivity and the negotiation of common ground in spoken discourse: Final particles in English. *Language & Communication*, 32(3), 182–204.

Haselow, Alexander. 2019. Discourse marker sequences: Insights into the serial order of communicative tasks in real-time turn production. *Journal of Pragmatics*, 146(1), 1–18.

Hawkins, John A. 1994. *A Performance Theory of Order and Constituency*. Cambridge: Cambridge University Press.

Hawkins, John A. 2004. *Efficiency and Complexity in Grammars*. Oxford: Oxford University Press.

Hedberg, Nancy. 1990. *Discourse Pragmatics and Cleft Sentences in English. Dissertation*. Minneapolis: University of Minnesota Press.

Hedberg, Nancy & Lorna Fadden. 2007. The information structure of *it*-clefts, *wh*-clefts and reverse *wh*-clefts in English. In Nancy Hedberg & Ron Zacharski, eds., *The Grammar–Pragmatics Interface: Essays in Honor of Jeanette K. Gundel*. Amsterdam and Philadelphia: John Benjamins, pp. 49–76.

Heine, Bernd, Gunther Kaltenböck, Tania Kuteva & Haiping Long. 2021. *The Rise of Discourse Markers*. Cambridge: Cambridge University Press.

Heine, Bernd & Heiko Narrog, eds. 2011. *The Oxford Handbook of Grammaticalization*. Oxford: Oxford University Press.

Hellermann, John & Andrea Vergun. 2007. Language which is not taught: The discourse marker use of beginning adult learners of English. *Journal of Pragmatics*, 39(1), 157–79.

Herring, Susan C., ed. 1996. *Computer-Mediated Communication: Linguistic, Social, and Cross-Cultural Perspectives*. Amsterdam and Philadelphia: John Benjamins.

Herring, Susan C. 2019. The coevolution of computer-mediated communication and computer-mediated discourse analysis. In Patricia Bou-Franch & Pilar Garcés-Conejos Blitvich, eds., *Analyzing Digital Discourse: New Insights and Future Directions*. Cham: Palgrave Macmillan, pp. 25–67.

Heyd, Theresa & Cornelius Puschmann. 2017. Hashtagging and functional shift: Adaptation and appropriation of the #. *Journal of Pragmatics*, 116, 51–63.

Hoffmann, Christian R. 2012. *Cohesive Profiling: Meaning and Interaction in Personal Weblogs*. Amsterdam and Philadelphia: John Benjamins.

Holler, Anke & Katja Suckow, eds. 2016. *Empirical Perspectives on Anaphora Resolution*. Berlin and Boston: De Gruyter.

Huddleston, Rodney & Geoffrey K. Pullum. 2002. *The Cambridge Grammar of the English Language*. Cambridge: Cambridge University Press.

Huddleston, Rodney & Geoffrey K. Pullum. 2005. *A Student's Introduction to English Grammar*. Cambridge: Cambridge University Press.

Hundt, Marianne, Melanie Röthlisberger & Elena Seoane. 2018. Predicting voice alternation across academic Englishes. *Corpus Linguistics and Linguistic Theory*, 17(1), 189–222.

Iyeiri, Y., M. Yaguchi & Y. Baba. 2010. Coordinating and subordinating conjunctions in spoken American English. In O. J. Askedal, I. Roberts & T. Matsushita, eds., *Noam Chomsky and Language Descriptions*. Amsterdam: John Benjamins, pp. 179–96.

Johansson, Stig. 1997. A corpus study of English existential clauses: Register variation and discourse function. In Terttu Nevalainen, Matti Rissanen & Leena Kahlas-Tarkka, eds., *To Explain the Present: Studies in the Changing English Language in Honour of Matti Rissanen*. Helsinki: Société Néophilologique, pp. 303–18.

Jucker, Andreas H. & Yael Ziv. 1998. *Discourse Markers: Descriptions and Theory*. Amsterdam and Philadelphia: John Benjamins.

Kaiser, Elsi. 2011. Focusing on pronouns: Consequences of subjecthood, pronominalisation, and contrastive focus. *Language and Cognitive Processes*, 26(10), 1625–66.

Kaltenböck, Gunther. 2000. *It*-extraposition and non-extraposition in English discourse. In Christian Mair & Marianne Hundt, eds., *Corpus Linguistics and Linguistic Theory: Papers from the Twentieth International Conference on English Language Research on Computerized Corpora (ICAME 20)*. Amsterdam: Rodopi, pp. 157–75.

Kaltenböck, Gunther. 2004. Using non-extraposition in spoken and written texts. In Karin Aijmer & Anna-Brita Stenström, eds., *Discourse Patterns in Spoken and Written Corpora*. Amsterdam and Philadelphia: John Benjamins, pp. 219–42.

Kaltenböck, Gunther. 2005. *It*-extraposition in English: A functional view. *International Journal of Corpus Linguistics*, 10(2), 119–59.

Kaltenböck, Gunther, Bernd Heine & Tania Kuteva. 2011. On thetical grammar. *Studies in Language*, 35(4), 852–97.

Kaltenböck, Gunther, Evelien Keizer & Arne Lohmann, eds. 2016. *Outside the Clause: Form and Function of Extra-Clausal Constituents*. Amsterdam and Philadelphia: John Benjamins.

Kehler, Andrew & Hannah Rohde. 2013. A probabilistic reconciliation of coherence-driven and centering-driven theories of pronoun interpretation. *Theoretical Linguistics*, 39(1–2), 1–37.

Keizer, Evelien. 2015. *A Functional Discourse Grammar for English*. New York: Oxford University Press.

Keizer, Evelien. 2018. Modal adverbs in FDG: Putting the theory to the test. *Open Linguistics*, 4(1), 356–90.

Koch, Peter and Wulf Oesterreicher. 1985. Sprache der Nähe – Sprache der Distanz. Mündlichkeit und Schriftlichkeit im Spannungsfeld von Sprachtheorie und Sprachgeschichte. *Romanistisches Jahrbuch*, 36, 15–43.

Koops, Christian & Arne Lohmann. 2015. A quantitative approach to the grammaticalization of discourse markers: Evidence from their sequencing behavior. *International Journal of Corpus Linguistics*, 20(2), 232–59.

Kreyer, Rolf. 2006. *Inversion in Modern Written English: Syntactic Complexity, Information Status and the Creative Writer*. Tübingen: Narr.

Kytö, Merja & Päivi Pahta, eds. 2016. *The Cambridge Handbook of English Historical Linguistics*. Cambridge: Cambridge University Press.

Labov, William. 2013. *The Language of Life and Death: The Transformation of Experience in Oral Narrative*. Cambridge: Cambridge University Press.

Lambrecht, Knud. 1994. *Information Structure and Sentence Form: Topic, Focus, and the Mental Representations of Discourse Referents*. Cambridge: Cambridge University Press.

Lange, Claudia & Tanja Rütten. 2017. Non-canonical grammar!? *Zeitschrift für Anglistik und Amerikanistik*, 65(3), 243–7.

Leech, Geoffrey & Nicholas Smith. 2006. Recent grammatical change in written English 1961–1992: Some preliminary findings of a comparison of American with British English. In Antoinette Renouf & Andrew Kehoe, *The Changing Face of Corpus Linguistics*. Amsterdam: Rodopi, pp. 186–204.

Leech, Geoffrey, Marianne Hundt, Christian Mair & Nicholas Smith. 2009. *Change in Contemporary English*. Cambridge: Cambridge University Press.

Lenker, Ursula. 2010. *Argument and Rhetoric: Adverbial Connectors in the History of English*. Berlin and New York: De Gruyter Mouton.

Leuckert, Sven. 2019. *Topicalization in Asian Englishes: Forms, Functions and Frequencies of a Fronting Construction*. London: Routledge.

Lindquist, Hans & Magnus Levin. 2018. *Corpus Linguistics and the Description of English*, 2nd edn. Edinburgh: Edinburgh University Press.

Lohmann, Arne & Christian Koops. 2016. Aspects of discourse marker sequencing: Empirical challenges and theoretical implications. In

Gunther Kaltenböck, Evelien Keizer & Arne Lohmann, eds., *Outside the Clause: Form and Function of Extra-Clausal Constituents*. Amsterdam and Philadelphia: John Benjamins, pp. 417–46.

Lohse, Barbara, John A. Hawkins & Thomas Wasow. 2004. Domain minimization in English verb-particle constructions. *Language*, 80(2), 238–61.

Macaulay, Monica. 2011. *Surviving Linguistics: A Guide for Graduate Students*, 2nd edn. Somerville, MA: Cascadilla Press.

Mair, Christian. 2006. *Twentieth-Century English: History, Variation and Standardization*. Cambridge: Cambridge University Press.

Mair, Christian & Marianne Hundt, eds. 2000. *Corpus Linguistics and Linguistic Theory: Papers from the Twentieth International Conference on English Language Research on Computerized Corpora (ICAME 20)*. Amsterdam: Rodopi.

Mair, Christian & Geoffrey Leech. 2020. Current changes in English syntax. In Bas Aarts, April McMahon & Lars Hinrichs, eds., *The Handbook of English Linguistics*. Malden, MA: Wiley, pp. 249–76.

McCulloch, Gretchen. 2019. *Because Internet: Understanding the New Rules of Language*. New York: Riverhead.

McEnery, Tony & Andrew Hardie. 2012. *Corpus Linguistics: Method, Theory and Practice*. Cambridge: Cambridge University Press.

McWhorter, John. 2013. *Txtng is killing language. JK!!!* [Video]. TED Conferences. https://bit.ly/mcwhorter_tedtalk

Megherbi, Hakima, Alix Seigneuric, Jane Oakhill & Steve Bueno. 2019. Children's understanding of pronouns that differ in scope of reference. *Journal of Child Language*, 46(5), 1012–24.

Mitkov, Ruslan. 2014. *Anaphora Resolution*. Hoboken, NY: Taylor and Francis.

Müller, Simone. 2005. *Discourse Markers in Native and Non-Native English Discourse*. Amsterdam and Philadelphia: John Benjamins.

Nariyama, Shigeko. 2004. Subject ellipsis in English. *Journal of Pragmatics*, 36(2), 237–64.

Newmeyer, Frederick J. 2001. The Prague School and North American functionalist approaches to syntax. *Journal of Linguistics*, 37(1), 101–26.

Newmeyer, Frederick J. 2003. Grammar is grammar and usage is usage. *Language*, 79(4), 682–707.

Oakhill, Jane & Alan Garnham. 1988. *Becoming a Skilled Reader*. Oxford: Blackwell.

Ogden, Charles K. & Ivor A. Richards. 1972. *The Meaning of Meaning: A Study of the Influence of Language Upon Thought and of the Science of Symbolism*, 10th edn. London: Routledge.

O'Grady, William D. 1997. *Syntactic Development*. Chicago: University of Chicago Press.

Oh, Sun-Young. 2000. *Actually* and *in fact* in American English: A data-based analysis. *English Language and Linguistics*, 4(2), 243–68.

Oh, Sun-Young. 2005. English zero anaphora as an interactional resource. *Research on Language and Social Interaction*, 38(3), 267–302.

Oh, Sun-Young. 2006. English zero anaphora as an interactional resource II. *Discourse Studies*, 8(6), 817–46.

Patten, Amanda L. 2014. The historical development of the *it*-cleft: A comparison of two different approaches. In Nikolas Gisborne & Willem Hollmann, eds., *Theory and Data in Cognitive Linguistics*. Amsterdam and Philadelphia: John Benjamins, pp. 87–114.

Pennebaker, James W. 2011. *The Secret Life of Pronouns: What Our Words Say About Us*. New York: Bloomsbury Press.

Pinker, Steven, David S. Lebeaux & Loren A. Frost. 1987. Productivity and constraints in the acquisition of the passive. *Cognition*, 26(3), 195–267.

Polat, Brittany. 2011. Investigating acquisition of discourse markers through a developmental learner corpus. *Journal of Pragmatics*, 43(15), 3745–56.

Prado-Alonso, Carlos & J. Carlos Acuña-Fariña. 2010. A comprehensive account of full-verb inversion in English. *Folia Linguistica*, 44(2), 509–54.

Prince, Ellen F. 1978. A comparison of *wh*-clefts and *it*-clefts in discourse. *Language*, 54(4), 883–906.

Prince, Ellen F. 1981. Toward a taxonomy of given-new information. In Peter Cole, ed., *Radical Pragmatics*. New York: Academic Press, pp. 223–54.

Puschmann, Cornelius. 2010. *The Corporate Blog as an Emerging Genre of Computer-Mediated Communication: Features, Constraints, Discourse Situation*. Göttingen: Universitätsverlag Göttingen.

Quirk, Randolph, Sidney Greenbaum, Geoffrey Leech & Jan Svartvik. 1985. *A Comprehensive Grammar of the English Language*. London: Longman.

Rasinger, Sebastian M. 2013. *Quantitative Research in Linguistics: An Introduction*, 2nd edn. London: Bloomsbury.

Renkema, Jan & Christoph Schubert. 2018. *Introduction to Discourse Studies: New Edition*. Amsterdam and Philadelphia: John Benjamins.

Rezvani Kalajahi, Seyed A., Steve Neufeld & Ain Nadzimah Abdullah. 2017. The discourse connector list: A multi-genre cross-cultural corpus analysis. *Text & Talk*, 37(3), 283–310.

Rohdenburg, Günter & Britta Mondorf, eds. 2003. *Determinants of Grammatical Variation in English*. Berlin and New York: De Gruyter Mouton.

Rosenbach, Anette. 2014. English genitive variation – the state of the art. *English Language and Linguistics*, 18(2), 215–62.

Sanders, Ted. 1997. Semantic and pragmatic sources of coherence: On the categorization of coherence relations in context. *Discourse Processes*, 24 (1), 119–47.

Sanders, Ted J. M. & Morton A. Gernsbacher. 2004. Accessibility in text and discourse processing. *Discourse Processes*, 37(2), 79–89.

Sarda, Laure, Shirley Carter-Thomas, Benjamin Fagard & Michel Charolles, eds. 2014. *Adverbials in Use: From Predicative to Discourse Functions*. Louvain-La-Neuve: UCL, Presses Universitaires de Louvain.

Schaub, Steffen. 2016. The influence of register on noun phrase complexity in varieties of English. In Christoph Schubert & Christina Sanchez-Stockhammer, eds., *Variational Text Linguistics*. Berlin and Boston: De Gruyter Mouton, pp. 251–70.

Schiffrin, Deborah. 1987. *Discourse Markers*. Cambridge: Cambridge University Press.

Schiffrin, Deborah. 1990. *Approaches to Discourse*. Oxford: Blackwell.

Schilk, Marco & Steffen Schaub. 2016. Noun phrase complexity across varieties of English: Focus on syntactic function and text type. *English World-Wide*, 37, 58–85.

Schourup, Lawrence. 1999. Discourse markers: Tutorial overview. *Lingua*, 107(3–4), 227–65.

Schubert, Christoph & Christina Sanchez-Stockhammer. 2016. *Variational Text Linguistics*. Berlin and Boston: De Gruyter Mouton.

Seoane, Elena. 2006. Changing styles: On the recent evolution of scientific British and American English. In Christiane Dalton-Puffer, Dieter Kastovsky, Nikolaus Ritt & Herbert Schendel, eds., *Syntax, Style and Grammatical Norms: English from 1500–2000*. Bern: Peter Lang, pp. 191–211.

Shaw, Philip. 2009. Linking adverbials in student and professional writing in literary studies: What makes writing mature. In Maggie Charles, Diane Pecorari & Susan Hunston, eds., *Academic Writing: At the Interface of Corpus and Discourse*. London: Continuum, pp. 215–35.

Short, Mick. 1996. *Exploring the Language of Poems, Plays and Prose*, 1st edn. Harlow: Pearson.

Smith, Sara W. & Andreas H. Jucker. 2000. *Actually* and other markers of an apparent discrepancy between propositional attitudes of conversational partners. In Nancy Hedberg & Ron Zacharski, eds., *The Grammar–Pragmatics Interface: Essays in Honor of Jeanette K. Gundel*. Amsterdam and Philadelphia: John Benjamins, pp. 207–38.

Spooren, Wilbert & Ted Sanders. 2008. The acquisition order of coherence relations: On cognitive complexity in discourse. *Journal of Pragmatics*, 40 (12), 2003–26.

Squires, Lauren, ed. 2016. *English in Computer-Mediated Communication: Variation, Representation, and Change*. Berlin and Boston: De Gruyter Mouton.

Stefanowitsch, Anatol. 2020. *Corpus Linguistics: A Guide to the Methodology*. Berlin: Language Science Press.

Strunk, Jr., William & E. B. White. 2000. *The Elements of Style*. Fourth edition. New York: Allyn and Bacon.

Swales, John M. 1990. *Genre Analysis: English in Academic and Research Settings*. Cambridge: Cambridge University Press.

Swales, John M. 2004. *Research Genres. Exploration and Applications*. Cambridge: Cambridge University Press.

Tagliamonte, Sali. 2005. *So who? Like how? Just what?* Discourse markers in the conversations of young Canadians. *Journal of Pragmatics*, 37(11), 1896–915.

Teddiman, Laura & John Newman. 2007. Subject ellipsis in English: Construction of and findings from a diary corpus. Paper presented at the 26th International Conference on Lexis and Grammar, Bonifacio, France. 2–6 October. Online. https://bit.ly/3JtNKTI

Tenbrink, Thora. 2020. *Cognitive Discourse Analysis: An Introduction*. Cambridge: Cambridge University Press.

The American Heritage Dictionary of the English Language. 2000. Boston: Houghton Mifflin. Online. www.ahdictionary.com

Thornton, Rosalind, Hirohisa Kiguchi & Elena D'Onofrio. 2018. Cleft sentences and reconstruction in child language. *Language*, 94 (2), 405–31.

Tieken-Boon van Ostade, Ingrid. 2014. *In Search of Jane Austen: The Language of the Letters*. New York: Oxford University Press.

Tizón-Couto, David. 2012. *Left Dislocation in English: A Functional-Discoursal Approach*. Bern: Peter Lang.

Toolan, Michael. 2013. *Language in Literature: An Introduction to Stylistics*. London: Routledge.

Traugott, Elizabeth C. & Richard B. Dasher. 2009. *Regularity in Semantic Change*. Cambridge: Cambridge University Press.

Travis, Catherine E. & Amy M. Lindstrom. 2016. Different registers, different grammars? Subject expression in English conversation and narrative. *Language Variation and Change*, 28(1), 103–28.

Turkle, Sherry. 2015. *Reclaiming Conversation: The Power of Talk in a Digital Age*. New York: Penguin Books.

Turner, Elizabeth A. & Ragnar Rommetveit. 1967. Experimental manipulation of the production of active and passive voice in children. *Language and Speech*, 10(3), 169–80.

van Dijk, Chantal N., Merel van Witteloostuijn, Nada Vasić, Sergey Avrutin & Elma Blom. 2016. The influence of texting language on grammar and executive functions in primary school children. *PLoS ONE*, 11(3), e0152409.

van Silfhout, Gerdineke, Jacqueline Evers-Vermeul & Ted Sanders. 2015. Connectives as processing signals: How students benefit in processing narrative and expository texts. *Discourse Processes*, 52(1), 47–76.

Verstraete, Jean-Christophe. 2004. Initial and final position for adverbial clauses in English: The constructional basis of the discursive and syntactic differences. *Linguistics*, 42(4), 819–53.

Virtanen, Tuija. 1992. Given and new information in adverbials: Clause-initial adverbials of time and place. *Journal of Pragmatics*, 17(2), 99–115.

Virtanen, Tuija, ed. 2004. *Approaches to Cognition Through Text and Discourse*. Berlin and New York: De Gruyter Mouton.

Virtanen, Tuija. 2008. Adverbials of 'manner' and 'manner plus' in written English: Why initial placement? *SKY Journal of Linguistics*, 21, 271–93.

Virtanen, Tuija. 2010. Variation across texts and discourses: Theoretical and methodological perspectives on text type and genre. In Heidrun Dorgeloh & Anja Wanner, eds., *Syntactic Variation and Genre*. Berlin and New York: De Gruyter Mouton, pp. 53–84.

Virtanen, Tuija. 2014. Sentence-initial adverbials in written texts: On discourse functions and cognitive motivations. In Laure Sarda, Shirley Carter-Thomas, Benjamin Fagard & Michel Charolles, eds., *Adverbials in Use: From Predicative to Discourse Functions*. Louvain-La-Neuve: UCL, Presses Universitaire de Louvain, pp. 103–32.

Vonk, Wietske, Lettica G. Hustinx & Wim H. Simons. 1992. The use of referential expressions in structuring discourse. *Language and Cognitive Processes*, 7(3–4), 301–33.

Wanner, Anja. 2009. *Deconstructing the English Passive*. Berlin and New York: De Gruyter Mouton.

Ward, Gregory & Betty J. Birner. 2006. Information structure and non-canonical syntax. In Laurence R. Horn & Gregory L. Ward, eds., *The Handbook of Pragmatics*. Oxford: Blackwell, pp. 153–74.

Wårvik, Brita. 1995. The ambiguous adverbial/conjunctions *þa* and *þonne* in Middle English: A discourse-pragmatic study of *then* and *when* in Early English Saints' Lives. In Andreas H. Jucker, ed., *Historical Pragmatics: Pragmatic Developments in the History of English*. Amsterdam and Philadelphia: John Benjamins, pp. 345–57.

Wasow, Thomas & Jennifer Arnold. 2003. Post-verbal constituent ordering in English. In Günter Rohdenburg & Britta Mondorf, eds., *Determinants of Grammatical Variation in English*. Berlin and New York: De Gruyter Mouton, pp. 119–54.

Waters, Cathleen. 2009. Actually, it's more than pragmatics, it's really grammaticalization. *Toronto Working Papers in Linguistics*. Online. https://bit.ly/3vYHzRo

Webber, Bonnie L. 1991. Structure and ostension in the interpretation of discourse deixis. *Language and Cognitive Processes*, 6(2), 107–35.

Weir, Andrew. 2012. Left-edge deletion in English and subject omission in diaries. *English Language and Linguistics*, 16(1), 105–29.

Wiechmann, Daniel & Elma Kerz. 2013. The positioning of concessive adverbial clauses in English: Assessing the importance of discourse-pragmatic and processing-based constraints. *English Language and Linguistics*, 17(1), 1–23.

Wulff, Stefanie & Stefan T. Gries. 2019. Particle placement in learner language. *Language Learning*, 69(4), 873–910.

Xiao, Richard, Tony McEnery & Yufang Qian. 2006. Passive constructions in English and Chinese: A corpus-based contrastive study. *Languages in Contrast*, 6(1), 109–49.

Yáñez-Bouza, Nuria. 2015. *Grammar, Rhetoric and Usage in English: Preposition Placement 1500–1900*. Cambridge: Cambridge University Press.

Yates, Simeon J. 1996. Oral and written linguistic aspects of computer conferencing. In Susan C. Herring, ed., *Computer-mediated Communication: Linguistic, Social, and Cross-cultural Perspectives*. Amsterdam and Philadelphia: John Benjamins, pp. 29–46.

Yuill, Nicola & Jane Oakhill. 2010. *Children's Problems in Text Comprehension: An Experimental Investigation*. Cambridge: Cambridge University Press.

Zappavigna, Michele. 2015. Searchable talk: The linguistic functions of hashtags. *Social Semiotics*, 25(3), 274–91.

Zhang, Guiping. 2015. *It is suggested that . . .* or *it is better to . . .?* Forms and meanings of subject *it*-extraposition in academic and popular writing. *Journal of English for Academic Purposes*, 20, 1–13.

## Primary Sources

Andželika. 2019. This dog was trained to respond to Harry Potter spells and he's probably the cutest Hogwarts student ever. boredpanda.com. Online. https://bit.ly/3xT39JE

Austen, Jane. 1985 [1815]. *Emma*. Harmondsworth: Penguin.

Axon, Rachel. 2013. Air apparent: Ayumu Hirano might challenge Shaun White. *USA Today Sports*. Online. https://bit.ly/axon_usatoday

Bauer, Laurie. 2020. Blackbirds and blue whales: Stress in English A+N constructions. *English Language and Linguistics*, 25(3), 581–600.

Brontë, Charlotte. 1981 [1847]. *Jane Eyre*. New York: Bantam.

Bruni, Frank. 2020. How to go to college during a pandemic. *The New York Times*. August 1. Online. https://bit.ly/bruni_nyt

Burroughs, Edgar Rice. 1972 [1923]. *The Moon Maid*. London: Tom Stacey Reprints Ltd.

Carroll, Lewis. 1991 [1865]. *Alice's Adventures in Wonderland*. Project Gutenberg. Online. https://bit.ly/3se4siz

Davies, Mark. 2004–. *British National Corpus*. Online. www.english-corpora.org/bnc/

Davies, Mark. 2008–. *Corpus of Contemporary American English (COCA)*. www.english-corpora.org/coca/

Davies, Mark. 2010–. *Corpus of Historical American English (COHA), 1810–2009*. www.english-corpora.org/coha/

Davies, Mark. 2011–. *Corpus of American Soap Operas*. www.english-corpora.org/soap/

Davies, Mark. 2013. *Corpus of Global Web-Based English (GloWbE)*. www.english-corpora.org/glowbe/

Davies, Mark. 2016–. *Corpus of Online Registers of English (CORE)*. www.english-corpora.org/core/

Davies, Mark. 2019-. *The TV Corpus, 1950–2018*. www.english-corpora.org/tv/

Easton, Lauren. 2017. Making a case for a singular "they". AP Style Blog. Online. www.apstylebook.com/blog_posts/7

Garunay, Melanie. 2016. President Obama speaks on the results of the election: "We are Americans first". The White House. Online. https://bit.ly/3LF974V

Geiger, A.W. & Nikki Graf. 2019. About four-in-ten U.S. adults say forms should offer more than two gender options. Pew Research Center. Online. https://bit.ly/pewresearch2019

Grieve, Jack, Andrea Nini & Diansheng Guo. 2017. Analyzing lexical emergence in Modern American English online. *English Language and Linguistics*, 21(1), 99–127.

Grimm, Jacob & Wilhelm Grimm. 2001. "The Frog-Prince" in *Grimms' Fairy Tales*. [Kinder und Hausmärchen]. Translated by Edgar Taylor and Marian Edwardes. Project Gutenberg. Online. https://bit.ly/project_gutenberg_the_frog_prince

Helsinki Corpus TEI XML Edition. 2011. First edition. Designed by Alpo Honkapohja, Samuli Kaislaniemi, Henri Kauhanen, Matti Kilpiö,

Ville Marttila, Terttu Nevalainen, Arja Nurmi, Matti Rissanen and Jukka Tyrkkö. Implemented by Henri Kauhanen and Ville Marttila. Based on *The Helsinki Corpus of English Texts* (1991). Helsinki: The Research Unit for Variation, Contacts and Change in English (VARIENG), University of Helsinki. Online. https://helsinkicorpus.arts.gla.ac.uk

Imperial War Museum. 2021. The peace treaties that ended the first world war. Online. https://bit.ly/3F24MWT

James, P. D. 2004. *Devices and Desires*. London: Vintage.

Lata, Ramina, James F. Conway, Naiqian Cheng et al. 2000. Maturation dynamics of a viral capsid: visualization of transitional intermediate states. *Cell*, 100(2), 253–63.

Lewis, Carolyn Herbst. 2018. At home, you're the most important thing: The Chicago maternity center and medical home birth, 1932–1973. *Journal of Women's History*, 30(4), 35–59.

Maduku, Richard. 2018. Logos on my mind. *The Guardian* (Nigeria). Online. January 1. https://bit.ly/maduku_theguardian

Martin, Jeff. 2020. John Lewis mourned as "founding father" of better America. *The Washington Post*. July 30. Online. https://bit.ly/martin_wsp

Martínez, Ignacio Palacios. 2015. Variation, development and pragmatic uses of *innit* in the language of British adults and teenagers. *English Language and Linguistics*, 19(3), 383–405.

Merriam-Webster. 2019. "They" is Merriam-Webster's word of the year 2019. Online. https://bit.ly/they_MW2019wordoftheyear

Rosa, Amanda. 2020. Finally, N.Y.C. beaches are open for swimming. Thank god. *The New York Times*. July 7. Online. https://bit.ly/rosa_nyt

Rouse, W. H. D. 2019. *The Crocodile and the Monkey*. The Story Hut. Online. https://bit.ly/the_crocodile_and_the_monkey

Schitt's Creek. 2020. Season 6, Episode 2: The incident transcript. Online. https://bit.ly/3y92fc1

Shakespeare, William. 2003 [1597]. *Romeo and Juliet*. Online. https://bit.ly/shakespeare_romeo_and_juliet

Shakespeare, William. 1981 [1623]. *The Comedy of Errors*. New York: Penguin Classics.

Shelley, Mary Wollstonecraft. 1993 [1818]. *Frankenstein*. Project Gutenberg. Online. https://bit.ly/3kGYL8A

Tagliamonte, Sali & Jennifer Smith. 2005. No momentary fancy! The zero 'complementizer' in English dialects. *English Language and Linguistics*, 9 (2), 289–309.

Tolkien, J. R. R. 1991 [1937]. *The Hobbit*. New York: HarperCollins.

van den Heuvel, Cor. 2000. *The Haiku Anthology: Haiku and Senryu in English*, 3rd edn. New York: Norton.

will.i.am. 2013. *Mona Lisa Smile*. Lyrics available at www.lyricfind.com

# Index

abstract, scientific, 8, 255, 256, 261, 281, 283
accessibility, referential, 202, 203, 213, 215, 220
*actually*, 167, 168, 235–6, 245, 246, 247, 250, 251
adjunct
  adjunct, clause-oriented, 54, 57, 58, 81
  adjunct, connective, 54, 164, 175–82
  adjunct, initial, 52, 58
  adjunct, position of, 86
  adjunct, temporal, 54, 57, 223, 235
  adjunct, VP-oriented, 54, 58, 81
agent, 8, 20, 22, 88–112, 260–5
Aijmer, Karin, 245–6, 252
*and*, turn-initial, 165, 168, 182, 186, 251
animacy, 90, 103
argument (of verb), 71, 88, 89
argument, realization of, 89, 90, 94, 96, 97, 104, 111, 113, 114

backgrounding, 112
*because X*, 256, 272, 275–81
Bell, David M., 170, 188
Biber, Douglas, 6, 16, 35, 38, 180, 206, 221, 254–9, 287
Birner, Betty, 48, 61, 75, 86, 87
blog, 21, 168, 209, 219, 243
Bohmann, Axel, 276–81, 287
bracketing, 178, 233–43
Brinton, Laurel, 226–9, 244, 245
Buysse, Lieven, 248
*by*-phrase, 90, 97–112, 124

*Cambridge Grammar*, 6, 7, 55
CARS model, 256, 262
CHILDES, 113, 162, 166
clause, canonical, 22, 51, 104, 130, 144

CLAWS, 31, 32
cleft construction
  *it*-clefting, 119, 130–58
Clift, Rebecca, 245, 287
COCA, 3, 26, 31
coherence, 14, 198, 220, 226
cohesion, 163, 187, 191, 192, 199, 200, 209, 221
coindexing, 191
comment clause, 51, 244, 245
communication, computer-mediated, 271, 288
complement clause, 16, 34, 35, 38–42
complement, predicative, 71, 151
complementizer, 33–42, 47, 244
complexity, NP, 267, 269, 270, 285, 286
complexity, syntactic, 90, 109, 110
conjunction
  conjunction, additive, 164–74, 178–82
connective
  connective, additive, 168, 170, 176, 179, 223
  connective, adversative, 164, 179, 188
  connective, pure/impure, 176, 184
  connective, temporal, 164, 175, 179, 223
Conrad, Susan, 6, 21, 38, 221, 254, 256, 258, 266
context, situational, 18, 44
conversation analysis, 173, 259, 287
coordination, 103, 161–4, 169, 183, 188, 259
core clause, 51, 54, 89, 162, 225, 228
co-reference, 189–93
corpus data, 9, 15, 26, 48, 87, 107, 115, 123, 126, 128, 138, 152, 170, 239

320

CPSIA information can be obtained
at www.ICGtesting.com
Printed in the USA
LVHW022103301122
734228LV00005B/413

9 781108 471053